Psychology: What's in It for Us?

PSYCHOLOGY
what's in it for us?

LEWIS M. ANDREWS
and
MARVIN KARLINS

UNIVERSITY OF SOUTH FLORIDA

random house **new york**

Second Edition
987654321
Copyright © 1975 by Random House, Inc.

Library of Congress Cataloging in Publication Data
Andrews, Lewis M
  Psychology: what's in it for us?
  1. Behavior modification. 2. Biofeedback training. 3. Psychol-
ogy. I. Karlins, Marvin, joint author. II. Title.
BF637.B4K38 1975   158   74-30029
ISBN 0-394-31850-1

11Sep'79

Manufactured in the United States of America

Cover art: Terry Lamb

For My Father

L. M. A.

To Steve and Sue

M. K.

contents

viii
Contents

Psychology: What's in It for Us?

introduction

> We have had religious revolutions, we have had political, industrial, economic, and nationalistic revolutions. All of them, as our descendents will discover, were but ripples in an ocean of conservatism—trivial by comparison with the psychological revolution toward which we are so rapidly moving.—Aldous Huxley

It should come as no surprise to any American that he lives in a "psychological" society. After all, the names of Sigmund Freud and B. F. Skinner are more familiar to us than, say, the names of many past presidents (Franklin Pierce? John Tyler?), and words like *id*, *ego*, and *conditioning* are almost as well known as Kentucky Fried Chicken. Most literate parents have read enough popularized psychology to feel they can make a thorough analysis of their own children. And what sophisticated young adult doesn't love to impress his friends with excerpts from *Open Marriage; I'm O.K., You're O.K.; How to be Your Own Best Friend*; or some such best seller?

What is truly intriguing, however, is not the popularity of psychology per se, but the fact that behind the social veil of glib and sometimes spurious phrases a *powerful psychotechnology is actually evolving*. Effective methods for curing physical ailments, for correcting behavior disorders, for improving performance, and for elevating the quality of life already exist, and more are being tested in the laboratory.

In the following pages it is our pleasant task to outline these methods in detail and then to share with you an understanding of the promise they hold for the betterment of the human condition. Unfolding will be the story of psychologists joined in a partnership for human progress, working both to overcome the multitude of problems confronting all of us and to expand our potential for a longer, more satisfying life.

1

avoid an altercation: use behavior modification

A child is dying. He lies motionless on the hospital bed, his gaunt face swathed in tape where the feeding tube protrudes from his nose. His body is sunken, little more than a skeleton outlined with little folds of skin. For months this infant has been starving to death by regurgitating his meals immediately after eating them. The attending physicians are frustrated; extensive tests have failed to uncover an organic cause for the child's condition. The doctors have fought his vomiting with dietary changes, anti-nauseants, intensive nursing care, even force feeding. To no avail. With precious little time remaining, two University of Wisconsin scientists are called onto the case. In the space of a few days, without drugs, force feeding, or surgery, they are able to halt the regurgitation. A few months later the child is fully recovered, happily celebrating his first birthday.

This is not fiction. It is a true story. But to understand

how this child's life was so suddenly saved, we must first understand a technique called *behavior modification*.

WHAT IS BEHAVIOR MODIFICATION?

It doesn't take a keen eye to see that many Americans need psychological help to live satisfying lives in today's kaleidoscopically changing world. In this situation, where 10 percent of the citizenry can expect to encounter severe psychological disorders sometime in their lives and hundreds of thousands more will seek aid, or should, to cope with lesser problems, effective therapy becomes a vital factor in the mental health of the community.

Let us inquire, then: What is therapy? If you asked the man in the street such a question, he would probably mutter something about Freud, castration complexes, and couches. To many people, Freudian psychoanalysis is synonymous with therapy, the *only* kind available. Nothing could be further from the truth; in fact, it has been recently reported that fewer than ½ of 1 percent of Americans seeking professional help for psychological problems are treated by qualified psychoanalysts. Today, other forms of therapy are gaining popular support among clinical psychologists and psychiatrists. One of the more recent and promising of these is behavior modification, a scientific procedure for systematically changing behavior through the use of rewards or punishments or both.

Defined in such a manner, free of scientific jargon, the method seems, to some people, to offer nothing new, and in one way these people are correct: The man who purchases flowers for his wife or spanks his child is practicing a rudimentary form of behavior modification ("rudimentary" in comparison with the more sophisticated, more effective behavior modification used by scientists). On the other hand, these people are incorrect in assuming that behavior modification is old hat. What makes the approach novel (and effective) is the use of psychological learning principles in the reinforcement of behavior.

Although the major thrust of behavior modification is a product of the last fifteen years, the impetus for the movement came from investigations in the earlier decades of this century. One classic and influential study was performed in 1920 by John Watson, father of psychological behaviorism and advocate of human behavior control. Watson was convinced that such control was feasible and, not one to hide his convictions, once boasted:

> Give me a dozen healthy infants, well formed, and my own specified world to bring them up in and I'll guarantee to take any one at random and train him to become any type of specialist I might select—doctor, lawyer, artist, merchant-chief, and, yes, even beggar-man and thief, regardless of his talents, penchants, tendencies, abilities, vocations, and race of his ancestors.[1]

Unlike many of his contemporaries, who speculated on such matters but went no further, Watson set out to substantiate his claims in the laboratory. His proof was gathered at the expense of Albert, a normal, healthy infant. Albert was basically stolid and unemotional. He cried infrequently, didn't scare easily, and except when confronted with loud sounds, showed no signs of fear. At nine months of age, he was suddenly presented with objects he had never seen before, including a white rat, a rabbit, a dog, a monkey, cotton, and wool, and he approached these objects without apprehension.

At this juncture Watson set out to prove his point: that he could control Albert's behavior at will and, specifically, make him afraid of the white rat he now approached fearlessly. The animal was admitted into Albert's playroom, as it had been before, but now each time the child reached for the animal, a loud gong was struck nearby. After a very few of these encounters, Albert began to cry and scurry away whenever he saw the rat, even when the gong did *not* sound. Furthermore, the child showed fear of other objects that resembled a rat, for example, the white rabbit he had earlier approached without fear. By a few pairings of a negative reinforcer (loud sound) with an initially attractive plaything, Watson was effectively able to condition little Albert's behavior and make him afraid of a whole class of objects similar to, and including, a white rat.[2]

Another classic study, by Paul Fuller in 1949, reports an attempt to teach a "vegetative human organism" a simple response.[3] As reported in the *American Journal of Psychology*, Fuller worked with an institutionalized eighteen-year-old patient who could neither walk nor talk. Day after day he lay flat on his back, unable to turn over, unable even to chew his food. According to hospital personnel, the patient had never learned to perform the simplest of tasks. Fuller set out to see if the young man could learn to raise his right arm to receive food. First, the patient was deprived of food for fifteen hours; then, whenever he raised his right arm, he was syringe-fed a sugar-milk solution. After a few sessions the patient was raising his right hand regularly to receive a food reward. When the food was taken away, the hand-raising response *extinguished*, or gradually disappeared in the absence of reinforcement.

The Watson and Fuller experiments share one important characteristic: the use of reinforcement to change behavior. Behavior modification works by increasing or decreasing the likelihood of a specified behavioral response through systematic reward and punishment. Little Albert received negative reinforcement (loud sound), and it is assumed that such punishment should eventually lead to cessation of the negatively reinforced behavior. In the case of the bedridden patient, the reinforcement was positive (food), and it is expected that rewarded behavior will be maintained (and often will increase in frequency). The process by which reinforcement becomes associated with certain behaviors is called *conditioning*. The psychologist uses his knowledge of conditioning principles to make his efforts more effective.

One can get a feeling for the power of conditioning procedures and for how such methods can systematically change a wide variety of human actions by reading B. F. Skinner's novel *Walden Two*. Although it is labeled a work of fiction, it is grounded in scientific facts, using the established learning principles underlying behavior modification to regulate human behavior and create a utopian community. In reality, the book is a reflection of Skinner's scientific thinking from start to finish, an application of his operant conditioning methods to the design of a society created and governed by psychologists.

In *Walden Two* every person is well-behaved, happy, and productive. Citizens are controlled, but they are not aware of being controlled. Control is achieved by procedures similar to those employed by Watson with little Albert and by Fuller with the vegetative patient. Explains the novel's psychologist-hero: "When he behaves as we want him to behave, we simply create a situation he likes, or remove one he doesn't like. As a result, the probability that he will behave that way again goes up, which is what we want. Technically, it's called 'positive reinforcement.' "[4]

In the years since the early work of Skinner, Watson, and Fuller, scientists have made behavior modification a far more powerful system for controlling behavior. At the same time they have used it to change increasingly complex and diverse types of human activity. A large proportion of current behavior modification takes place in clinical settings, where it is used to eliminate or modify dysfunctional personal behavior. The ability of behavior modification to change entrenched, highly resistant forms of human activity reminds us of its potency as a behavior control device.

USING BEHAVIOR MODIFICATION
TO HELP PEOPLE OVERCOME PROBLEMS

Consider the work described by A. B. Goorney, a specialist in neuropsychiatry at the RAF Hospital in Wroughton, England.[5] Dr. Goorney used behavior modification to treat a highly complex adult behavior: compulsive gambling. His patient was a thirty-seven-year-old man who had been playing the horses for thirteen years. Unhappy at home and unlucky at the track, this gambler faced a dissolving marriage and a depleted bankroll. It was, in fact, his wife, concerned that his continuing losses would bring financial ruin, who referred the man for therapy.

Treating the gambler required, first, a full understanding of his problem. Dr. Goorney obtained this through interviews with the patient. Discussion revealed a man who began gambling shortly after the start of a disappointing marriage, a compulsive bettor who wagered until his funds evaporated (he always lost) or his wife intervened. During gambling bouts the patient spent most of his waking hours thinking about the horses. Mornings were spent picking selections from the racing forms; afternoons, daydreaming about winning; and evenings, anxiously listening to broadcast results of the races.

Once apprised of the patient's gambling pattern, Dr. Goorney was able to proceed with behavior modification therapy. The treatment chosen was negative reinforcement: a total of 675 brief but unpleasant electric shocks administered to the patient's upper arms during nine days of therapy. Each treatment day consisted of six ten-minute shock sessions, each session occurring during a time when the patient was involved in some phase of his gambling pattern (e.g., studying the racing form). The strategy behind this approach was straightforward: To cure the patient of his compulsion, it was necessary to treat *all* behaviors related to gambling.

The results of this aversion reinforcement were shocking, to say the least. Halfway through therapy the patient indicated a decreasing interest in some of the activities related to his habit; by the seventh treatment day he was essentially cured, showing no desire even to hear the results of the races. One month after therapy had been terminated, the patient claimed that all interest in horse racing had disappeared and that harmony was beginning to appear in his marriage. A follow-up one year later found the patient reporting a continued lack of interest in horse racing and maintained progress in his marital situation.

Here then is an amazing therapeutic triumph. In the space of nine days, a compulsive gambling habit of thirteen years' duration is broken. Such is the power of behavior modification when it is skillfully used to regulate the actions of man.[6] But compulsive gambling is also relatively rare in our society—rare, that is, compared with instances of other social problems. Let us examine the role of behavior modification in coping with a more common difficulty: marital discord.

THE CASE OF H AND W

By any standard, this couple's marriage of six years was in trouble.[7] (We'll call the husband H and the wife W.) Not only had H, at one point, moved out of the house to live with another woman, but even worse, the communication between H and W had broken down completely. This sad fact became obvious as each described to therapist Herbert Fensterheim a different version of an incident involving sex that had taken place just prior to the separation. Fensterheim records each side of the story:

W's version: For several nights in a row the husband ate his dinner quickly and said that he had to go back to work. Even during dinner he acted uninterested in her conversation and completely ignored her admittedly tepid objections to his working every night. Her resentments caused by this rejection and lack of consideration grew and she increasingly ruminated throughout the day about his unjust treatment of her. On the night in question, the husband returned home after midnight, woke the wife, and with no exchange of words began to make love to her. With an overwhelming feeling of sullenness she passively allowed him to complete the sex act, at which point he exploded with rage.

H's version: He had been involved in a project important for the financial success of his firm. As there were great problems and a deadline approaching, he had been working very hard, under great pressure, and with considerable anxiety. During this period he needed comfort and support from his wife but found her remote and taciturn. On the night in question he returned home tired and dispirited, and his sexual advances this time were more with the intent of making a needed tender contact than for purely sexual reasons. Instead he found his wife more distant than ever and he became overwhelmed with rage.[8]

When Fensterheim asked H why he hadn't communicated his frustrations to his wife, the husband replied matter-of-factly that she "should have known." Similarly, when Fensterheim asked W why she hadn't asked what was bothering her husband, she responded blankly that such a question simply never occurred to her.

It soon became clear to Fensterheim that relations between H and W would not improve until they had learned to express their feelings, their likes and dislikes, openly and directly. To achieve this, the therapist instructed each partner to replay the scene, acting out their respective roles as if each were free to speak whatever he and she truly felt. This initial step demonstrated forcefully to both patients how the perceptions and responses of one person can change when he knows what the other person is experiencing and vice versa. During this and later sessions, H and W gradually acquired the ability to understand their communication blocks in terms of inhibition of feelings; this awareness, in turn, encouraged them to improve their out-of-therapy communication. Finally, and most importantly, each success was reinforced both by praise from the therapist and, later, "by their own feeling of accomplishment."

To accelerate this process, Fensterheim prescribed a simple but effective conditioning program which required each partner to phrase his or her statements to the other person as often as possible in "feeling talk," that is, to make each sentence explicit in its emotional content. Sentences were to be "started with the first person pronoun . . . followed immediately by a feeling verb, and . . . directed toward the other person." Examples would be "I like what you did"; "I don't like what you did"; "I like what you said"; or "I don't like what you said." Additionally, Fensterheim instructed H and W to keep a record of how many times they actually used such phrases. The therapist's interest in this scorekeeping was more than academic; he knew that the tally would operate as a reinforcement system. Each "check" was, in effect, a self-administered positive reinforcement which encouraged further feeling talk.

At this point therapy had reached the "half-successful" mark. H and W were certainly expressing their feelings more, but only their positive feelings. Daily resentments remained unsaid—and therefore unresolved. Each partner was still afraid to express negative feelings, apparently for fear of offending the other.

To solve this problem, Fensterheim employed another aspect of conditioning called *systematic desensitization*. With this method a behavior is encouraged, not through positive reinforcement, but by allowing the anxiety associated with the behavior to diminish gradually through increasing familiarity (much like a child learning to swim in deep water by first sticking his foot in the pool, then wading in shallow water, and finally venturing over to the adult side of the pool). In this case H and W gradually accustomed themselves in the security of the therapist's office to speaking and hearing statements of negative feelings.

Fensterheim also encouraged each partner, through positive reinforcement, to practice *role reversal*. W, for example, would describe a current situation in their relationship as she saw it; then H would repeat what she had just said, but in his own words. In this way the couple became immediately aware of the glaring omissions of intended meaning in even their most trivial verbal exchanges.

H and W were seen only fourteen times, yet this relatively short encounter with behavior therapy was enough to save their marriage and, more significantly, for them to develop a happy and creative relationship. "A year's follow-up indicates no thought of dissolving the marriage," writes Fensterheim.

> . . . the general marital relationship is now better than it ever has been. More important, they each have the feeling of a personal closeness between them. As ancilliary benefits, the wife's depression is gone and the husband reports better relations with his business partners.[9]

THE TOKEN ECONOMY

What about behavior modification in the classroom? Might it be used to aid learning and to regulate classroom behavior? Current research suggests that it can. A team of investigators headed by Robert Hamblin, a professor at Washington University, has implemented a token-exchange system to calm aggressive children, to train two-year-olds to read as well as five-year-olds are able to, to encourage shy ghetto children to become above-average talkers, and to start autistic youths on the road to recovery. In a recent article[10] these scientists reported that children (in good capitalistic fashion) will perform specific behaviors to "earn" tokens that they can exchange for valued prizes: Playdoh, movie admissions, snacks, and so forth. The teacher, by controlling the tokens, controls the behavior of the class. Reading Hamblin's report, one is amazed at how quickly and efficiently the teacher was able to produce the results he desired.

Consider, for example, the use of token reinforcement in calming aggressive behavior. For this phase of the research, the Hamblin team assembled a teacher's nightmare: a group of four-year-old boys so aggressive that psychiatrists and social workers had failed to tame them. An instructor was then asked to use her previous training and experience to teach the five boys; that is, she was asked to fulfill the role of "typical teacher," using "typical educational procedures" in the classroom. The poor woman tried every tactic in her repertoire, to no avail: After eight days of nerve-rattling effort, she was stymied by children who committed an average of 150 aggressive acts per day. Here is a four-minute segment of activity in the classroom under such conditions. It should give you a graphic feeling for what the teacher had to confront.

Mike, John and Dan are seated together playing with pieces of Playdoh. Barry, some distance from the others, is seated and also is playing with Playdoh. The children, except Barry, are talking about what they are making. Time is 9:10 A.M. Miss Sally, the teacher, turns toward the children and says, "It's time for a lesson. Put your Playdoh away." Mike says, "Not me." John says, "Not Me." Dan says, "Not Me." Miss Sally moves toward Mike. Mike throws some Playdoh in Miss Sally's face. Miss Sally jerks back, then moves forward rapidly and snatches Playdoh from Mike. Puts Playdoh in her pocket. Mike screams for his Playdoh, says he wants to play with it. Mike moves toward Miss Sally and attempts to snatch the Playdoh from Miss Sally's pocket. Miss Sally pushes him away. Mike kicks Miss Sally on the leg. Kicks her again, and demands the return of his Playdoh. Kicks Miss Sally again. Picks up a small steel chair and throws it at Miss Sally. Miss Sally jumps out of the way. Mike picks up another chair and throws it more violently. Miss Sally

cannot move in time. Chair strikes her foot. Miss Sally pushes
Mike down on the floor. Mike gets up. Pulls over one chair.
Now another, another. Stops a moment. Miss Sally is picking
up chairs. Mike looks at Miss Sally. Miss Sally moves toward
Mike. Mike runs away.

John wants his Playdoh. Miss Sally says "No." He joins
Mike in pulling over chairs and attempts to grab Playdoh
from Miss Sally's pocket. Miss Sally pushes him away
roughly. John is screaming that he wants to play with his
Playdoh. Moves toward phonograph. Pulls it off the table;
lets it crash onto the floor. Mike has his coat on. Says he is
going home. Miss Sally asks Dan to bolt the door. Dan gets
to the door at the same time as Mike. Mike hits Dan in the
face. Dan's nose is bleeding. Miss Sally walks over to Dan,
turns to the others, and says that she is taking Dan to the
washroom and that while she is away, they may play with
the Playdoh. Returns Playdoh from pocket to Mike and John.
Time: 9:14 A.M.[11]

At this point the hapless teacher was told of behavior
modification techniques and instructed to (1) ignore aggression when possible (turn her back when it occurred) and
(2) to reinforce, with tokens, any child who performed an
act of cooperation. By the end of the experiment, the boys'
behavior had undergone marked change: Cooperative acts
had increased from approximately 55 to 180 per day, whereas aggressive sequences plummeted from roughly 150 to 10.
Here is an example of classroom activity after behavior modification procedures had taken effect. The sequence takes
place during rest period, a time when the most aggressive
acts had occurred in the past.

All of the children are sitting around the table drinking their
milk; John, as usual, has finished first. Takes his plastic mug
and returns it to the table. Miss Martha, the assistant teacher,
gives him a token. John goes to the cupboard, takes out his
mat, spreads it out by the blackboard, and lies down. Miss
Martha gives him a token. Meanwhile, Mike, Barry, and Jack

have spread their mats on the carpet. Dan is lying on the carpet itself since he hasn't a mat. Each of them gets a token. Mike asks if he can sleep by the wall. Miss Sally says "Yes." John asks if he can put out the light. Miss Sally says to wait until Barry has his mat spread properly. Dan asks Mike if he can share his mat with him. Mike says "No." Dan then asks Jack. Jack says, "Yes," but before he can move over, Mike says "Yes." Dan joins Mike. Both Jack and Mike get tokens. Mike and Jack get up to put their tokens in their cans. Return to their mats. Miss Sally asks John to put out the light. John does so. Miss Martha gives him a token. All quiet now. Four minutes later—all quiet. Quiet still, three minutes later. Time: 10:23 A.M. Rest period ends.[12]

Commenting on the marked behavior change in the young boys, Hamblin says: "In 'normal' nursery schools, our observations have shown that five boys can be expected to have 15 aggression sequences and 60 cooperation sequences per day. Thus, from extremely aggressive and uncooperative, our boys had become less aggressive and far more cooperative than 'normal' boys."[13]

The token-exchange system has been used in mental institutions as well as classrooms. In general, behavior modification is being employed with increasing frequency with the mentally ill and retarded. One such application is presented by James Lent in his discussion of Mimosa Cottage, where behavior modification is used to train mentally retarded young women to become functioning members of society.[14] The therapy does not cure retardation, but it does provide the means for motivating the patients to learn the skills necessary to leave the hospital and live in the community. The goal of Lent's work is to teach Mimosa girls behaviors expected of normally functioning individuals, skills most people take for granted: physical cleanliness, proper dress and grooming, and correct posture and verbal behavior. All this is accomplished by reinforcing desired behavior with tokens, rewards that can be cashed in for items at the cottage store or for trips into town. Speaking of several girls who have been successfully trained by the reinforcement procedure and have left Mimosa Cottage to live in the community, Lent concludes: "They are not fully independent, but they are able to take care of most of their personal needs and to move about the community alone. . . . All of them lead simple but productive lives. Those around them may even forget, at times, that they were ever labeled 'mentally retarded.' "[15]

Medical problems can also be treated through behavior modification, as we saw with the case of the starving infant at the beginning of this chapter. To review: The baby was starving to death by regurgitating his meals immediately after eating them. All medical attempts to halt this behavior (dietary changes, anti-nauseants, intensive nursing care, force feeding) were unsuccessful. The child was near death when he was visited by two scientists who began a new treatment to combat his vomiting. The method worked, and the baby's life was saved. Psychologist Peter Lang, one of the scientists who successfully treated the young child, described what happened:

> I measured the muscle potentials along the infant's esophagus and found that on the graph paper I could detect the first wave of reverse peristalsis that just preceded regurgitation. I arranged an apparatus to give aversive electric shocks to his leg whenever his esophagus started to back up, which continued until vomiting had ceased. After only a few meals with this therapy the infant ceased to vomit. He is now a healthy toddler.[16]

MIGHT BEHAVIOR MODIFICATION BE USED TO ENSLAVE OUR MINDS?

Developments in behavior modification represent a dramatic advance in the technology of behavior control and, as such, arouse the fears of those who see such control as a threat to human freedom. The citizen can hardly be blamed for his unrest. His fear of scientific behavior control has been nurtured on a diet of exaggerations and half-truths from overzealous reporters, flamboyant scientists, and government alarmists. He hears vague references to brainwashing, truth serums, and hypnosis. He reads novels like *1984* by George Orwell and *Brave New World* by Aldous Huxley, which describe awesome behavior control procedures such as socialization by aversive conditioning, chemical "stunting" of normal brain growth, mass use of lobotomy operations, and the attachment of human brains to computers by microsurgery. If he prefers nonfiction, *The Hidden Persuaders*, *Battle for the Mind*, *The Rape of the Mind*, and *The Brain Watchers* treat him to some unsettling prophecies. The "danger" of behavior control is constantly exploited on television and in feature films. For example, Mary Shelley's *Frankenstein*, which is literally revived every few years by Hollywood, is a constant reminder to audiences of the "evil" inherent in behavioral engineering.

But could a clique of unscrupulous scientists or politicians *really* use behavior modification to *deliberately regulate* social and political activities? Probably not, for this behavior control technique, as powerful as it is, has one self-limiting factor: It requires careful, personalized administration. A small clique of scientists or politicians would find it very difficult to carefully construct and manipulate the environmental reinforcement contingencies necessary to control millions of people simultaneously.

The only significant abuse of behavior control techniques in the foreseeable future will occur on a person-to-person basis. It is at this local level of interpersonal politics that regulatory procedures difficult to employ on a mass scale become effective. This problem is particularly acute now that psychology teachers and behavior therapists are attempting to present the principles of behavior modification in simple terms that students, parents, and other laymen can readily understand.

A case in point concerns a psychologist and seventeen students. The students were told to reinforce any statement made to them by friends and relatives that began with an expression of personal conviction: "I think," "I believe," "It seems to me," or "I feel." They did this by smiling or paraphrasing the statement in an agreeable fashion. In every case the friend or relative increased the rate at which he stated personal convictions. *In no case were the friends or relatives aware that they were being conditioned.* The psychologist had the additional shock of discovering that he himself was being conditioned by a colleague to whom he was describing the results of his work.[17]

Another example concerns two students who decided to change an athletic roommate, by means of behavior modification, into an art lover. They hung various pictures around the walls and, knowing their friend liked attention, deprived him of it. They ignored him completely, unless he happened to be noticing a picture. Within a week the roommate was talking about the pictures all the time. The conversion was complete when he got up one morning and said, "Hey, fellows, how about going to the museum?"[18] If students can accomplish such a dramatic change outside the laboratory, what might a worker be able to do to his boss, or a young man to his prudish girl friend?

Fortunately, the number of people that one man could control through such conditioning techniques is limited for the reason that we have just discussed. It is also likely (at least we can hope) that as behavior modification receives more publicity, people will develop a sensitivity for how and when someone else is trying to manipulate them. Actually, the truly radical upshot of behavior modification is not the power it gives an individual to control others, but the power it gives an individual to control himself. Ponder, if you will, the situation of a young man we'll call P, a person whose obsessional thought about being "unattractive, stupid and brain damaged" were so severe that clinical tests indicated he was schizophrenic. Yet he was cured—and with a psychological program of marvelous simplicity. Supervising psychologist Michael Mahoney explains:

> After he [P] had determined the initial frequency of these maladaptive thoughts through self-observation, the man was instructed to punish himself by snapping a heavy-gauge rubber band against his wrist whenever he engaged in obsessional thoughts. When the negative thoughts had been drastically reduced, positive self-thoughts were established and gradually increased through use of a . . . self-reward. That is, the individual was asked to write down three positive things about himself on small cards that were then attached to his cigarette package. He was instructed to read a positive self-statement whenever he wanted to smoke and then to reward himself with a cigarette. A "wild card" was alternated with the other three, and it required the young man to think of an original positive self-statement. Soon he began to generate complementary self-thoughts . . . in the absence of smoking stimuli. The treatment techniques were gradually decreased, and the young man was able to resume a normal and adaptive life without lengthy hospitalization or extended therapy.[19]

That P was coached by a therapist should not allow us to overlook one very significant consideration: *P conducted his own therapy.* P, not the psychologist, calculated the nature and frequency of his own disorder. It was P who administered his own reinforcement and who determined the appropriate positive self-statements. Indeed, if P had known the basis of behavior modification in the beginning, he probably could have done without Mahoney! In simplest terms, effective self-modification is nothing more than (a) stating in clear and exact terms the behavior to be eliminated or encouraged, (b) finding an appropriate reinforcement that is easy to administer, and (c) applying the reinforcement to the behavior with some degree of consistency. (More complex self-modification methods involve managing environmental cues, as indicated in Chapter 2, and developing rigorous systems for the self-monitoring of one's own behaviors.)

This option for increased self-control has not escaped the attention of academic psychologists and is currently the source of great excitement at some universities. For not only has psychology discovered a workable technique for the cure of neurotic and dysfunctional behaviors; it has also discovered a technique that can be easily transferred to the layman for his own use *at his own discretion.* Several self-help books based on behavior modification have appeared on the market in the last two years, and we can expect more in the near future.[20]

The growing focus on self-control is a sign that behavior modification will become an even more important force for regulating human conduct in the coming years. The power of reinforcement to modify human behavior is one of the most pervasive and documented findings in modern psychology, and behavior modification is the first *truly effective* system to harness the power of reinforcement in regulating man's actions. In some ways it is strange that scientists didn't hit on behavior modification sooner; after all, the principles on which it is based are operative all around us. (Just consider what people will do for money.[21]) Perhaps it is a case of the fish being the last organism to discover water.

BEHAVIOR MODIFICATION: WHAT'S IN IT FOR US?

After some of the dramatic and useful applications of behavior modification have been spelled out, this may seem like a superfluous question. Yet there is one remaining advantage to conditioning that even professionals overlook. Behavior modification is such a blatantly potent methodology that most psychologists focus their energies on finding new ways to *apply it directly*—that is, to use it for creating specific changes or for alleviating specific problems. But we do well to remember that behavior modification is more than a technique; it is a philosophy as well. It reflects the simple but persuasive notion that no behavior pattern is haphazard, that even the most bizarre habits and inclinations are the logical product of environmental conditioning.

Viewed in this broader perspective, behavior modification becomes an important tool, not only for systematic control, but for *analysis* as well. Once schooled in the theories of behavior modification, the psychologist acquires the ability to spot and to define the causes of even the most "inexplicable" behaviors.

A case in point is Dr. Martin Seligman's approach to the subject of depression.[22] At a surface level this well-known psychiatric disorder poses a profound contradiction. On the one hand, we see ample evidence that the quality of life has improved in the United States over the last thirty years; there are more appliances, conveniences, freedoms, and recreational opportunities than ever before. On the other hand, incidences of depression continue to accelerate out of proportion to gains in population, particularly among the young. How can this be?

Some will argue, and perhaps quite rightly, that material rewards do not nourish the spirit. But Seligman, versed in reinforcement theories, is able to see another explanation. If a person is going to adopt a given behavior pattern, Seligman reminds us, that behavior must be rewarded, at least occasionally. In modern society, however, people often reap the benefits of the good life independently of their actions. This is particularly true of American children who receive snacks, records, and money so randomly from their parents that these goodies "might as well have fallen from the sky." Seligman argues that the effect of such directionless reinforcement is just that—"directionlessness." People develop the vague feeling that their actions do not make a difference because they are not reinforced for doing anything *in particular*. Some people then lapse into states of passivity and helplessness; in sum, they become depressed.

Seligman believes that this syndrome accounts for the so-called *success depression*. After many years of seeking and finally achieving a difficult goal, such as earning a Ph.D. or becoming president of a large company, an individual suddenly becomes sulky and withdraws. This depression occurs, according to Seligman,

> because reinforcers are no longer contingent upon present responding. After years of goal directed activity, a person now gets his reinforcers because of who he *is* rather than because of what he is *doing*. Perhaps this explains the number of beautiful women who become depressed and attempt suicide. They receive abundant positive reinforcement not for what they do but for how they look.[23]

Having *understood* a problem through his knowledge of conditioning, the psychologist is now in a better position to employ behavior modification for effective and lasting *change*. Seligman's analysis of depression, for example, would call for a conditioning program in which the desired behavior is immediately reinforced. It matters not so much what the depressed person does, but that he (or she) is able to connect his action to a discernible reinforcement—that he is able to see his actions having an effect. Therapy for depression based on this conclusion has been quite successful:

> In an Alabama hospital, for instance, E. S. Taulbee and H. W. Wright have created an "anti-depression" room. They seat a severely depressed patient in the room and then abuse him in a simple manner. He is told to sand a block of wood, then is reprimanded because he is sanding against the grain of the wood. After he switches to sanding with the grain, he

is reprimanded for sanding with the grain. The abuse continues until the depressed patient gets angry. He is then promptly led out of the room with apologies. His outburst, and its immediate effect on the person abusing him, breaks up his depression.[24]

Behavior modification as an analytical tool may even help to solve difficult political and economic problems, particularly by pointing out the hidden payoffs, or positive reinforcements, that serve to perpetuate social ills.

Consider inflation. Most government officials regard inflation as a heinous curse on the economy and would, they say, do anything to curb it. Yet, as one astute editorial writer has observed,[25] the government reaps a major advantage (reward) from inflation: increased income. How? Because in an inflationary economy, people tend to earn more money, which automatically puts them into higher income tax brackets. This enables the Internal Revenue Service to collect greater revenues which, in turn, are spent by congressmen for various pet projects. The rub, of course, is that while people are earning more dollars, the real purchasing power of their money has not changed; what *has changed* is that people are now paying a higher percentage of their income to Uncle Sam. Seeing this, a behavior modifier would immediately advocate some kind of remedial measure, such as adjusting tax rates to compensate for inflation. If nothing else, this action would make inflation "less reinforcing" to government officials and further encourage economic reform.

Understandably, suggestions like this one do not always make federal officials very happy, but they do show the potential power of 'behavior modification for resolving even the most complex and global of problems. It is not farfetched to expect that the use of behavior modification as an analytical tool will become a creative, revolutionary force in the service of free and efficient government.

26

Psychology: What's in It for Us?

NOTES

1. J. Watson, *Behaviorism* (New York: People's Institute, 1924), p. 82.
2. J. Watson and R. Rayner, "Conditioned Emotional Reactions," *Journal of Experimental Psychology* 3 (1920): 1–14.
3. P. Fuller, "Operant Conditioning of a Vegetative Human Organism," *American Journal of Psychology* 62 (1949): 587–590.
4. B. Skinner, *Walden Two* (New York: Macmillan, 1948).
5. A. Goorney, "Treatment of a Compulsive Horse Race Gambler by Aversion Therapy," *British Journal of Psychiatry* 114 (1968): 329–333.
6. There is a problem with behavior modification, however, when the therapist uses negative (rather than positive) reinforcement in changing behavior, as Dr. Goorney did. During his nine days of therapy, the compulsive gambler suffered recurrent anxiety attacks. At one point, Dr. Goorney states, "the patient expressed the opinion that it was only the realization that he must obtain a cure that was keeping him going." Would less motivated or more anxious individuals have continued in therapy? It could well be that negative reinforcement is limited in therapeutic usefulness to people who are highly motivated to overcome their problems.
7. A. Fensterheim, "Assertive Methods and Marital Problems," *Advances in Behavior Therapy* (New York: Academic Press, 1972), pp. 13–18.
8. Ibid., pp. 14–15.
9. Ibid., p. 17.
10. R. Hamblin et al., "Changing the Game from 'Get the Teacher' to 'Learn,'" *TransAction* (January 1969): 20–31.
11. Ibid., p. 22.
12. Ibid., p. 24.
13. Ibid.
14. J. Lent, "Mimosa Cottage: Experiment in Hope," *Psychology Today* (June 1968): 51–58.
15. Ibid., p. 58.
16. P. Lang, "Autonomic Control—or Learning to Play the Internal Organs," *Psychology Today* (October 1970): 37. For the complete report of the experiment, see P. Lang and B. Melamed, "Case Report: Avoidance Conditioning Therapy of an Infant with Chronic Ruminative Vomiting," *Journal of Abnormal Psychology* 74 (1969): 1–8.
17. J. Mann, *Changing Human Behavior* (New York: Scribner, 1965).
18. G. Wald, "Determinancy, Individuality, and the Problem of Free Will," in *New Views of the Nature of Man*, ed. J. Platt (Chicago: University of Chicago Press, 1965), pp. 16–46.
19. M. Mahoney and C. Thoresen, *Self-Control: Power to the Person* (Monterey, Calif.: Brooks/Cole, 1974), p. 25.

20. The text by Mahoney and Thoresen, though a bit academic, is one of the better books on this subject.

21. When you study the use of token economies in behavior modification work, you see just how close the relationship between money and tokens is. Dr. J. Atthowe and Dr. L. Krasner describe how they have used a token economy to help patients learn proper behaviors in a mental hospital. In their article, "Preliminary Report on the Application of Contingent Reinforcement Procedures (Token Economy) on a 'Chronic' Psychiatric Ward," *Journal of Abnormal Psychology* 73 (1968): 37–43, they describe in some detail how their token system worked. So well developed was this system that some patients had "the ultimate in reinforcement"—a kind of "carte blanche" that entitled them to all the privileges of the token economy. In our cash economy these patients had the equivalent of a good "credit rating" and could use a credit card approach to the expenditure of tokens.

22. M. Seligman, "Fall into Helplessness," *Psychology Today* (June 1973): 43 ff.

23. Ibid., p. 45.

24. Ibid., p. 108.

25. "De-Indexing the Government," *Wall Street Journal*, 6 May 1974, p. 16.

SUGGESTED READINGS

FULLER, P. "Operant Conditioning of a Vegetative Human Organism." *American Journal of Psychology* 62 (1949): 587–590.

GOOREY, A. "Treatment of a Compulsive Horse Race Gambler by Aversion Therapy." *British Journal of Psychiatry* 114 (1968): 329–333.

HAMBLIN, R.; BUCKHOLDT, D.; BUSHELL, D.; ELLIS, D.; and FERRITOR, D. "Changing the Game from 'Get the Teacher' to 'Learn.'" *Trans-Action* (January 1969): 20–31.

LANG, P., and MELAMED, B. "Case Report: Avoidance Conditioning Therapy of an Infant with Chronic Ruminative Vomiting." *Journal of Abnormal Psychology* 74 (1969): 1–8. See also White, J., and Taylor, D. "Noxious Conditioning As a Treatment for Rumination." *Mental Retardation* (February 1967): 30–33.

LENT, J. "Mimosa Cottage: Experiment in Hope." *Psychology Today* (June 1968: 51–58. For two additional articles on behavior modification in the treatment of the mentally ill and retarded, see Ayllon, T. "Intensive Treatment of Psychotic Behavior by Stimulus Satiation and Food Reinforcement." *Behavior Research and Therapy* 1 (1963): 53–61; and Atthowe, J., and Krasner, L. "Preliminary Report on the

Application of Contingent Reinforcement Procedures (Token Economy) on a 'Chronic' Psychiatric Ward." *Journal of Abnormal Psychology* 73 (1968): 37–43.

MAHONEY, M., and THORESEN, C. *Self-Control: Power to the Person,* Monterey, Calif.: Brooks/Cole, 1974.

SKINNER, B. *Walden Two.* New York: Macmillan, 1948.

———. "Contingencies of Reinforcement in the Design of a Culture." *Behavioral Science* 11 (1966): 159–166.

WATSON, J., and RAYNER, R. "Conditioned Emotional Reactions." *Journal of Experimental Psychology* 3 (1920): 1–14.

2

environmental design

The next time you board a bus or enter an airport terminal, note the way people have distributed themselves in the available seats. If it is not very crowded, you will observe a consistency in the way individuals maintain spatial distance between themselves and their neighbors. One general rule that seems to hold is that strangers will never take adjoining seats if other empty seats are available. Thus, when strangers board a bus containing, for example, ten double seats, you can be relatively certain that no double seat will be filled (two passengers sitting abreast) until *each* has been occupied by one person first.

There seem to be definite consistencies in the ways humans govern the space around them, that is, the manner in

Consulting Editor: Terri Snow, Interior Designer, Reid and Tarics Associates, San Francisco which they regulate the distance between themselves and other persons. The term for such spatial regulation is *territoriality*, and the territorial imperative is practiced by humans and lower animals alike. The underlying principle of territoriality is that many species of life desire and attempt to maintain a specified amount and *quality* of space for themselves. Return again to our example of strangers on a bus: If you don't believe that the territorial imperative operates strongly among humans, get on a bus or subway car occupied by only one other passenger and plop yourself down next to him.

Psychological research is valuable in the service of man only insofar as it reveals insights or suggests solutions concerning human problems. The study of territoriality has been vitally important to man's destiny because it has focused attention on problems basic to the very survival of human life. From the investigation of the territorial imperative has come the understanding that the prolonged violation of spatial requirements (e.g., overcrowding) leads to behavioral pathology in the affected organisms and (in lower animals) sometimes even to death. Fortunately, though, this research also suggests ways to avoid such consequences and even to improve on the quality of living through *environmental design*. Let us begin our survey of this subject with an unusually colorful, if bizarre, experiment.

THE IMPACT OF OVERCROWDING

From the observation loft of psychologist John Calhoun's barn, you could easily look down into the four interconnecting pens that constituted a sort of "rat city."[1] Calhoun built the pens so that he could study the impact of overcrowding on animal behavior, and as one gazed into the pens, the results of that overcrowding were graphically, almost pornographically, apparent.

In the two end pens, farthest from the "center-city" area, a sense of tranquillity prevailed, enforced by a dominant male rat, who guarded the only runway into the pen, keeping all but a harem of females out of the area. Thus, the number of animals in these two end pens was kept at a low level of population density. This was not the case, however, in the middle pens, where you observed what can best be described as an inner-city slum. Here, in pens with unguardable accesses, masses of rats moved freely about, feeding, feuding, and fornicating in terribly overcrowded conditions.

The tragic impact of this overcrowding was apparent in almost every phase of the rats' daily lives and was expressed in almost every kind of social pathology possible. Consider, for example, the constellation of behaviors involved in proper maternal behavior. In the end pens females continued to function normally in birth and post-birth functions, but it was a totally different story in the densely crowded middle pens. There, normal nest-building activities were disrupted and eventually terminated; the infant mortality rate soared to over 90 percent (as compared with 50 percent in the end pens); pups that did survive birth were often abandoned or, worse, eaten; and half the females themselves died of pregnancy-related difficulties.

Social relations among rats in the middle pens also suffered. Bizarre behavior predominated: pansexualism, cannabalism, rape—you name it; these rats probably performed it. Out of this social turmoil, a strange male class system emerged, one very different from that existing in rat colonies where population density is normal.

At the top of this class system were a few dominant, aggressive animals (about one for every dozen males), but unlike their dominant counterparts in normal rat populations, who hold their dominion for lengthy periods of time, the middle-pen aggressive rats were periodically ousted from their position, often in free-for-all battles with their pen mates. Calhoun emphasizes that these aggressive, dominant males were the most normal males in the middle pens, yet "even they exhibited occasional signs of pathology, going berserk, attacking females, juveniles and the less active males, and showing a particular predilection—which rats do not normally display—for biting other animals on the tail."[2]

Below these dominant rats, a second class of adult males could be identified, the "pansexuals." Seemingly unable (or unwilling) to differentiate between appropriate and inappropriate sex partners, these moderately active animals made overtures to literally everything that moved: male rats, female rats, even juvenile rats. These pansexuals were often the target of attack by the dominant males (who would, however, accept their sexual attention), but they would seldom embroil themselves in the status free-for-alls that erupted in the middle pens.

A third class of rats might best be labeled the "outcasts." These animals presented something of an enigma to the observer: In the densely populated middle pens, they walked alone. They were the isolates in the crowd, the friendless, never befriending. They ignored their fellow rats (even females in heat) and were ignored in return. In appearance, these rats were the healthiest animals around, "fat and sleek," their bodies unscarred by battle; yet they "moved through the community like somnambulists," and "their social disorientation was nearly complete."[3]

Then there were the "probers." This fourth class of rats was, to Calhoun, the strangest class of all. Like the outcasts, the probers were subordinate, resigned from the struggle for dominance; but unlike the outcasts, who were inactive (somnambulistic), the probers were hyperactive, more so than any class of animals in the pens. They were also far from being hermits; they desired contact with other rats, particularly sexual contact, and they would go to extreme lengths to get it.

The prober was, in every sense of the words, a furry sexual pervert. Pity the hapless estrous female who crossed his path. There is, in normal rat mating behavior, a certain etiquette involved, a series of little niceties that add a romance to the act. First, the male pursues the female to her home. Then he waits patiently outside while she retires into her burrow. When she finally emerges, then, and only then, does the courtship ritual culminate in sexual relations. The prober observes the first step of courtship behavior: He chases the female to her burrow entrance. But that is where chivalry ends. The prober has no patience for the rigors of delay. Instead, he follows the female inside the burrow, copulating with her in a final burst of hypersexual frenzy. Then, if there are any dead rat pups in the nest area, he eats them.

It is difficult to convey in words the degree of social pathology exhibited in the densely populated middle pens. Calhoun came about as close as one can when he described what he saw as a "behavior sink. . . . The unhealthy connotations of the term are not accidental," he wrote. "A behavioral sink does act to aggravate all forms of pathology that can be found within a group."[4]

John Calhoun is not the only scientist to find a relationship between animal overcrowding and social pathology. Other investigators, using other animals, have reported similar findings.[5] But what do these findings portend for *human* behavior? Are they applicable? At the least, they seem to suggest that if lower animals are so powerfully affected by population density, possibly man, the highest animal, might be influenced to some degree also. Just *how* affected will be determined by studies concentrating on human overcrowding, and it is to these studies that we now turn.

In many ways Chicago is a unique American city. No other metropolis has a State Street, a John Hancock center, a major league ball park without lights. Yet in one sense Chicago is no different from its sister cities. It has an overpopulation problem. Recently, a team of investigators examined the impact of overcrowding on Chicago's inhabitants.[6] These scientists wanted to know if packing individuals into a limited amount of space might lead to various kinds of pathology, the kinds of dysfunctional behavior exhibited by animals living in behavioral sinks. In order to find out, they examined the relationship between population density (the number of persons per acre) and five measures of pathology:

1. *Standard mortality ratio.* Does overcrowding lead to shorter life?
2. *General fertility rate.* Does overcrowding lead to a reduction in the birth rate?
3. *Public assistance rate.* Does overcrowding lead to ineffectual parental care of the young?
4. *Juvenile delinquency rate.* Does overcrowding lead to asocial, aggressive behavior?
5. *Admissions to mental hospitals.* Does overcrowding lead to psychological breakdowns?

What did they discover? Something unexpected. When appropriate statistical controls were implemented,[7] no relationship was found between population density (people per acre) and the various measures of pathology. Did this mean that at the human level overcrowding did not lead to the kinds of dysfunctional behaviors found in densely populated animal colonies? The results seemed to indicate that such was the case. But wait a moment, reasoned the investigators. Possibly the number of individuals per acre was not an appropriate measure for determining the impact of overcrowding in an urban setting. After all, with the advent of high-rise apartment buildings (and other new forms of urban multiple-dwelling units), the number of people living on an acre might not be so important as the way they are living in structures distributed throughout that space. For example, 350 people living on a block of two-story dwellings might be more overcrowded than 1,500 individuals living in a high-rise apartment complex.

With this consideration in mind, the scientists devised four new measures of population density, all based on structural factors rather than on simple head count per acre: (1) the number of persons per room, (2) the number of rooms per housing unit, (3) the number of housing units per structure, and (4) the number of residential structures per acre. When the five measures of pathology are examined in relation to these new definitions of population density, a whole new picture emerges. Now there is a noticeable statistical relationship between pathology and overcrowding. The persons-per-room measure shows a particularly strong relationship with four of the five pathologies—mortality, fertility, public assistance, and juvenile delinquency—suggesting that when one's living quarters become overcrowded, the chances of behavioral sink activity increases. (Most recent studies suggest that the psychological state of a population may impose its own peculiar spatial imperatives. Prisoners, for example, require more personal space than college students do.[8]) Back in 1966, Edward Hall, the well-known author of *The Hidden Dimension*, had already foreseen that the number of persons per room would be a crucial variable in determining the well-being of city dwellers:

> Proper screening can reduce both . . . disruptions and . . . overstimulation, and permits much higher concentrations of populations. Screening is what we get from rooms, apartments, and buildings in cities. Such screening works until several individuals are crowded into one room; then a drastic change occurs. The walls no longer shield and protect, but instead press inward on the inhabitants.[9]

ENVIRONMENTAL DESIGN AND TERRITORIALITY

Think about Hall's comment for a moment. Is there not a seed of an intriguing idea lurking there? He states that "Proper screening . . . permits . . . higher concentrations of populations. Screening is what we get from rooms, apartments, and buildings in cities." Doesn't this observation suggest that *architecture* might be used to combat urban overcrowding and its potential for behavior pathology? Might not architects, by developing new screening designs, create structures that would provide city dwellers with a sense of adequate personal space, even in densely populated areas? A whole new discipline called *environmental design* has evolved, in which architectural know-how is applied in the service of man. The basic premise underlying environmental design is that spatial arrangements in architectural design can regulate human behavior. Proceeding from this assumption, the psychologist and the architect can work together in creating environments that will benefit man.

Because the products architects design are so much a part of everyday life, we often fail to realize how effectively they can regulate our behavior. This fact was driven home forcefully to one of the authors and a friend during a trip to New York. Forced to wait an hour at one of the terminals at Kennedy International Airport, they sat down in the waiting room to talk. Unfortunately, the chairs were so uncomfortable that they had to get up and spend their time walking and browsing around the gift shops. The author clearly remembers grumbling at the time about the "stupid designer who could build such useless pieces of furniture." You can imagine his chagrin, then, when, a few months later, he discovered the chairs had *purposely* been built to be uncomfortable. Robert Sommer, professor of psychology at the University of California, explains:

> In most [airline] terminals it is virtually impossible for two people sitting down to converse comfortably for any length of time. The chairs are either bolted together and arranged in rows theater style facing the ticket counters, or arranged back-to-back, and even if they face one another they are at such distances that comfortable conversation is impossible.

> The motive for the . . . arrangement appears the same as that in hotels and other commercial places—to drive people out of the waiting areas into cafes, bars, and shops where they will spend money.[10]

Sommer points out that one designer has gone as far as developing a chair that "exerts disagreeable pressure upon the spine if occupied for over a few minutes. . . ." The chair is being purchased by American businessmen who don't want their customers to get too comfortable for too long in one place.

As we pointed out earlier, the major concern of environmental designers is not to produce uncomfortable chairs but, rather, to design environments that will allow man to live a happier, healthier, more meaningful life in the space allotted to him. They are already making progress. You can see the fruits of their labor in the "New Towns" springing up across America, in the contained community buildings like the Marina Towers in Chicago, in the judicious use of greenery and recreational areas in apartment complexes and suburban housing developments. You may suspect that the environmental design movement will be even more significant in the years ahead, particularly as the citizenry becomes increasingly ecology conscious.

In an intriguing article Sommer even suggests that the principles of environmental design might be used to create more satisfying environments for people living in institutions. To make his point, he draws a contrast between an effectively designed playland for children (Storyland Park in Pennsylvania) and two mental hospitals in New York, both designed to conform to the needs of the state rather than those of the patients.

> Storyland is intended as a childhood imagination come true. Besides the junior fire engine, there is a Western town with a real jail where each child can be sheriff. There are tunnels

to crawl through, walls to climb, things to take apart, an absence of no-nos—in short, everything to delight and interest the child. Buildings are child-sized, with small doors and windows, tiny tables and chairs, all to the child's scale.

One cannot say the same of Rockland or Pilgrim State Hospital, each located in progressive New York State. . . . It would be possible, although somewhat difficult, to design a large state hospital as a Utopia for schizophrenics. . . . This would require that society recognize the legitimacy of the patient's way of life. For a patient who happens to be labeled schizophrenic, it means explicit recognition that withdrawal from social intercourse is a legitimate *modus vivendi*, acceptance of the fact that some people find no place to hide in society and turn within themselves for solace. Strange mannerisms, bizarre dress, and crazy talk are all means for keeping other people at a distance.

Knowing the schizophrenic's need for isolation, it is possible to design mental institutions that make it easy for him to withdraw. Instead of long corridors and open dayrooms, we could provide many private areas, lockers, and dressers where he could keep his belongings, and wooded areas where he could be secluded or build a shanty. A good architect can design for isolation and solitude just as creatively as he designs for custody and enforced behavior change.[11]

Sommer doesn't believe that economic considerations are keeping such hospitals from being built; he makes a convincing argument that they would be less costly than traditional hospitals. Rather, he believes the reason is "society's reluctance to underwrite an institution that is basically subversive to society's own values." After all, where would society be if everyone chose to live isolated and alone, abhorring social contact with his fellows?

Would it be wise to use architectural design to construct a mental institution affording patients complete social isolation? This is a difficult question to answer, involving as it does many issues, including the right of the patient versus the needs of the society and the conflict over whether a schizophrenic is "sick" and should be "cured." There is no question, however, that environmental design can be, and has been, used to improve the lot of the mentally ill and the retarded. Reports in the psychological journals attest to the role of color patterns and spatial design of wards in making patients happier. Individuals in other types of institutions have also been helped by environmental design. In hospitals, for instance, architectural and medical knowledge have been combined to produce entire rooms that are best described as therapy enclosures:

> The hyperbaric chamber where barometric pressure and oxygen content are regulated to treat circulatory disorders and gas gangrene; metabolic surgery suites where body temperature can be reduced to slow metabolic rates before difficult surgery; the use of saturated atmospheres for serious cases of burns; artificially cooled, dry air to lighten the thermal stress on cardiac cases; and the use of electrostatic precipitation and ultraviolet radiation to produce completely sterile atmospheres for difficult respiratory ailments and prevention of cross-infection from contagious diseases.[12]

In a related study of hospital architecture, it was found that corridor design plays a significant role in determining the amount of time a nurse spends with her patients. The researchers discovered that nurses working in radial, or circular, corridors gave patients "significantly more" attention than did the nurses in charge of straight, perpendicular, or parallel corridors.[13] This finding has obvious implications for future hospital construction.

Investigations of office designs also suggest applications. One English experimenter, who examined the floor plans of an insurance company in Manchester, discovered that the "small office arrangement produces the best possibility for the formation of a group with clear identity and concepts of itself as a discrete and simple entity. On the other hand, the [large] 'open plan' office allows for more *possibilities* of interpersonal contact and group formation."[14] Another study, this one at an engineering division of the Ford Motor Company, showed that attractive landscaping will instill a sense of community between workers and managers, reduce the clutter of "out-of-date and unnecessary" paperwork, and promote office efficiency in general.[15]

Another aspect of environmental design is called *cue management*: controlling a given behavior by strategically arranging the critical stimuli that elicit it. To appreciate how this technique works, we'll first have to go back a decade.

OBESITY HAS ITS PLACE, ALSO ITS TIME AND TASTE

In 1964 a researcher named A. Stunkard reported the results of a simple but important study.[16] He asked a group made up of obese and normal-weight subjects to visit his laboratory at breakfast time. They were given only one previous instruction: Do not eat any food in the early morning hours before the visit to the laboratory. When they arrived, Stunkard had each visitor swallow a gastric balloon that continuously recorded their stomach contractions. Then, at regular fifteen-minute intervals, he asked the subjects, "Do you feel hungry?" They, in turn, answered "yes" or "no," giving Stunkard a measure of how stomach contractions correlate with subjective experiences of hunger. The results for normal subjects were predictable: Their reports of hunger correlated directly with their stomach contractions. "For the obese, on the other hand, there [was] little correspondence between gastric motility and self-reports of hunger." In other words, "whether or not the obese subject [describes] himself as hungry seems to have almost nothing to do with the state of his gut."[17]

If the obese person does not experience hunger as a result of stomach contractions, then what does motivate him to eat and then overeat? This question intrigued Columbia University psychologist Stanley Schachter. Through a series of experiments, he came to the following conclusion: "Eating by the obese seems unrelated to any internal, visceral state, but is determined by external, food-related cues such as the sight, smell, and taste of food." Schachter recognized, of course, that everyone's eating is, to some extent, influenced by his immediate environment. Most tourists, for example, are not hungry for meat after watching a gory bullfight. For normal people, however, situational factors are not dominant, whereas for the obese "internal state is irrelevant, and eating behavior is determined largely by external cues."[18]

One of the most interesting experiments to document Schachter's beliefs took place at Saint Luke's Hospital in New York, where two researchers worked with an unstimulating, liquid nutritional supplement, similar to Metrecal or Nutrament. Eleven subjects (six very obese and five normal) were restricted to this diet for periods extending from one week to many months. The results, reports Schachter, were

> dramatic and startling. The food consumption of [a typically obese] subject dropped precipitately the moment she entered upon the experimental regimen, and it remained at an incredibly low level for the duration of the experiment. . . . On the other hand, the food consumption of the normal subject dropped slightly on the first two days, then returned to a fairly steady [level].[19]

In other words, the eating behavior of the obese subject went down when the food was presented in an unappetizing manner whereas the normal subject continued to eat according to his physiological needs.

Taste is not the only external cue for obese eating behavior. Even the perception of time will have an impact on whether a fat person judges himself to be hungry. To demonstrate this, Schachter studied the relationship between obesity and rapid time-zone changes. He hypothesized that fat people, being externally directed, would quickly adjust to local eating schedules when flying from one time zone to another, whereas normally weighted people (eating in response to internal, visceral cues) would experience discordance between their internal clocks and external time changes. A study of over 200 Air France flight personnel proved Schachter correct. Only 11.9 percent of the obese employees complained of time changes on the European run, but 25.3 percent of normal-weight subjects were disturbed by the discrepancy between American mealtimes and their physiological states. "It does appear," concludes Schachter, "that fatter flying Frenchmen are less troubled by the effects of time changes on eating."[20]

The findings of Schachter and other investigators shed light on the problem of why past approaches to treating obesity have often been long-term failures. Many doctors prescribe amphetamines or noncaloric bulk-producing substances for their overweight patients in order to reduce the physiological symptoms of food deprivation. "Unfortunately," notes Schachter, "these symptoms appear to have little to do with whether or not a fat person eats." Instead, Schachter recommends a diet based on *environmental management of cues.*

> Restricted, low-calorie diets should be effective as long as the obese dieter blinds himself to food-relevant cues or as long as he exists in a world barren of such cues. [In the Saint Luke's Hospital study], the subjects did, in fact, live in such a world. Restricted to a bland liquid diet in a small hospital ward, the fat subjects lost impressive amounts of weight. Back in real life, however, the subjects quickly regained their original weights.[21]

Although Schachter's technique of managing environmental cues to combat obesity has not yet been attempted on a mass scale, accumulating scientific evidence suggests that, once it is tried, such a procedure should be valuable in weight control. Tardiness in use of the technique is a consequence of its newness rather than of difficulty in its implementation. As a matter of fact, once the pound-conscious reader is made *aware* of Schachter's findings, he can begin to use environmental cue management in the service of his own weight reduction. Beginning a diet in a house devoid of attractive, high-calorie foods; keeping away from gourmet shops and steering a wide path around favorite Italian restaurants; making a commitment not to prepare rich, enticing meals—these are just a few of the numerous ways a person can make his environment a less attractive place in which to get fat.

Environmental cue management appears today to be a potent design technique with a wide variety of practical uses. For example, Dr. David Shapiro of the Harvard Medical School has suggested that smoking is actually a conditioned response to specific environmental cues. Heavy smokers, he notes, are more likely to light up in certain situations than in others (e.g., while watching TV, when driving a car, directly after meals, and during any period of stress). In one experiment Shapiro attempted to break the causal link between these cues and smoking by conditioning volunteer subjects to smoke on a new cue, presented at random intervals by a portable, hand-operated watch timer. For one week the timer presented cues at each smoker's normal smoking rate. Every week thereafter the number of programmed cues per day was cut by four. The results were encouraging. Shapiro writes: "Out of the 40 volunteers, all of whom showed some reduction during the program, 27 decreased their smoking rate to twelve or fewer cigarettes and 19 to eight or fewer cigarettes."[22] Other studies show that cue management can strengthen study habits, reduce neurotic behaviors, and help us to maintain an organized life.[23]

ENVIRONMENTAL DESIGN: WHAT'S IN IT FOR US?

The possible applications of environmental design have been highly touted in the media of late, and we suspect that the field will grow rapidly, especially now that architects, engi-

44

Psychology: What's in It for Us?

neers, and even politicians are becoming interested. Just recently, the California State Legislature approved the budget for a plan to train police to evaluate different city locations, specifying what environmental factors encourage crime (e.g., poor street lighting). This information could then be made available to urban planners, who, in turn, can take design steps to make the buildings or parks in these areas safer. Current research on environmental design will touch all aspects of our society, from improving the educational atmosphere in the classroom to making resort areas as pleasant as possible, from structuring home interiors that facilitate family communication to building museums that help us to better appreciate art.

NOTES

1. J. Calhoun, "Population Density and Social Pathology," *Scientific American* 206 (1962): 139–148.
2. Ibid., p. 146.
3. Ibid.
4. Ibid., p. 144.
5. See, for example, E. Hall, *The Hidden Dimension* (New York: Doubleday, 1966) and V. Wynne-Edwards, "Population Control in Animals," *Scientific American* 211 (1964): 68–74.
6. O. Galle, W. Gove, and J. McPherson, "Population Density and Pathology: What Are the Relations for Man?" *Science* 176 (1972): 23–30.
7. Controls for social class and ethnic status.
8. J. Dabbs et al., "Personal Space When 'Cornered': College Students and Prison Inmates," *APA Proceedings* (1973): 213–214.
9. E. Hall, *The Hidden Dimension* (New York: Doubleday, 1966), p. 175.
10. R. Sommer, *Personal Space: The Behavioral Basis of Design* (Englewood Cliffs, N.J.: Prentice-Hall, 1969).
11. R. Sommer, "Planning Notplace for Nobody," *Saturday Review*, 5 April 1969, pp. 68–69.
12. Ibid., p. 68.
13. D. Trites et al., "Influence of Nursing-Unit Design on the Activities and Subjective Feelings of Nursing Personnel," *Environment and Behavior* 2 (1970): 303–334.
14. W. Ittelson et al., *An Introduction to Environmental Psychology* (New York: Holt, 1974), p. 360.
15. Ibid., p. 361.

16. A. Stunkard and C. Loch, "The Interpretation of Gastric Motility," *Archives of General Psychiatry* 11 (1964): 74–82.
17. S. Schachter, "Some Extraordinary Facts About Obese Humans and Rats," *American Psychologist* 26 (1971): 129.
18. Ibid., p. 130.
19. S. Schachter, "Obesity and Eating," *Science* 161 (1968): 753.
20. S. Schachter, "Eat, Eat," *Psychology Today* (April 1971): 79.
21. Ibid.
22. D. Shapiro, G. Schwartz, B. Tursky, and S. Shnidman, "Smoking on Cue: A Behavioral Approach to Smoking Reduction," *Journal of Health and Social Behavior* (June 1971): 111.
23. M. Mahoney and C. Thoresen, *Self-Control: Power to the Person* (Monterey, Calif.: Brooks/Cole, 1974).

SUGGESTED READINGS

ARDREY, R. *African Genesis.* London: Colins, 1961.

———. *The Territorial Imperative.* New York: Atheneum, 1966.

———. *The Social Contract.* New York: Atheneum, 1970.

CALHOUN, J. "Population Density and Social Pathology," *Scientific American* 206 (1962): 139–148.

GALLE, O.; GOVE, W.; and MCPHERSON, J. "Population Density and Pathology: What Are the Relations for Man?" *Science* 176 (1972): 23–30.

HALL, E. *The Silent Language.* New York: Doubleday, 1959.

———. *The Hidden Dimension.* New York: Doubleday, 1966.

HALL, E., and WHYTE, W. "Intercultural Communication: A Guide to Men of Action." *Human Organization* 19 (1960): 5–12.

MAHONEY, M., and THORESEN, C. *Self-Control: Power to the Person.* Monterey, Calif.: Brooks/Cole, 1974.

MORRIS, D. *The Naked Ape.* New York: McGraw-Hill, 1967.

———. *The Human Zoo.* New York: McGraw-Hill, 1969.

SOMMER, R. *Personal Space: The Behavioral Basis of Design.* Englewood Cliffs, N.J.: Prentice-Hall, 1969.

———. "Planning Notplace for Nobody." *Saturday Review.* 5 April 1969, pp. 67–69.

STUDER, R., and STEA, D. "Architectural Programming, Environmental Design, and Human Behavior." *Journal of Social Issues* 22 (1966): 127–136.

WYNNE-EDWARDS, V. "Population Control in Animals." *Scientific American* 211 (1964): 68–74.

3

biofeedback:
turning on the power
of your mind

If you had walked into Dr. David Shapiro's laboratory at the Harvard Medical School awhile back and looked around, you might have thought you were witnessing a patient's physical examination. After all, the young man seated nearby was obviously having his blood pressure checked, the inflatable cuff already wrapped snugly around his upper arm. If, however, you lingered in the room awhile, you'd soon realize that this examination was like no other you had ever seen. Whoever heard of a patient having his blood pressure tested twenty-five times in one sitting, and this to the accompaniment of flashing red lights, strange tones, and even an occasional slide of a *Playboy* nude? Better yet, who ever heard of a patient's blood pressure going *down* under such conditions? Yet that is exactly what happened when Shapiro and his colleagues asked a group of young men to lower their blood pressure using *biofeedback*.[1] How did they do it?

To learn the answer to this, you first have to know what biofeedback is.

WHAT IS BIOFEEDBACK?

Imagine that you are visiting your first English pub and that your host challenges you to a game of darts. Never having played, you graciously decline and then, in the finest American spirit, run out, buy a set, and begin practicing in your hotel. After the first hundred tosses, you begin getting a feel for the game; by the next day you're ready to go out and challenge the queen's finest.

You have learned your dart game well. But suppose you were forced to practice your throws blindfolded, with plugs in your ears. Could you ever perfect your toss under these conditions? No. Improvement would be impossible because you lack the vital component of learning: *feedback* concerning your performance. Deprived of visual feedback, unable to gain *knowledge of results* concerning your throwing accuracy, your plight would be hopeless.

We use feedback so regularly in our everyday lives that we seldom realize how pervasive and important it is. Yet as one eminent scholar has pointed out, "Every animal is a self-regulating system owing its existence, its stability and most of its behavior to feedback controls."[2] It is only when we are suddenly deprived of our normal opportunity to receive feedback (e.g., in the case of sudden blindness) that we come to understand its momentous value for our very survival.

The term *feedback* is of relatively recent origin, coined around the beginning of this century by pioneers in radio. Mathematician Norbert Wiener, a founding father of research in feedback, concisely defined it as "a method of controlling a system by reinserting into it the results of its past performance."[3] Thus, a dart player learns to control his performance by observing and acting upon the results of his previous tosses.

What, then, is biofeedback? It is simply a particular *kind* of feedback, feedback from different parts of the body: the brain, the heart, the circulatory system, the different muscle groups, and so on. Biofeedback training is the procedure that allows a person to tune in to his bodily functions and, eventually, to control them. Without such training, most of us would never be able to receive feedback from our internal worlds, feedback that is absolutely necessary if we wish to gain mastery over all aspects of our behavior. Without it, we are no better off than the blindfolded dart thrower, unable to observe the results of our probes into inner space.

In a typical biofeedback training session, a subject obtains information about his inner world by hooking up with equipment (biofeedback machines) that can amplify one or a number of his body signals and translate them into readily observable signals: a flashing light, the movement of a needle, a steady tone, the squiggle of a pen. Even unconscious body states give off energy that can be measured. Small increases in hand temperature, for example, will cause more heat to be released from the hand. Similarly, increases in muscle tension will accelerate electrical activity at the surface of the skin. Just as a stethoscope amplifies heartbeat sound waves, biofeedback machines monitor these subtle energy shifts and translate them into flashing lights, clicking noises, or some other signal accessible to our normal senses. When several functions are monitored at once, the results can be aesthetically pleasing. Subjects hooked up to special equipment are actually able to produce a light and sound show with their body waves, to "watch the 'music' of their minds and bodies flicker across various screens in a dazzling matrix of colors, each coded to a different function."[4]

Once a person is able to recognize his body waves, he soon learns to *control* them at will. Nobody knows why this happens; it just does. And the machines are only a temporary necessity; after a little practice—the time varies, depending on what body function the person is trying to control—he is able to carry on without mechanical aids. When used in this manner, instrumentation is analogous to the training wheels on a child's bicycle, which are discarded once the youngster has learned to keep his balance. If you prefer a more exotic description, think of a biofeedback machine as a "space-time demolisher," allowing a person to achieve control over his nervous system in a shorter period of time than would be possible without it. A yogi spends many years learning to control his brain waves; the average person using biofeedback training can learn to begin controlling *his* in a matter of hours.

AN EXAMPLE OF HOW
BIOFEEDBACK TRAINING WORKS

If it weren't for the metal disks on Eric's throat, he might be mistaken for an ordinary student preparing for exams. In Eric's case, however, the test he is studying for is taking place while he reads: He is being examined for *subvocalization*, the tendency to mouth words silently while reading. Such a habit limits reading speed to a ceiling of about 150 words per minute while it increases reader fatigue.

The metal disks on Eric's neck are electrodes, small microphones designed to record the minute bioelectric potentials generated by the movement of his vocal muscles. These potentials are fed into an amplifier known as an *electromyograph*, or *EMG machine*, and translated into a signal. The signal will tell Dr. Curtis Hardyck, director of the project, whether Eric is subvocalizing. (Before the advent of advanced electromyographic techniques, it was literally impossible to detect subvocalization.) When the muscles of Eric's larynx are relaxed, the amplitude of the signal is low. However, when he talks at a conversational level, the amplitude of the signal rises appreciably. Thus, if the amplitude of the EMG signal is high while Eric is reading silently, he can be diagnosed as a subvocalizer.

If Eric's EMG results indicate subvocalization, he will learn to overcome it via biofeedback training. Hardyck has utilized such an approach with dozens of subvocalizers, and in an overwhelming number of cases, the results have been dramatic and swift: Patients learn to kick the subvocalization habit in one to three hours.[5]

The method of treatment is relatively simple. The patient is seated in a comfortable chair; electrodes are placed on each side of his Adam's apple; and he is given a book to read. He is informed that a tone will come on if certain speech-muscle activity is present. In order to demonstrate this, the patient is asked to whisper. As he does, the tone comes on. He is then told to relax. When he does, the tone terminates. The patient is encouraged to turn the tone on and off until satisfied that he can control its activation at will. Once he believes he can, the biofeedback session begins. The patient is instructed to read but to keep the tone off as much as possible. In short order, the tone remains off, and the subvocalization problem is overcome.

It should be emphasized that biofeedback plays the central role in helping readers overcome subvocalization. Hardyck observes that "attempts to reduce the speech muscle activity by instruction alone were not successful. In the majority of cases the subjects were not aware of their subvocal activity even when told they were subvocalizing, and they were unable to reduce or to control it without the auditory feedback."[6]

Consider the components of Hardyck's biofeedback blueprint. A patient has a problem. It is determined that the problem has a clearly defined basis in some specified activity of the body. Through instrumentation the patient is permitted to monitor that specific behavior, to tune in to his inner world. The activity is represented by a signal of some kind, and the patient is instructed to change the signal while he observes it. If the patient is able to do as he is asked, the inappropriate bodily activity will be modified or eliminated. *It is important to note that the patient is never told to "slow down his muscles" or "speed up his heart"; instead, he is asked to "keep the tone off" or "make the light dimmer."* People are so out of touch with themselves that direct attempts to change a subtle behavior will frequently achieve the opposite of the desired result.

BIOFEEDBACK TRAINING IN THE EXPLORATION OF HUMAN CONSCIOUSNESS

Until recently man could catch only fleeting glimpses of the unlimited universe that is his mind. William James, the eminent turn-of-the-century psychologist, spent a major portion of his life studying altered states of consciousness, yet lamented that "my own constitution shuts me out from their enjoyment almost entirely."[7] Like so many explorers of the mind, James was relegated to the role of secondhand observer. For more than fifty years since James, research into altered states of consciousness has consisted of little more than scattered reports of mystical experiences, reminiscences of spaced-out drug users, and a lot of speculation.

Biofeedback training has created a major revolution in the study of human consciousness, for no longer is consciousness a hapless victim of chance, mood, or chemistry. Through biofeedback training, man is learning to *choose* his state of being, is able to explore new experiences in a systematic, controlled way *without* relying on unstable and often dangerous drugs. You might say that he can change his mind without losing his head.

Although biofeedback training of consciousness is a recent development, credit for pioneering work should go to Hans Berger, a German scientist who discovered the existence of brain waves in the period following World War

I. After sticking two electrodes from a crude galvanometer onto the scalp of a seventeen-year-old mental patient, Berger noticed that the meter indicator registered an electrical response. After five more years of research, Berger was able to establish conclusively the existence of two distinct brain-wave patterns, which he named *alpha* and *beta*. He also showed a relationship between brain-wave patterns and mental states: Beta seemed to be associated with concentration, such as that involved in doing an arithmetic problem, whereas alpha seemed to accompany states of nonconcentration or passivity.

Since Berger's first successful experiment, the technology for studying brain waves has improved enormously. Researchers now use what is commonly called an *EEG machine*, or more technically, an *electroencephalograph*. In simplest terms the EEG machine consists of three parts: a set of electrodes, which are attached to the scalp with a harmless paste; a brain-wave amplifier, and finally, a device for recording or displaying changes in brain-wave patterns. This recording device is usually a row of inked pens pressing against a continuously unwinding roll of graph paper. The pens oscillate in tune with the brain's changing electrical rhythm, tracing out a brain-wave picture that can be studied, analyzed, or hung on the wall as pop art.

Using this advanced machinery, science has expanded Berger's original description of brain-wave activity from two to four patterns: alpha and beta, plus *theta* and *delta*. Beta is the highest brain wave (meaning that it has a frequency greater than 14 cycles per second) and is usually associated with normal waking experience, such as reading this book. Just below beta is alpha (8 to 13 cycles per second), a state most often described as pleasant, passive, and relaxed. Next down the psychic scale is theta (4 to 7 cycles per second), an intriguing rhythm because it is associated with both creative thought and, occasionally, anxiety. Delta (½ to 6 cycles) occurs almost exclusively during sleep.[8]

Like so many important innovations, the discovery that man could control his brain waves came almost by accident. In 1958 at the University of Chicago, where Dr. Joseph Kamiya was conducting sleep research, he decided to try an unusual experiment. "I became fascinated by the alpha rhythms that came and went in the waking EEG's," said Kamiya, "and wondered if, through laboratory experiments with this easily traced rhythm, a subject could be taught *awareness* of an internal state."[9] What the doctor found provided quite a surprise: Not only could the human guinea pigs learn to identify the alpha and nonalpha states but "they were able to control their minds to the extent of entering and sustaining either stage upon our command."[10]

Kamiya's findings precipitated a minor revolution in experimental psychology. To identify your brain-wave states— that was interesting. But to *control* them—that was downright fascinating. The problem now was finding a simple system for teaching subjects brain-wave control. Kamiya himself hit on the answer: biofeedback training. He devised circuitry that would translate the occurrence of alpha waves, as measured by the EEG machine, into a tone. Each time a subject produced alpha waves, he would simultaneously generate a tone. When he stopped, the tone would also stop. The subject had only one task: to find some way to keep his alpha tone on as long as possible. As it turns out, many people trained in this manner can learn to produce alpha at will in a relatively short period of time (three to ten hours).

In the decade since Kamiya's pioneering experiment, the research on training brain waves has accelerated geometrically. Not only alpha, but beta, theta, and even delta have come under voluntary control, at least in the laboratory. The machinery has also been modified. The tone can be amplified to indicate increases in brain-wave intensity, or it can be replaced by another form of feedback, such as a light. The basic technique, however, remains the same: The brain-wave impulses that elude normal consciousness are piped through

EEG machine electrodes, amplified by delicate circuitry, and finally translated into light, sound, or some other medium that is accessible to the senses. Once tuned into himself, almost anyone can learn to identify specific brain-wave states and, in a relatively short period of time, start to control them.

From the beginning of brain-wave biofeedback training, most people have been interested in learning to control their alpha brain waves, for obvious reasons. Alpha is a relatively *easy* frequency to monitor and control. In addition, the relationship between alpha and experiences of pleasure was (and is) an incentive to imaginative scientists. (Some individuals find alpha so exciting that they try hard to become alpha subjects in university research projects. Biofeedback investigator Erik Peper once received a phone call at 2:00 A.M. from an excited would-be volunteer. Peper was perturbed but not surprised. "Whenever EEG feedback is studied," he claims, "unpaid, uninvited volunteers go to great lengths for the opportunity to tune in to alpha." Peper also reports sighting students walking around New York City with headsets and earphones firmly clamped on, monitoring their own brain waves.) Recent evidence indicates, however, that theta is an even *more* intriguing brain-wave state. Zen masters, for example, go *past* alpha into theta during deep meditation. Theta is also the state people reach just before sleep, a time when writers and artists occasionally get some of their best ideas. Some creative people habitually keep a pencil and paper near their bedside in order to record insights that occur during presleep theta states (Chapter 11).

Experiments at the Menninger Foundation in Topeka, Kansas, have convinced Dr. Elmer Green that people who travel into theta are able to experience psychic events that are normally *buried* in the unconscious mind. He believes that theta training may be very useful for analytic therapy. "Through the use of feedback techniques for deep relaxation, psychiatrists will be able to develop in many patients a deep reverie in a short time [and] with selected cases . . . normally unconscious material of analytic value should be recoverable."[11] Green also believes that theta training will enable man to explore higher levels of awareness, including creative consciousness, without the use of drugs.

What is theta training like? One woman who participated in a three-month program at Green's lab describes it this way: Each day she would go into a darkened, empty room, casually place electrodes on her head, and then plug the wires into an EEG feedback circuit. Guided only by the cool, dim lights from the surrounding machines, she made her way to a nearby couch. "I would attempt to get into a quiet, relaxed, blank mind state, and yet not fall asleep," she recalls with a smile. "And that's not easy to do!" She would proceed to stretch out, calm herself, and wait for a tone to indicate that she was in theta. Her task was to become aware of her experience while the tone was sounding. "Fifty percent of the time . . . I couldn't pull into consciousness what was just under the level of consciousness, and I probably would have gone to sleep if it weren't for the tone." At other times, however, she experienced sensations and images "so very personal that I wouldn't want to discuss it except with a psychiatrist or guru." The material she *would* discuss went something like this:

> I saw fantastic images. . . . There was an American Indian with a feather headdress on a long refectory table. . . . There were some images that were reminiscent of my own night-time dreams. . . . On a couple of occasions an eye, just a very large eye . . . pulsating with light and life. . . . There were also differences in body sensations . . . feeling my body rising as if a tingling, buzzing from inside the core of my limbs was making me rise from the table. . . .[12]

Somewhere between waking consciousness and sleep lies a wealth of unexplored images and experiences. By learning to control our brain waves, we are beginning to gain access to these fascinating mental products. As biofeedback training gives us the means to prolong the period of time we can remain in the theta state, we might well come even closer to understanding and experiencing creative thought.[13]

RATIONAL OR AESTHETIC CONSCIOUSNESS?

If you take a human brain and surgically cut the corpus callosum, which connects the left and right hemispheres, an interesting thing happens: The two sections begin to operate independently. This was amply demonstrated by a bizarre experiment in which a scientist first severed the two hemispheres of a monkey's brain, then conditioned each side to perform contradictory tasks. One section had learned that when a bar was pressed, a banana would be given as a reward; the other had learned to expect a shock when the bar was touched. When both hemispheres were in the presence of a bar, a grotesque fight ensued between the right paw (controlled by the left side of the brain) and the left paw (controlled by the right side). One part of the monkey's brain tried to press the bar; the other struggled desperately to prevent the bar from being pressed.[14] A similar phenomenon is exhibited in humans who have undergone split-brain surgery in order to curb uncontrollable seizures. Although capable of leading a normal life, a split-brain patient will frequently find himself doing unusual things, such as "buttoning his shirt with one hand and unbuttoning it with the other."[15]

Apart from calming seizures in patients, split-brain research has provided dramatic evidence that man can experience at least two, and possibly more, levels of consciousness *simultaneously*. Investigations show that the hemispheres operate semi-independently even when connected. Roger Sperry, a biologist, notes that each hemisphere "seems to have its own separate and private sensations, its own perceptions, its own concepts, and its own impulses to act, with related volitional, cognitive, and learning experiences."[16] Furthermore, each hemisphere tends to specialize. One side of the brain, generally the left, is usually associated with verbal activities, and the right hemisphere with spatial activities such as drawing and designing. Researcher Joseph Bogen has described the left as "rational, digital, and objective," the right as "emotional, analogical and subjective."[17]

In our linear, ordered culture, the left hemisphere, or rational brain, clearly dominates our thinking, but its rule is not absolute. At times, during some of our waking hours and perhaps during most of sleep, the right hemisphere, or nonrational brain, takes over.

It seems that domination by one hemisphere occurs by default; the adjacent hemisphere simply turns off. Physiologically this means that one side remains in the busy beta state while the other slows down into the rhythmic, less active alpha state. An aesthetic awareness would indicate that the rational brain is resting in alpha; conversely, a logical consciousness would mean that the nonrational brain has shifted to a lower frequency.

Further experiments using biofeedback from the rational and artistic brains should yield interesting results, perhaps even destroy some myths. For example, are women really less rational than men? Preliminary evidence already indicates that there is more hemispheric integration in women than in men. Women are more likely to emerge from left hemisphere surgery with less pronounced speaking difficulties than men. Similarly, "right hemisphere brain surgery seems to impair women's art aptitude less than it does men's."[18]

The big breakthrough will come when man learns through biofeedback training to switch into rational or artistic consciousness at will, simply by turning off the interfering hemisphere of the brain. This is exactly the goal that Bob Ornstein is trying to achieve at the Langley Porter Neuropsychiatric Institute. Is it possible for man to gain voluntary control of his artistic and rational thought processes? "The equipment we need is just at the area of being put together," Ornstein says.[19]

Ornstein believes that learning to generate brain waves in specific areas of the brain, rather than producing gross alpha or theta, is a quantum jump in brain research. More precise control of brain waves, he predicts, will enable man to master a greater repertoire of moods, emotions, and experiences. He also believes that man will discover more than two simultaneous consciousnesses. "I think we've got many more than two," he says.[20]

BIOFEEDBACK TRAINING IN THE TREATMENT OF MEDICAL PROBLEMS

Biofeedback training has opened a doorway into our minds. It has given us a technology and a procedure for exploring our innermost thoughts and feelings while allowing scientists to peek over our shoulders and record what we experience. Yet we do not want to give the impression that the only value of biofeedback training is in taking "the inner trip." One of the most exciting applications of this new scientific development is in the field of medicine. One of the major contributions of biofeedback research has been demonstrating that patients can and should play a more active role in achieving better health through the voluntary control of their own nervous systems. Using biofeedback training, doctor and patient can cooperatively mount an assault against human illness, an assault in which the patient becomes his own prescription for good health. Some medical problems will, of course, still have to be treated by traditional procedures (drugs, surgery, and so forth), but those people who are amenable to treatment by biofeedback procedures will be afforded the opportunity to acquire more responsibility for, and power over, their own health.

Consider, for example, biofeedback training in the treatment of anxiety. For most people anxiety is one of two kinds. There is the anxiety that is *free-floating*, a general feeling of apprehension that is not attached to any specific type of activity. It is best characterized by the person who says, "I've felt uneasy all day, and I don't know why." A second and more *specific* anxiety occurs while a person is undertaking or anticipating certain types of behavior he dreads, like making a speech or looking down from high places. This kind of anxiety is reflected in the comments of a man waiting for an elevator: "Every time I get into one of these damn things I feel closed in . . . as if I'm not able to breathe." Anyone who suffers from claustrophobia understands what it means to be anxious.

Most doctors agree that one way to reduce both free-floating and specific anxiety is to get patients to relax. The problem, of course, is how? Instructing the person to relax sometimes backfires: Asked to relax particular muscles, the patient may respond by unintentionally tensing them instead. A procedure is needed whereby the patient can receive feedback about his relaxation efforts, and Dr. Thomas Budzynski, at the University of Colorado Medical School, is providing information about such a procedure.[21]

In a typical Budzynski biofeedback training session, electrodes are attached to a patient's forehead so that any movement in the frontalis (forehead) muscle can be detected, amplified, and fed back to the patient through an EMG machine. The task of the patient is to keep the frontalis muscle relaxed. He does this by controlling a tone that rises when the muscle contracts and falls when it relaxes.

Budzynski has chosen the frontalis muscle for biofeedback work because it is a crucial barometer of the patient's relaxation level. Once a person learns to relax his forehead muscle, he will also usually relax his scalp, neck, and upper body, areas of the body that are crucial to a sense of calm.

In addition to its value in helping patients learn to relax, the Budzynski biofeedback training procedure can be used to help a patient overcome specific forms of anxiety. In one remarkable case Budzynski reported to Gay Luce and Erik Peper that he

> liberated a 22-year-old girl from an unbelievable list of phobias, including panic attacks, fear of heights, fear of crowds, fear of riding in cars, and claustrophobia. When systematically confronted with the feared images in a relaxed state, she gradually lost her intense feelings about them. It is almost impossible to remain highly anxious when deeply relaxed.[22]

In two recent case studies Budzynski and his colleague Johann Stoyva used EMG biofeedback successfully to help a forty-two-year-old management consultant combat his public-speaking anxiety (previously this had forced him to refuse several lucrative speaking engagements) and to assist a forty-five-year-old woman in overcoming extreme anxiety at social gatherings.[23] The Budzynski research team has also used EMG biofeedback training in treating tension headaches and insomnia.

Where will all this work lead us? Budzynski gives this buoyant response: "I think doctors are going to lend patients an EMG machine instead of handing out sleeping pills in the future."[24]

At the Baltimore City Hospital, Dr. Bernard Engel and his colleague Dr. Theodore Weiss are using heart-rate biofeedback training to help patients combat coronary problems. In their major study[25] Weiss and Engel were interested in seeing whether eight heart patients could learn to control dangerous irregularities in heartbeat by force of mental discipline alone. The irregularities, called *premature ventricular contractions* (PVCs), are dangerous and their control important because, as Weiss and Engel note, "the presence of PVCs is associated with an increased probability of sudden death."[26]

The heart-rate training took place in a quiet, windowless laboratory, with the patient lying comfortably on a hospital bed. There he was hooked up to a cardiotachometer, which converted his heartbeat into electric signals. These, in turn, were fed into a computer, analyzed, and translated into red, yellow, and green lights on a panel at the foot of his bed. While he was watching his light panel "traffic signal," the patient was told to "drive" his own heart by following the "rules of the road": slow his heartbeat when the red light was on and increase it when the green light appeared. The patient's goal was to keep his heartbeat at a safe "middle speed," signaled by a steady yellow light.

Using his biofeedback traffic signal, the patient first learned to speed his heart, then to slow it, and finally, to keep it beating within narrow normal limits. Most patients cannot describe in words just *how* they accomplish their cardiac control, but by watching the visual display (which gives them feedback about their heartbeat control efforts), they come to "get a feeling" for when they are regulating their heartbeat correctly. One man said he imagined pushing his heart to the left to slow it down, and a woman pictured herself swinging back and forth in attempting to adjust the speed of her heartbeat. Engel explains the control this way: "It's like an athlete who does something well. He's grooving."[27]

Perhaps the most exciting part of the Weiss and Engel work is what happens when the patient is disconnected from his training equipment and sent home to fend for himself. After extensive training on the machines, he finds he *can* take his lessons home with him and regulate his heartbeat without the need for artificial feedback. One of the eight patients has sustained her low PVC rate for almost two years, reporting that she is able to detect and modify her irregular heartbeat without a machine for guidance. Three other patients have also been able to use their biofeedback training to regulate PVC activity away from the hospital.

Learning to regulate cardiac arrhythmias through the power of the mind is not an easy task. Many hours must be spent in getting a feel for PVCs and how to control them. Weiss and Engel are optimistic about reducing training time in the future. "As more nearly optimal conditioning techniques are employed it should be possible to accomplish comparable results in much shorter periods of time," they claim.[28] Even now, however, the many hours spent in training seem worth it. As science writer Gay Luce and biofeedback researcher Erik Peper emphasize:

> training may be fundamentally tedious, and may require a long time, but unlike drugs it gives the patient a sense of mastery over his own body. One of the women in Dr. Engel's group was elated when she could report that she no longer had dizzy spells or thumping in her chest because of her own ability to cope with the symptoms.[29]

There is something about man learning to "drive his own heart" that seems to bespeak the ultimate adventure and, in this sense, a patient who can control his heart seems more intriguing than a doctor who can transplant one. The initial findings of researchers like Weiss and Engel are promising and point to the day when biofeedback training might be used as part of a treatment regimen to aid patients in preventing and combating certain kinds of heart disease.

It seems that individuals can control their blood pressure as well as their heart rate, as we noted in the opening passage of this chapter. To demonstrate this, Dr. Shapiro and his Harvard colleagues conducted the following experiment: A subject was ushered into a light- and sound-controlled cubicle and seated, and a cuff for measuring blood pressure was attached to his arm. A crystal microphone was placed inside the cuff to amplify blood pressure activity from the subject's brachial artery. Once he was comfortable, the patient was told to watch for a blue light signal. This would signify the beginning of a test trial in which he was expected to keep a flashing red light and a tone on as long as possible. The more frequently the light flashed, the better the subject was at controlling his blood pressure. Every time the subject accumulated twenty light flashes, he was rewarded with a five-second peek at a *Playboy* pinup. Under such experimental conditions, subjects rapidly learned to lower their blood pressure.[30]

Why is Shapiro so concerned about teaching persons to lower their blood pressure through biofeedback training? To provide them with a possibly effective method for treating hypertension. It is estimated that approximately one out of every eight Americans suffers from hypertension (elevated blood pressure without a demonstrable cause), a condition that doctors implicate in strokes and heart attacks. Because prolonged periods of high blood pressure can damage the blood vessels and arteries, it is important to find ways to lower the pressure. Drugs have been used for this purpose in the past, but dosage levels and side effects can be problems. It is the hope of men like Shapiro and his colleagues that in the future biofeedback training will augment or replace drug therapy in the treatment of high blood pressure.[31]

Anxiety, heart disease, high blood pressure, and insomnia are some of the important medical problems being treated through biofeedback training. Such training is also used in the treatment of migraine headaches, epilepsy, and the rehabilitation of muscles paralyzed by strokes.[32] Dr. Peter Wellgan envisions the day when ulcers will be controlled or eliminated by training patients to limit the secretion of their gastric juices. This psychologist has good reason to be optimistic. In his study at the University of California (Irvine), thirty-five ulcer patients were able to reduce their stomach acid levels through biofeedback training.[33] There is even evidence that biofeedback can correct dysfunctional muscle spasms. In a recent experiment conducted by Dr. J. Brudny and his colleagues, nine patients were trained to progressively decrease spasms causing distortions in the position of the head and neck. All nine improved discernibly, three "to the point of remaining symptom-free for from several months to over a year."[34]

Just how much of a contribution will biofeedback make to the improvement of the human condition? As of this writing, speculation runs rampant. Some scientists suggest that voluntary starvation and absorption of cancerous growths through blood-flow control might be found feasible.[35] Others see a future where biofeedback training may be used by men to achieve erections and by women to control ovulation, a rather advantageous combination. Then there is composer David Rosenboom, who regulates his mental states to create brain-wave music and who predicts a future for biofeedback in the performing arts. (Rosenboom, the composer of the seventy-two-hour piece "How Much Better If Plymouth Rock Had Landed on the Pilgrims," reported to *The New York Times* that he composed by controlling the emission of certain brain waves and making them into music. He recently gave a brain-wave concert at New York's Automation House.[36]) Even these scenarios are minor, however, compared with the implications of recent studies by Los Angeles researcher Dr. Barry Sterman.

His experiments began innocently enough. Curious to explore the nature of certain isolated, unlabeled brain-wave patterns, Sterman successfully trained laboratory cats, with milk reinforcements, to increase their output of these unusual rhythms.[37] One pattern—the "sensorimotor rhythm"— seemed to make the animals motionless, "freezing" them into rigid positions. This may not seem like much, but closer inspection revealed that this training had some remarkable side effects:

. . . it led to unusually peaceful, unbroken sleep, slowed down the cats' heart rates, and gave them exceptional resistance to certain drugs. Instead of going into convulsions after being exposed to a poisonous compound used in rocket fuels, for instance, these cats took on odd, rigid postures that seemed to ward off the seizures—even three months after their training. This is a clear indication that epileptics may someday learn to control their seizures through biofeedback.[38]

Yet this discovery was only the prelude to a more intriguing sequence of events. As Sterman worked with the cats, he noticed that their feelings of satisfaction, which accompanied the milk rewards, were *characterized by a distinctive brain-wave pattern:* the "post-reinforcement rhythm." Did this mean that the cats could self-induce a feeling of contentment by gaining voluntary control over this rhythm? The experiment was performed, and Sterman soon found himself the owner of some very happy felines. Indeed, the more the animals manufactured this post-reinforcement pattern, "the less they cared about their milk rewards. They just lay down in the conditioning chamber, their eyes closed, purring, as if in a state of bliss."[39]

If such training can be duplicated in humans, the possibilities for "the pursuit of happiness" are enormous. It is not far-fetched to think that someday we may be able to self-induce the beneficial experiences associated with the electrical stimulation of the brain, but without the surgery. Noted science journalist Maya Pines elaborates,

> For people who experience little pleasure in life, such training might be a revelation. It could lead to profound changes in personality, turning a normally tense or grouchy person into one who is fulfilled and well disposed. Possibly this sort of training in early childhood might also reduce the . . . reactions that so often cause aggressive behavior and violence in later life.[40]

BIOFEEDBACK: WHAT'S IN IT FOR US?

Not long ago one of the authors attended a biofeedback
training session at which several persons were learning to
increase their output of alpha brain waves, the state of consciousness that some people find relaxing and pleasant. After
the session a few of the participants were informally asked
to describe what for them was the major value of biofeedback training. "It made me feel good" was the first respond-
ent's reply. "A chance to experience something new, something I might not be able to experience any other way," suggested a second person. "Without the necessity for drugs,"
added a third participant. "It's kind of a personal ecology
trip—you don't despoil your internal environment with artificial ingredients; you use only what you already have."

The achievement of a pleasurable state; an opportunity to
explore untapped frontiers; the chance to practice personal
ecology—all are important advantages of biofeedback training. But perhaps the greatest advantage is one we don't normally think about. It was described most aptly by a fourth
participant, who said simply, "It gave me a sense of dignity."

It is difficult to capture on paper the sense of exhilaration
felt by the person who, through biofeedback training, is able
to master his body through his own power. All his life he
has been taught he cannot control his "involuntary" nervous
system. All his life he has been encouraged to "let the pill
do the job" or "go ask Mr. Jones for the answer." All his life
his capacity to control his own body, his own mind, his own
fate has been challenged, deprecated, even ridiculed. And
then, suddenly, there he is controlling his own nervous system, a man on his own magical mastery tour. "My God, I
really did it by myself, didn't I?" one patient proudly an-
nounced after she had learned to control her own nervous
system. "Yes," answered the doctor, "and that's the beauty
of it."

Biofeedback is important to man because it challenges the simplistic view of human behavior held by many contemporary scientists. Biofeedback-training findings support an alternative concept of human behavior that emphasizes the efficacy of self-control over external control and the need to recognize that man's potential has been sadly underestimated by the scientific community.[41] For the first time experimenters are demonstrating that man can be the master of his own destiny rather than the slave of his juices. Every new disease, every mental state, every "involuntary" behavior brought under conscious control through biofeedback training is a step toward revitalizing man's tarnished self-image. Biofeedback training not only promises to enhance man's control of his internal states, but also offers him a renewed sense of freedom and dignity that will make this control both satisfying and fulfilling.

To be free, one must want to be free. If self-determination is to survive and prosper, people must come to believe— not merely hope or wish—that man is more than a biological automaton, that he is capable of controlling himself, by himself and for himself. People must believe that man has the intuitive wisdom to move in ways that are beneficial both for himself and for others. Biofeedback research is an important scientific enterprise because it is validating these optimistic beliefs with empirical evidence. Even if biofeedback training does not develop as rapidly as anticipated, its value to our democracy—indeed, to the perpetuation of the free spirit everywhere—will still be incalculable.

NOTES

1. A more extensive discussion of biofeedback can be found in M. Karlins and L. Andrews, *Biofeedback* (Philadelphia: Lippincott, 1972). A good article on the topic is G. Luce and E. Peper, "Biofeedback: Mind over Body, Mind over Mind," *The New York Times Magazine*, 12 September 1971, pp. 34 ff.
2. O. Mayr, "The Origins of Feedback Control," *Scientific American*

223 (1970): 111.
3. Ibid.
4. D. Rorvik, "The Wave of the Future: Brain Waves," *Look*, 6 October 1970, p. 91.
5. C. Hardyck and L. Petrinovich, "Treatment of Subvocal Speech During Reading," *Journal of Reading* 12 (1969): 361–368 ff.
6. Ibid., p. 367.
7. W. James, *The Varieties of Religious Experience* (New York: New American Library, Mentor Books, 1958), p. 292.
8. The borders between brain states are somewhat arbitrary. Some researchers, for example, will define alpha as 7 to 14 cycles per second.
9. J. Kamiya, "Conscious Control of Brain Waves," *Psychology Today* (April 1968): 57.
10. Ibid., p. 58.
11. E. Green, A. Green, and E. Walters, "Self-regulation of Internal States," in *Progress of Cybernetics: Proceedings of the International Congress of Cybernetics*, London, 1969, ed. J. Rose (London: Gordon & Breach, 1970), p. 1316.
12. Personal communication, 1971.
13. For a good discussion of the theta brain waves and creativity, see E. Green, A. Green, and E. Walters, "Voluntary Control of Internal States: Psychological and Physiological," *Journal of Transpersonal Psychology* 2 (1972): 1–26 (relevant pages are 12–22).
14. B. Hoebel, Personal communication, 1971.
15. *Newsweek*, 21 June 1971, p. 65.
16. P. Bakan, "The Eyes Have It," *Psychology Today* (April 1971): 64.
17. Ibid., p. 67.
18. Ibid., p. 69.
19. R. Ornstein, Personal communication, 1971.
20. Ibid.
21. See, for example, T. Budzynski, J. Stoyva, and C. Adler, "Feedback-induced Muscle Relaxation: Application to Tension Headaches," *Journal of Behavior Therapy and Experimental Psychiatry* 1 (1970): 205–211.
22. Luce and Peper, "Biofeedback: Mind over Body, Mind over Mind," p. 132.
23. Ibid., p. 136.
24. T. Budzynski and J. Stoyva, "Biofeedback Techniques in Behavior Therapy and Autogenic Training" (unpublished manuscript, University of Colorado Medical Center, 1971).
25. T. Weiss and B. Engel, "Operant Conditioning of Heart Rate in Patients with Premature Ventricular Contractions," *Psychosomatic Medicine* 33 (1971): 301–321.
26. Ibid., p. 319.

27. *Newsweek*, 21 June 1971, p. 62.
28. Weiss and Engel, "Operant Conditioning of Heart Rate in Patients with Premature Ventricular Contractions," p. 320.
29. Luce and Peper, "Biofeedback: Mind over Body, Mind over Mind," p. 134.
30. D. Shapiro et al., "Effects of Feedback and Reinforcement on the Control of Human Systolic Blood Pressure," *Science* 163 (1969): 588–590.
31. Initial results look promising. In an experiment involving actual patients, Dr. Aimee Christy and Dr. John Vitale of the San Francisco Veterans Administration Hospital report that blood pressure biofeedback training was successful with two labile hypertensive patients. At Harvard Dr. Herbert Benson has helped five of his seven patients lower their blood pressure in the laboratory using biofeedback. "Nevertheless," as Benson notes, "to generalize this training—and keep blood pressure down at home and at the office—may require some revision of behavior and even re-evaluation of life style, as well as some professional behavior therapy."
32. Work with migraine headaches has been carried on by Dr. Sargent and Dr. E. Green; epilepsy studies have been conducted by Dr. J. Korein and his colleagues and also by Dr. M. Sterman; a report of biofeedback training being used in the rehabilitation of muscles paralyzed by strokes appeared in *Medical World News*, 10 December 1971, p. 35, under the title "Muscles Retrained at Home."
33. P. Wellgan, Personal communication of prepublication data, 1974.
34. N. Miller, "Applications of Learning and Biofeedback to Psychiatry and Medicine," in *Comprehensive Textbook of Psychiatry*, 2nd ed., eds. H. Kaplan and B. Sadock (Baltimore: Williams & Wilkins, in press).
35. Green, Green, and Walters, "Voluntary Control of Internal States: Psychological and Physiological," p. 23.
36. Karlins and Andrews, p. 140.
37. M. Pines, *The Brain Changers* (New York: Harcourt, 1973), pp. 83–85.
38. Ibid., pp. 83–84.
39. Ibid., p. 84.
40. Ibid.
41. The humanistic psychology movement is aimed at scientifically demonstrating man's potential for functioning at levels traditional psychologists have denied or ignored.

SUGGESTED READINGS

BROWN, B. "Recognition of Aspects of Consciousness Through Association with EEG Alpha Activity Represented by a Light Signal." *Psychophysiology* 6 (1970): 442–452.

BUDZYNSKI, T.; STOYVA, J.; and ADLER, C. "Feedback-induced Muscle Relaxation: Application to Tension Headaches." *Journal of Behavior Therapy and Experimental Psychiatry* 1 (1970): 205–211.

DICARA, L. "Learning in the Autonomic Nervous System." *Scientific American* 222 (1970): 30–39.

GREEN, E.; GREEN, A.; and WALTERS, E. "Voluntary Control of Internal States: Psychological and Physiological." *Journal of Transpersonal Psychology* 2 (1972): 1–26.

HARDYCK, C., and PETRINOVICH, L. "Treatment of Subvocal Speech During Reading." *Journal of Reading* 12 (1969): 361–368 ff.

HENAHAN, D. "Music Draws Strains Direct from Brains." *The New York Times*. 25 November 1970.

KAMIYA, J. "Conscious Control of Brain Waves." *Psychology Today* (April 1968): 56–60.

KARLINS, M., and ANDREWS, L. *Biofeedback: Turning on the Power of Your Mind*. Philadelphia: Lippincott, 1972.

KASAMATSU, A., and HIRAI, T. "An Electroencephalographic Study of the Zen Meditation (Zazen)." In *Altered States of Consciousness*, edited by C. Tart, pp. 489–501. New York: Wiley, 1969.

KIEFER, D. "Meditation and Bio-Feedback." In *The Highest State of Consciousness*, edited by J. White. New York: Doubleday, Anchor Books, 1972.

LUCE, G., and PEPER, E. "Biofeedback: Mind over Body, Mind over Mind." *The New York Times Magazine*. 12 September 1971, pp. 34 ff.

MILLER, N. "Learning of Visceral and Glandular Responses," *Science* 163 (1969): 434–445.

PINES, M. *The Brain Changers*. New York: Harcourt, 1973.

SHAPIRO, D.; TURSKY, B.; GERSHON, E.; and STERN, M. "Effects of Feedback and Reinforcement on the Control of Human Systolic Blood Pressure." *Science* 163 (1969): 588–590.

WEISS, T., and ENGEL, B. "Operant Conditioning of Heart Rate in Patients with Premature Ventricular Contractions." *Psychosomatic Medicine* 33 (1971): 301–321.

4

electrical stimulation
of the brain

José Delgado is a man who does some very interesting things with electricity. Once he used electric power to fix a bull-fight, a wise move, considering he was in the ring at the time and, as a Yale professor of medicine, not exactly an accomplished matador. Why did Dr. Delgado undertake such a Plimptonesque assignment? To demonstrate the behavior control potential of a scientific procedure known as *electrical stimulation of the brain* (*ESB*). The demonstration was possible because the bull was doctored before it entered the ring; tiny electrodes, capable of delivering minute electrical pulses when activated by remote-control radio signals, were surgically implanted into its brain. Once this was accomplished, Delgado could engage his adversary without fear. When the bull began his charge, the Yale surgeon simply pressed a button on his radio transmitter and watched as the bull, properly stimulated, halted abruptly and lost interest in the flashing red cape.

James Olds is a man who does some very interesting things with rats. Back in the 1950s this psychologist also used electric power and discovered the wellspring of Elysium in a most unexpected place. Olds had wondered what would happen if he electrically stimulated the brain of a rat. To find out, he placed an electrode inside the rodent's head and "turned on the juice" whenever the animal approached a designated spot on a large table. How did the rat respond? Did it stay clear of the area where the intercranial stimulation had been delivered (meaning the electrical pulse had been aversive), or did it approach the locale again (meaning the electrical stimulus had been rewarding)? Olds found that his experimental subjects seemed to "get a charge" from the electricity. That is, they approached the area where they had received the electrical stimulation and centered their activities on that spot.

In order to clarify his rather unexpected findings, Olds conducted a series of experiments, the results of which pointed to a series of "pleasure and pain centers" in the rat's brain.[1] When the rat was electrically stimulated in a pleasure center, it performed acts aimed at reproducing the stimulation. Conversely, when it was stimulated in a pain center, it tried to avoid further stimulation. The reinforcement value of ESB is awesome, indeed. Rats, for example, have been known to press a lever up to 7,000 times an hour to get an intercranial electric jolt, ignoring food, sleep, and sex in the process. One story (unconfirmed) tells of a rat that was allowed to electrically stimulate itself overnight. Upon returning to the laboratory the next morning, the experimenters found the furry rodent flat on his back, exhausted, his paw reaching toward the lever for one last electrical satisfaction.

The pioneering work of José Delgado and James Olds has generated enough scientific interest to make ESB research one of the major investigative fields of contemporary psychology. Has any of this work included brain stimulation with humans? Yes. ESB scientists have not ignored their fellow men. Reading Delgado's milestone book *Physical Control of the Mind*, one gets a feeling for the power of brain implants in influencing human behavior. Delgado begins by stating that brain stimulation in man has "blocked the thinking process, inhibited speech and movement, or in other cases has evoked pleasure, laughter, friendliness, verbal output, hostility, fear, hallucinations, and memories."[2] He then draws on his own work to support such a claim.

Some of Delgado's research reports read like science fiction scenarios. In one set of experiments, for example, electrical stimulation of the brain produced pleasurable sensations in three epilepsy patients. One patient, a bright and attractive thirty-year-old woman, experienced a pleasant feeling of relaxation when stimulated. Her talking increased, as did the intimacy of her subject matter. Her enjoyment must have been intense. Normally reserved and poised, the patient "openly expressed her fondness for the therapist (who was new to her), kissed his hands, and talked about her immense gratitude for what was being done for her."

A second female patient was not to be outdone. Reporting that she liked the stimulation "very much" and that it caused an "enjoyable tingling sensation in the left side of her body 'from my face down to the bottom of my legs,' " the patient became increasingly talkative and flirtatious as stimulation continued, finally expressing her desire to marry the therapist.

Even a young male patient seemed emotionally attached to the doctor. After receiving several electrical stimulations which he fully enjoyed ("hey!" he exclaimed, "you can keep me here longer when you give me these; I like those"), he expressed fondness for the male interviewer, one such expression accompanied by a "voluptuous stretch." Further stimulation got the patient talking about sexual activity. At one point he said, "I was thinkin' if I was a boy or a girl—which one I'd like to be." Following another stimulation, he remarked with evident pleasure, "You're doin' it now," and then he said, "I'd like to be a girl."

Delgado has used ESB to elicit more than sexual responses. In one patient stimulation in the motor cortex section of the brain evoked a flexion of the right hand. Even at the doctor's request, the patient was unable to keep his fingers extended when stimulation was administered. Unable to control his fist-clenching response, the patient commented aptly: "I guess, Doctor, that your electricity is stronger than my will."

In another patient, a female, stimulation of the brain produced an acute sense of fear. The fear, which lasted for the duration of the electrical stimulation, was perceived as real and involved the woman's belief that a horrible disaster was about to befall her.

Finally, assaultive behavior was elicited in a young female with a history of uncontrollable violent rage. Her electrically induced fits of pique were similar to those she experienced spontaneously. One such stimulation occurred while the patient was happily playing a guitar. After a few seconds of the stimulation, she hurled the guitar away and attacked a nearby wall.

Delgado is not alone in reporting rather dramatic behavior alterations as a function of brain stimulation. At Tulane Medical Center, for example, Dr. Robert Heath has published studies that lend further support to the hypothesis that pleasure centers exist in the brains of men as well as in those of rats. In an experiment of particular interest, Heath implanted a series of electrodes into the brains of two patients.[3] The first, a twenty-eight-year-old man, suffered from narcolepsy, a condition that caused him to go from a state of total wakefulness to deep sleep in a matter of seconds. In an attempt to combat the narcolepsy, Heath outfitted the patient with a self-contained, transistorized brain-stimulation unit that he could wear on his belt and operate by himself.

The stimulation unit had three buttons. Each one, when depressed, triggered an electrical stimulus in a different segment of the patient's brain. After pushing the various buttons several times, the patient reported he felt "good" when he depressed button number 1, "lousy" when he pushed button 2, and "OK" when he held down button 3. From his button-pressing pattern it became obvious that button number 1 "must be doing something right": The patient pressed it to the exclusion of buttons 2 and 3. (The feeling aroused by button 2 was so distasteful that the patient placed a modified hairpin under the button so that it could not be depressed.) When asked why he pushed button 1 so frequently, he replied that it gave him a good feeling, "as if he were building up to a sexual orgasm."

Button number 1 had a bonus value. The electrical stimulation it triggered did more than please the patient; it also alerted him, thereby giving him the means to fight his narcolepsy. Now each time he felt himself "going under," he pushed button number 1 and literally jolted himself out of sleep.

Sometimes, when the narcoleptic state approached so suddenly that the patient didn't have time to press the button before he fell asleep, fellow patients and friends would arouse him by pushing the button for him. Because the patient could control his symptoms with the belt stimulator, he was able to return part time to his job as a nightclub entertainer.

Heath's second patient, a psychomotor epileptic with impulsive behavior problems, also tended to concentrate his self-stimulation activity on one button. This time, however, the button chosen delivered a stimulus that was irritating rather than pleasurable. When the patient was asked why he persisted in choosing the unpleasant stimulus, he explained that he wanted to bring into clearer focus a memory suggested by the stimulation.

The patient was also able to experience a pleasurable sensation by pressing a button triggering stimulation in the septal region of his brain. Upon experiencing this stimulation, the patient often made verbal reference to sexual topics. When asked why he spoke of sexual subjects during the pleasurable stimulation, he replied, "I don't know why that came to mind—I just happened to think of it." This finding—that pleasurable brain stimulation seems to be associated with a sexual-motive state—is similar to the results Delgado obtained with his three epileptic patients.

One of the most interesting findings of the Heath study is that a patient attempted to bring an elusive memory to awareness by vigorously stimulating one section of his brain. This has led experimenters to wonder if electrical stimulation of the brain might not be used to elicit the recall of memories in other people. Work conducted in Montreal by brain surgeon Wilder Penfield and his associates suggests it can be.[4]

William James once used the term *stream of consciousness* to refer to one aspect of man's cognitive behavior. Penfield's description of his patients' cognitive behavior when they were electrically stimulated is in metaphorical harmony with James:

> There is an area of the surface of the human brain where local electrical stimulation can call back a sequence of past experience. . . . It is as though a wire recorder, or strip of cinematographic film with a sound track, had been set in motion within the brain. The sights and sounds, and the thoughts, of a former day pass through the man's mind again.[5]

Penfield went fishing in the human stream of consciousness for memories. His fishing pole was a thin wire; his hook, an electrode; his bait, an electrical stimulus. And he was successful. When he stimulated the cerebral cortex, his patients recalled moments from the past. What they recalled was not very significant (one young boy heard his mother on the phone), but the memories were so vivid that the patients had difficulty believing the events weren't actually taking place. One woman who heard an orchestra playing every time the electrode was activated "believed that a Gramophone was being turned on in the operating room on each occasion, and she asserted her belief stoutly in a conversation some days after the operation."[6] Another patient, a male, clearly heard his cousins laughing, a somewhat disquieting experience, since his cousins were in South Africa and he was on an operating table in Canada.

ESB: WHAT'S IN IT FOR US?

Penfield's findings concerning the electrical elicitation of memories have fascinated many contemporary writers. Some of them feel that such work might be of great benefit to man in the not-to-distant future. Author and scientist Arthur C. Clarke has suggested one benefit. People who reach old age and have no interest in the future may have an opportunity to relive the past and to create again those they knew and loved when younger. "Even this . . . might not be a preparation for death, but the prelude to a new birth."[7] Even more provocative is Clarke's suggestion that artificial memories could be composed, taped, and then fed into the brain by electrical or other means. This ultimate form of entertainment has been imagined in D. C. Compton's novel *Synthajoy*.[8]

It is not necessary to travel into the realm of science fiction, however, to discover the benefits of ESB for man. Already, this procedure has been successfully employed to control involuntary movements in victims of cerebral palsy and Parkinson's disease, to alleviate intractable pain in cancer patients, and to help epileptic patients head off seizures.

ESB has also been used in treating psychological problems such as schizophrenia and excessive anxiety. ("One doctor, treating a woman whose chronic depression had led to several suicide attempts, found that he could control the level of her anxiety by turning a knob."[9]) And we have already discussed how Robert Heath outfitted one patient with a portable ESB unit so that he could combat his narcolepsy by self-administered electrical jolts.

In medicine's counterpart of a military "search and destroy" mission, ESB has also been used first to locate and then to eliminate small areas of the brain implicated in some patients' uncontrollable fits of rage. Consider the case of Thomas, a talented epileptic engineer who would brutally attack his wife or children during periods of rage he couldn't control. He was given ESB treatment by Harvard neurosurgeon Vernon Mark and his colleagues Frank Ervin (psychiatrist) and William Sweet (surgeon). "First, Mark and Ervin sent electric current into different parts of Thomas' brain; when the current sparked his rage, the doctors knew they had found the offending cells [during such a procedure, one patient struck a technician in the jaw.[10]] Surgeons Mark and Sweet then destroyed them, and in the four years since, Thomas has had no violent episodes."[11]

There is even preliminary evidence that ESB might help some individuals overcome certain sexual problems. Considering what we already know about Olds' self-stimulating rats and Heath's self-stimulating humans, such an application shouldn't come as much of a surprise. According to recent reports in the mass media, Heath helped a young homosexual attain his first successful heterosexual experience by first exposing him to weeks of repeated electrical stimulation in the "pleasure center" of his brain. *Newsweek* reports that "the patient's first orgasm with a woman was monitored by Heath and his associates on an EEG in the next room" and that according to Heath, "the machine registered violent spikes."[12]

A promising technology related, in spirit, to ESB is a method called *electrosleep*. Essentially, it is a process for inducing a relaxed state by applying a low-voltage electrical current (12-20 volts) across a person's skull. Because the method originated in the Soviet Union and because the term is so easily confused with high-voltage *electroconvulsive* (or *electroshock*) therapy, the first mention of electrosleep tends to inspire instant distrust, even among some psychiatric professionals. In fact, electrosleep is a painless, humane procedure without any observable negative side effects. Since the voltage is applied externally to the skull, electrosleep does not require surgery. More importantly, it appears to be quite successful in alleviating symptoms of anxiety and depression, even among patients resistant to drug therapy.

How does electrosleep treatment feel? Dr. Saul Rosenthal, an associate professor of psychiatry at the University of Texas Medical School and a prominent American researcher in the field, explains:

> The patient usually reclines for the treatment in a relatively quiet, semidarkened room. Two small disk electrodes wrapped in soft cloth and slightly dampened in [salt water] for better electrical connection are placed over the eyes and serve as cathodes. Two similar electrodes over the mastoid processes serve as anodes. They are all held in place by a light mask. During the treatment, the patient feels a mild, tingling sensation under the electrodes that should not be uncomfortable. If it does produce discomfort, the current is turned down until it does no longer. The patient usually feels calm and relaxed during the treatment but does not necessarily fall asleep. He is not unconscious at any time, and one may speak to him during the treatment.[13]

Normally there are five to ten treatments. They last about thirty minutes and are given on successive days. Although no two people respond to electrosleep in exactly the same way, Rosenthal is able to make these generalizations:

In the afternoon after the first treatment, [the patient] may note that he feels very sleepy, will nap for a few hours if this is possible, and then reports feeling quite relaxed and calmed with a marked decrease in anxiety. He will fall asleep readily at night and will report sleeping soundly and waking up alert. During the second day and from then on, the patient will report an increase in energy and in subjective feelings of alertness. He will report more tendency to sleep during the treatments but less of a sedated feeling following the treatment. Accompanying the decrease in anxiety and increase in energy, an elevation of mood is often seen that is variously described as "contentment" or a "happy high" and often seems to be a very mild euphoria. Subjects ranging from poverty-group housewives to practicing physicians report a subjective increase in ability to perform daily tasks (for the housewife, this may mean an increase in energy to do her cleaning and cooking and a regained ability to enjoy these functions, while a physician may report increased ability to handle his practice because of decreased background anxiety). Many report a decreased level of frustration with inconsequential irritations. For example, a secretary reported her reaction at getting off at the wrong exit of an expressway as "so what, I can always get back on and turn around," while a physician reported that he did not get aggravated at being served a mistaken order in a restaurant, but just felt it wasn't consequential enough to be irritated about. Nighttime sleep usually continues to be good. Follow-ups after periods of a few weeks to six months reveal that patients continue to report a decreased level of background anxiety and improved nighttime sleep.[14]

One experiment to test the effects of electrosleep involved twenty-two psychiatric patients who suffered primarily from anxiety, depression, and insomnia.[15] "They had been referred specifically for electrosleep treatment," recalls Rosenthal, because they had not responded to the usual medications "including minor tranquilizers, tricyclic antidepressants, hypnotics, and . . . phenothiazines." After completing a battery of psychological questionnaires, half the patients were actually given electrosleep treatments; the other eleven, a control group, were given simulated treatments; that is, "the electrodes and mask were applied and the machine timer was started, but no electricity was applied." All the subjects went through five half-hour sessions which were administered, as usual, on successive days.

The results were striking, even by Rosenthal's expectations. The clinical ratings of neurotic symptoms for those who actually received electrical stimulations fell sharply from 11.3 to 3.2, while ratings for the control group went from 12.2 to 9.5, a relatively small decline. Reductions in levels of anxiety and insomnia were particularly noticeable. While Rosenthal is cautious about touting such findings, he obviously believes that electrosleep provides us with a valuable therapeutic tool. Electrosleep is not as specific in its effects as ESB can be, but it does have the advantage of being both simple to administer and free from postoperative effects. In addition, the technology of electrosleep is already developed to the point where it can soon be available on a large-scale basis.

Perhaps the most exciting use of electrosleep will not be to cure people with psychological complaints, but to make happy people feel even better. During a recent experiment Rosenthal and psychiatrist Lynn F. Calvert gave a series of low-voltage shocks to seven normal subjects. What the researchers expected to find was "a mild sedative effect . . . and no particular effect on mood."[16] Instead, four subjects evidenced reactions ranging from increased activity and alertness to "a mild, comfortable euphoric tranquility" to "a feeling about not worrying about . . . usual daily irritations."[17] One female subject reported after her second treatment: "During the day I would smile for no real reason."[18]

How does electrosleep induce the brain to relax? No one knows for sure, though some scientists believe that the current triggers some kind of "balancing function" in our overstimulated, overanxious bodies. (*Some* effects may also be due to the power of suggestion, not to the electricity.) There is even speculation that electrosleep works directly on the hypothalamus, home of the "pleasure centers" discovered by Olds.[19] Whatever the reason for electrosleep's power, however, it is certain to become more popular, both as an object of psychological research and as a mode of psychotherapy.

ESB: A LOOK AHEAD

As amazing as current medical applications of ESB may seem, it is when we begin speculating on the future uses of this procedure that things really get interesting. As a case in point, let us return to ESB in the treatment of aggression. Vernon Mark and his associates used ESB to locate and destroy brain cells involved in uncontrollable human aggression. Even more dramatic ESB methods have been developed for controlling aggression in lower animals. The person most responsible for developing these methods is the person who risked his life to show how effective they could be. We are referring once again to José Delgado, who, you will remember, stopped the aggressive onslaught of a bull bred for fierceness with one application of ESB.

Delgado's research into the control of aggression through ESB almost has to be seen to be believed. Under the ubiquitous electrical probe, his subjects are little more than electrified automatons, becoming savage or docile at the push of a button. In one widely publicized experiment, Delgado made mother monkeys, who are normally gentle and loving parents, savagely attack their offspring under the influence of electrical brain stimulation. (They would hurl their babies across the cage, just as Thomas the epileptic engineer had hurled his children across the room during uncontrollable fits of rage.) After the stimulation had ceased, the mother monkey would retrieve her crumpled baby and once again hold it lovingly to her breast—until the next electrical stimulus, when she would again go into a violent rage, hurling the baby away once more.

In a more elaborate and even more incredible display of electrical behavior control, Delgado operated on several members of a monkey colony so that he could administer ESB to each one by remote radio control. Looking at the monkeys, with no wires trailing behind them, one found it difficult to tell they had been tampered with at all. It was not difficult to discern the results of the tampering, however. In one experiment the boss monkey of a colony could be made aggressive or passive toward his fellow monkeys by the flip of a switch. According to Delgado, "this demonstrates that peace and war—at least in monkey colonies— are within the control of the scientist."[20] Or within the control of a fellow monkey: In an experimental twist, a small female monkey learned to operate a lever that, when depressed, would deliver electrical stimulation to the brain of a "bullylike" boss monkey. Now when the monkey threatened her, she simply pressed the bar to inhibit his aggressive behavior.[21]

Delgado envisions a day when "cerebral pacemakers, operating in much the same way that cardiac pacemakers now do, will treat . . . violent behavior, by direct stimulation of the brain."[22] How would this work? An intriguing study with a chimp named Paddy suggests one possible way. Delgado outfitted Paddy with a "stimoceiver," an electrode-implantation package (weighing about an ounce) that allows the scientist to record electrical activity from the brain and also to stimulate the brain electrically by remote control. Paddy was then allowed to run free and mix with three other chimps. All the while, however, his brain activity was being monitored and fed into a computer that was programmed to detect specific brain waves associated with periods of excitement and aggressive behavior. Each time the computer picked up these specific brain waves, it automatically triggered a brief electrical stimulation to a section of Paddy's brain that caused a distinctly unpleasant sensation. The punishment had a dramatic effect on Paddy's behavior. Both his activity level and his aggressive acts were reduced. So was the brain-wave activity related to periods of excitement and aggression. Paddy became a very quiet, almost lethargic chimp. This new behavior persisted even after the experiment was terminated, and it was two weeks before Paddy's brain waves and behavior returned to normal.

Delgado fully appreciates the significance of this study for the ultimate control of aggression. "One of the implications of this study," he points out, "is that unwanted patterns of brain activity—for instance those correlated with assaultive or antisocial activity—could be recognized by the computer before they ever reached consciousness in order to trigger pacification of the subject."[23]

José Delgado's research with chimps is fascinating. Yet how relevant is it for understanding and controlling aggression in man? Quite relevant, it seems. The work of Mark and his Harvard colleagues with patients like Thomas and even Delgado's own ESB work with patients exhibiting uncontrollable fits of rage suggest that the basic mechanisms underlying aggression in man might be amenable to the kinds of control being exercised on lower animals. *How* amenable remains to be seen, but from our knowledge of comparative physiology, one speculative observation does seem in order. The brain structures underlying emotive behavior are basically the same in lower animals and man. The similarity of these primitive brain structures in lower and higher organisms makes one suspect that man's emotional behavior might be more open to regulation by brain stimulation than is his intellective functioning, which is controlled by a section of the brain unique to the human species.

Where will the research of men like José Delgado, James Olds, Robert Heath, and Wilder Penfield eventually lead us?

When it comes to assessing the future of brain stimulation, there is no dearth of commentators. Some make gloomy predictions of a *Brave New World* or *1984*; others, like science writer Albert Rosenfeld, are more optimistic:

> One can easily imagine people in the future wearing self-stimulating electrodes (it might even become the "in" thing to do) which might render the wearer sexually potent at any time; that might put him to sleep or keep him awake, according to his need; that might curb his appetite if he wanted to lose weight; that might relieve him of pain; that might give him courage when he was fearful, or render him tranquil when he was enraged.[24]

Author Herman Kahn looks ahead to the year 2000, where he envisions people wearing chest consoles with ten levers controlling electrical stimulation to the brain's pleasure centers. "Any two consenting adults might play their consoles together," Kahn speculates. "Just imagine all the possible combinations: 'Have you ever tried ten and five together?' couples would ask. Or, 'How about one and one?' 'But I don't think you should play your own console; that would be depraved.'"[25]

In the not-too-distant future, some scientists believe that man may use ESB to regain the use of limbs rendered useless by various forms of brain damage (e.g., the paralyzing effects of a stroke). At the Stanford Research Institute, Dr. Lawrence R. Pinneo and his colleagues are combining computer technology and ESB to create an "artificial brain" capable of directing limb movement by electrically stimulating specific segments of the brain stem in the proper sequence. In preliminary studies brain-damaged monkeys were able to accomplish basic motor responses (e.g., scratching, reaching out for food and bringing it to the mouth) when they were hooked up to the artificial brain.[26] If it were tied into different electrode-implantation sites, such an arti-

ficial brain might conceivably be programmed to afford the
user all sorts of visual, tactile, and auditory sensations without his ever having to leave the comfort of the living room
easy chair. "Molecular Biologist Leon Kass of the National
Academy of Sciences projects a world in which man pursues
only artificially induced sensation, a world in which the arts
have died, books are no longer read, and human beings do
not bother even to think or govern themselves."[27]

Researchers have already been successful in simulating a
primitive visual experience within the brain. In England, for
example, an elderly nurse suffering from glaucoma and
retinal detachment was helped with the aid of electronics to
"see again": Specifically, eighty small platinum electrodes
were placed strategically over the cortex of her right hemisphere. When stimulated, they produced the sensation of
"seeing" a spot of light. The British scientists who performed this operation are confident that such an electrode
display can be attached to a sensing device, analogous to a
photoelectric cell, thus enabling blind people "to avoid
obstacles when walking and possibly to read print or handwriting."[28] Meanwhile, Pinneo is currently developing computer programs that would enable artificial brains to "trigger" the actual experience of "seeing the outside world."
Such a device would, admittedly, be costly at first but
Pinneo is optimistic about the chances for making artificial
brains economically feasible:

> If our system should, in time, prove practical for human use,
> subsidization is a likely prospect from public clinics and
> national health organizations. Meanwhile, advances in com-
> puter hardware miniaturization (such as for NASA), and
> other electronic techniques, should ultimately lead to prac-
> tical, relatively low-cost, general-purpose computers small
> enough to be worn or carried by a human being as part of
> his clothing.[29]

José Delgado also has some predictions about the future

uses of brain stimulation, and they are tied up in his assessment of his own research goals. What are those goals? "I
would like to cure epilepsy, cure mental disturbances and
construct a better world. That's all."[30] He may be on the
way. It was recently reported that one monkey smiled 400,-
000 times in a row in response to consecutive stimulations in
the rhinal fissure of his brain. If these findings are applicable
to man, just think what a few key implantations could do in
a city like New York.

ESB: THE MORAL ISSUES

Of course, not all reactions to ESB have been as positive as
Delgado's. On the contrary, some people warn that ESB, or
any other form of surgery for psychological purposes (*psychosurgery*), will lead to dehumanizing, totalitarian, and even
sadistic practices. For these anxious observers, developments
in ESB conjure up all the anti-utopian visions of Huxley's
Brave New World or Orwell's *1984.*

How well founded are these fears? A few of the arguments against psychosurgery are clearly specious. It is highly
improbable, for example, that a dictator could ever use ESB
to conquer the minds of the citizenry on a massive scale.
Like behavior modification (Chapter 1), ESB requires such
careful and elaborate procedures that "massive implanta-
tion" could occur only in a society where totalitarian rule
was *already an accomplished fact.* As M.I.T.'s Seymour
Ketty has pointed out, "Anyone influential enough to get an
entire population to consent to having electrodes placed in
its head would have already achieved his goal without firing
a single volt."[31] Certainly, the protests against any type of
psychosurgery are illogical, at best. For some brain disorders, such as tumors and blocked blood vessels, psychosurgery is the only known remedy.

Yet there *is* the possibility that psychosurgery can be
abused—if not on a large scale, then in more controlled and

restricted settings such as prisons and mental hospitals. Not that psychosurgery is any more effective than traditional methods of repression (i.e., torture), but it does carry the authoritative stamp of science and, therefore, has the potential to be used as a mask for repression. Naturally, we'd like to think that instances of "psychosurgical repression" are impossible in our democracy; the sad fact, though, is that in 1973 the State of California almost initiated a project to quell the aggressive behavior of certain prison inmates through neurosurgery. Although the program was supposedly designed to detect and curb violence stemming from *physiological* abnormalities, psychologist Stephan Chorover hints that certain officials might have been interested in stifling *politically* motivated protests as well. As evidence, Chorover cites excerpts from an official affidavit describing one prisoner who, in theory, would have been eligible for the program:

_____ was 25, older and more mature than the bulk of the . . . inmates. He was aggressively outspoken, always seeking recruits for his views that the institution and its staff were oppressing all the inmates and particularly the black inmates. He was proficient at karate, and his files showed that he had been observed teaching other inmates karate techniques at another institution. . . . (He) had been one of a half-dozen men who led a work-stoppage and attempted general strike which had lasted for several days. . . . He was continuously in contact with friends and attorneys on the outside who encouraged his activities and provided him with books attacking society. He set a fire in May as a demonstration of his political views.[32]

Incidents such as the aborted California plan have sparked a heated debate among scientists as to the moral and ethical implications of ESB and other methods of psychosurgery. Those fearful of psychosurgery bring up the *Clockwork Orange* issue: Even if a person's behavior is antisocial in the extreme, do we have the right to limit his freedom by physically altering his brain, especially against his wishes? It's one thing, they argue, to operate on a willing patient's brain in order to repair some obvious physiological damage such as a tumor or a traumatic head injury; it's quite another for a scientist to arbitrarily decide that an individual's behavior is "undesirable" and to forcefully change that pattern by surgically implanting electrodes.

Then there is the *deception* question: Does the power of the psychosurgeon to create inner nirvana mislead us into thinking that all human problems are physiological? Will we, in other words, forget that some forms of deviance are more than brain dysfunctions, that they reflect a dissatisfaction with genuine economic and political inequities? Already "the Soviet Union has a notorious reputation for treating political dissenters as if they suffered from mental disorders."[33] The Russian government's treatment of Alexander Solzhenitsyn, as reported in his shattering essay *The Gulag Archipelago*, is one example; the abuse suffered by Zhores Medvedev is another:

> In 1969 the well-known biochemist and gerontologist was dismissed from his scientific post. In 1970 he was forcibly confined to a mental hospital where he underwent various "diagnosis" and "treatment" procedures. His only disorder was his insistence on writing and publishing strongly worded critiques of official Soviet policies. Yet psychiatrists diagnosed him schizophrenic, on the grounds that he engaged in two unrelated activities, gerontology and public criticism.[34]

Coercion and deception are important ethical issues which ought to concern scientists and laymen alike. But it should also remain clear that psychosurgery per se is not an intrinsic evil. On the contrary, for every potential disadvantage of psychosurgery, there seems to be a positive side. While the power of psychosurgery to induce specific and dramatic behavioral changes makes ESB a possible danger in the hands of insensitive men, it also provides humane doctors with a medical tool whose effects are far more specific, and therefore safer, than other modes of medication. (Drugs often have a scattered, damaging impact on the nervous system.[35]) Similarly, while ESB technology may cause us to ignore the political origins of individual deviance, it is equally true that ignorance of surgical therapies can lead to inadequate and even disastrous diagnoses. In one study it was found that eighteen patients who died in a mental hospital were actually suffering from neurological damage in the limbic system of the brain.[36] In theory, many of them could have been saved by psychosurgery.

The problem, then, is not psychosurgery itself, but how to be sure that it is used humanistically. Not an easy problem to solve, but experience to date suggests some helpful criteria: First, psychosurgery should be undertaken only "in cases where pathological disorders of the brain are well-defined."[37] Second, scientists and doctors "must observe strict rules of informed consent" from the patient.[38] Finally, the political and legal rights of those in prisons and other institutions must be reaffirmed in the clearest possible terms. Psychosurgery, like any psychological technique, serves us well only when it serves our inalienable rights.

NOTES

1. See J. Olds, "The Central Nervous System and the Reinforcement of Behavior," *American Psychologist* 24 (1969): 114–132.
2. J. Delgado, *Physical Control of the Mind* (New York: Harper & Row, 1969).
3. R. Heath, "Electrical Self-stimulation of the Brain in Man," *American Journal of Psychiatry* 120 (1963): 571–577.
4. W. Penfield, "The Interpretive Cortex," *Science* 129 (1959): 1719–1725.
5. Ibid., p. 1719.
6. Ibid., p. 1720.
7. A. Clarke, *Profiles of the Future* (New York: Harper & Row, 1963).
8. D. Compton, *Synthajoy* (New York: Ace, 1968).

9. K. Waggoner, "Psychocivilization or Electroligarchy: Dr. Delgado's Amazing World of ESB," *Yale Alumni Magazine* (January 1970): 22.

10. "Probing the Brain," *Newsweek*, 21 June 1971, p. 62.

11. "Man into Superman: The Promise and Peril of the New Genetics," *Time*, 19 April 1971, p. 47.

12. "Probing the Brain," p. 60.

13. S. Rosenthal, "Electrosleep," *World Biennial of Psychiatric Psychotherapy* 2 (1973): 381.

14. Ibid., pp. 383–384.

15. Ibid., pp. 382–383.

16. J. Miller, "Relax! The Brain Machines Are Here," *Human Behavior* (August 1974): 21.

17. Ibid.

18. Ibid.

19. Ibid.

20. Waggoner, "Psychocivilization or Electroligarchy: Dr. Delgado's Amazing World of ESB," p. 22.

21. M. Scarf, "Brain Researcher José Delgado Asks—What Kind of Humans Would We Like to Construct?" *The New York Times Magazine*, 15 November 1970, p. 166.

22. Ibid.

23. Ibid.

24. A. Rosenfeld, *Second Genesis* (Englewood Cliffs, N.J.: Prentice-Hall, 1969).

25. "Man into Superman: The Promise and Peril of the New Genetics," p. 47.

26. L. Pinneo, J. Kaplan, E. Elpel, P. Reynolds, and J. Glick, "Experimental Brain Prosthesis for Stroke," *Stroke* 3 (1972): 16–26.

27. "Man into Superman: The Promise and Peril of the New Genetics," p. 47.

28. L. Pinneo, "Development of a Brain Prosthesis," *Nonhuman Primates and Medical Research* (New York: Academic Press, 1973), p. 345.

29. Ibid., p. 350.

30. Waggoner, "Psychocivilization or Electroligarchy: Dr. Delgado's Amazing World of ESB," p. 21.

31. *Newsweek*, 21 June 1971, p. 67.

32. S. Chorover, "Big Brother and Psychotechnology," *Psychology Today* (October 1973): 48.

33. Ibid., p. 44.

34. Ibid.

35. V. Mark, "A Psychosurgeon's Case for Psychosurgery," *Psychology Today* (July 1974): 33.

36. Ibid., p. 84.

37. Ibid., p. 33.

38. Ibid.

Psychology: What's in It for Us?

SUGGESTED READINGS

DELGADO, J. *Physical Control of the Mind.* New York: Harper & Row, 1969.

DELGADO, J., *et al.* "Intracerebral Radio Stimulation and Recording in Completely Free Patients." *Journal of Nervous and Mental Disease* 147 (1968): 329–340.

HEATH, R. "Electrical Self-stimulation of the Brain in Man." *American Journal of Psychiatry* 120 (1963): 571–577.

"Man into Superman: The Promise and Peril of the New Genetics." *Time.* 19 April 1971, pp. 45 ff.

OLDS, J. "The Central Nervous System and the Reinforcement of Behavior." *American Psychologist* 24 (1969): 114–132.

OLDS, J., and MILNER, P. "Positive Reinforcement Produced by Electrical Stimulation of Septal Area and Other Regions of Rat Brain." *Journal of Comparative and Physiological Psychology* 47 (1954): 419–427.

PENFIELD, W. "The Interpretive Cortex." *Science* 129 (1959): 1719–1725.

PINNEO, L.; KAPLAN, J.; ELPEL, E.; REYNOLDS, P.; and GLICK, J. "Experimental Brain Prosthesis for Stroke." *Stroke* 3 (1972): 16–26.

"Probing the Brain." *Newsweek.* 21 June 1971, pp. 60–68.

ROSENTHAL, S. "Electrosleep." *World Biennial of Psychiatric Psychotherapy* 2 (1973): 377–389.

SCARF, M. "Brain Researcher José Delgado Asks—'What Kind of Humans Would We Like to Construct?'" *The New York Times Magazine.* 15 November 1970, pp. 46 ff.

WAGGONER, K. "Psychocivilization or Electroligarchy: Dr. Delgado's Amazing World of ESB." *Yale Alumni Magazine* (January 1970).

5

animal power

You have to hand it to B. F. Skinner. He hasn't become America's most distinguished psychologist by doing things the traditional way. There was, for instance, the time when he wrote a novel to express his scientific beliefs. Psychologists don't normally do that. Then, recently, he took dead aim at the cherished American notion of freedom, calling it an outmoded concept for modern man. Psychologists don't normally do that either. But in order to describe Skinner's most memorable excursion into the unconventional, we have to return to the days of World War II, when he approached the United States military with his better idea for a missile: using a pigeon as the guidance system (a new kind of homing pigeon).[1]

PIGEONS IN WAR, PIGEONS IN PEACE

It seems that in the early stages of the war American scientists were struggling to develop an effective air-to-ground missile but were stymied by the bulk of the proposed guidance systems, which took up so much space there wasn't enough room to house the explosives. Skinner's logic, under the circumstances, was impeccable. A compact, accurate guidance system was needed. All right, pigeons were compact, inexpensive, possessed the visual skills to "see their way to the target," and most important, were expendable. The problem was: How could a pigeon be trained to become a proficiently performing "feathered Kamikaze"? Skinner had the answer. He would teach the birds their job through his own system of *operant conditioning*, the same system that, you might recall, underlies behavior modification. His would be the first effectively functioning Pigeon Air Guidance (PAG) system.

In the basic training procedure, a pigeon learned to peck at the image of a target (e.g., submarine) projected on a screen. When he pecked correctly, he was rewarded with a portion of grain. From there on, things got more complex. The birds were taught to follow a variety of different land and sea targets, to distinguish these from irrelevant stimuli (e.g., patches that were used to represent clouds or flak), and to track a target for long periods of time without any reinforcement.

The equipment housing the pigeons also got more complex. What began as a crude block-and-hoist apparatus evolved into a sophisticated missile command center for the pigeon-bombardier. How did it work? Skinner explains:

> A lens in the nose of the missile threw an image on a translucent plate within reach of the pigeon in a pressure sealed chamber. Four air valves resting against the edges of the plate were jarred open momentarily as the pigeon pecked. . . . When the missile was on target, the pigeon pecked the center of the plate and all valves admitted equal amounts of air. . . .

But if the image moved as little as a quarter of an inch off-center [as if the missile were very slightly off-target], more air was admitted by the valves on one side.[2]

Nor did Skinner stop there. Deciding that "three heads are better than one," he designed a multiple-bird system to improve guidance accuracy. Three pigeons, each with its own lens and plate, were housed in the nose of the missile. With this arrangement, navigational decisions could be based on a majority decision among the birds, thus lessening the chance that any one bird might endanger the flight through erratic behavior.

The test came in 1944. After several setbacks and numerous design modifications, Skinner was called in to demonstrate his pigeons before a board of the top scientists in the country. He arrived confidently, offering a homing device "unusually resistant to jamming, capable of reacting to a wide variety of target patterns, requiring no materials in short supply, and so simple to build that production could be started in thirty days."[3] And how did the pigeons respond when the chips were down? Did they peck their way to the target? Perfectly. Too perfectly. As Skinner glumly recalls:

It was a perfect performance, but it had the wrong effect. . . . The spectacle of a living pigeon carrying out its assignment, no matter how beautifully, simply reminded the committee of how utterly fantastic our proposal was. I will not say that the meeting was marked by unrestrained merriment, for the merriment was restrained. But it was there, and it was obvious that our case was lost.[4]

Skinner's prophecy was accurate. A short time later word came that the project was to be officially terminated. As we will see (and discuss) later in this chapter, the scientists' prejudice toward using animals to accomplish tasks normally considered to be accomplishable by humans only is quite common and has severely curtailed the effective uses of animal power in the service of man.

Fortunately, in Skinner's case, the efforts of Project Pigeon were not wasted. At a later time the military showed a renewed interest in his ideas, leading to a new research program, Project ORCON (for organic control). Today, the idea of a feathered bombardier doesn't seem so far-fetched. Thanks in large part to the conditioning principles developed by Skinner, animals are currently performing tasks that would have boggled the imagination a few years ago. During the Vietnam War, for example, one of the authors heard a newscaster report that dolphins with knives attached to their snouts had been trained to stab North Vietnamese frogmen infiltrating South Vietnamese waters.

By presenting these examples, we don't want to give you the impression that the only applications of animal power are in warfare or other pursuits detrimental to human life. Once again, harnessing the power of an animal is like harnessing the power of the atom. Such power can be used to benefit or to destroy man. In this light, let us consider the pigeon again. We have discussed how it can be used as a weapon of destruction. But pigeons can also be trained to perform tasks that will free man from unpleasant duties and allow him to lead a happier, more productive life, as the research of Dr. Thomas Verhave suggests.[5]

In 1958, while employed as a psychopharmacologist at a major pharmaceutical company, Verhave took a tour of the plant, including the division where the pill capsules were made, inspected, and filled with medicine. Production took place in assembly-line fashion. At one end of the line, complex machines manufactured the capsules (the machines could turn out 20 million a day), which were then passed along a moving belt where seventy women employees (called capsule sorters) inspected them for imperfections. Those capsules that were dented, off-color, double-capped, or had gelatin sticking out were called skags and were discarded. Those capsules that passed the visual examination continued on to a second set of machines that filled them with the proper pharmaceuticals. As you might surmise from this description, the women pill sorters didn't exactly lead an exciting life at the office.

What he had observed at the pill-assembly section of the plant got Verhave to thinking: "On seeing those women and their simple monotonous task, and knowing about Skinner's pigeons . . . I said to myself, "Hell, a pigeon can do that!' "[6] A fellow scientist at the plant didn't seem to think so. When Verhave presented him with the idea, he "almost fell out of his chair and choked in a fit of laughter."[7] The laughter stopped, however, when Verhave told his colleague about Skinner's work. A short time later, with the approval of the company's director of research, Verhave and his friend set about constructing an apparatus that would facilitate the use of pigeon pill inspectors. Actually, the company had quite a stake in Verhave's research: At the time he had suggested his plan, the company had just finished spending a sizable amount of cash for an automated pill-inspecting machine that didn't work.

The pill-inspection apparatus Verhave and his colleagues developed was both imaginative and functional. The pigeon was placed in an enclosure and trained to peck at two spots: One spot was a small, transparent window; the other, an opaque window. A belt-driven mechanism brought an endless array of capsules, one at a time, into position behind the transparent window. When the pigeon pecked once at the transparent window, a bright light came on, allowing the bird a clear look at the illuminated pill. If the pigeon judged the capsule to be a skag, it pecked twice more on the transparent window. This caused the window light to go off, a new capsule to move into position, and a small food reward to drop into the pigeon's pecking range. However, if the bird decided the pill was acceptable, he pecked once on the opaque window. This action also turned off the transparent window light and moved a new capsule into position, but when the pigeon "accepted" a pill, he received no reinforcement. Incorrect pecks also received no reinforcement and led to a thiry-second blackout, making it impossible for the pigeon to work for further food.

Verhave started off his pigeons on a relatively simple discrimination task: differentiating between red and white pills. (One color was arbitrarily defined as a skag.) Within seven days his pigeons were inspecting on a 99 percent correct basis. Word of the pigeons' performance circulated through the plant rapidly, and in the following weeks a parade of company officials, from the director of research up to the president, came by for a demonstration look. They were followed by the chairman of the board and his brother, who raised the specter of possible adverse publicity centering around the use of pigeons on an assembly line. "Who would trust medicine inspected by pigeons?" they wanted to know. Verhave responded by claiming that "the use of pigeons was incidental, and that, for example, one could use hawks just as well; after all, what is better than a hawk's eye?"[8] The chairman and his brother "smiled wanly," asked a few more questions, and left.

A short time later Verhave's quality-control inspectors went the way of Skinner's feathered bombardiers. Out. After Verhave received official word that his pigeons were to be retired, he heard through the grapevine that the board of directors had voted thirteen to one against continuing the project. Reflecting upon the company decision, Verhave seems to echo Skinner's sentiments about man being the most serious obstacle to the effective use of animal power:

> Let me point out that the idea of using trained animals for the dubious purposes of Homo sapiens is very old indeed. . . . The obstacle in the way of such developments is not our ignorance of behavior, though it is still large, but mainly, it seems, the obstinate belief of man in his intellectual superiority over other creatures as well as a generalized fear of the imagined consequences of novel developments.[9]

There is a moral in the Verhave experiment: No matter how effectively you train an animal to perform human tasks, such efforts will go to waste if man is not ready to relinquish his labors to lower organisms. Man is a strange creature indeed. He thinks nothing of entrusting his life to a dog or horse, but recoils at the thought of a pigeon sorting pills on an assembly line. It would seem that man and beast must both be trained before scientists like Verhave can aid mankind with their efforts.

BRANDY AND THE BOMB

The pigeons on Verhave's assembly line represent one class of drug inspectors; man's best friend represents another. There is some evidence to suggest that dogs can be used to sniff out certain narcotics, a rather effective weapon against drug smuggling if the dogs live up to their trainers' expectations. Dogs can also be used to sniff out other things, like explosives, and on March 7, 1972, a canine named Brandy definitely lived up to his trainer's expectations.

On this particular March 7, Federal Aviation Agency officials had gathered at Kennedy International Airport in New York to watch Brandy (a German shepherd) and Sally (a black Labrador retriever) demonstrate how their sense of smell could be used to sniff out explosives or narcotics. Little did anyone realize just how powerful that demonstration would be.

As the dogs prepared to go through their paces, a drama was unfolding in another section of the airport, where air controllers were telling Captain William Motz that his airborne jetliner, with fifty-two people aboard, might contain a live bomb. Banking his plane around, Motz calmly and safely piloted his craft back to the airport, where passengers and crew were hurriedly evacuated. Meanwhile, word of the bomb threat had circulated, bringing Brandy, Sally, and members of the New York City bomb squad to the threatened jet.

The two dogs were rookies, but you wouldn't have guessed it from the way they boarded the plane. Brandy took the lead, moving swiftly and confidently in quest of the bomb, stopping finally in front of a large, black briefcase in the aircraft's cockpit. It didn't take bomb squad Detective William F. Schmitt long to discover that Brandy had been successful. He didn't have long. Cutting delicately into the case, Schmitt discovered a device with enough explosive power to blow the plane apart. A few tense moments later, he had deactivated it—five minutes before it was due to detonate.[10]

Brandy and Sally are two of six dogs graduated from a unique program headed by Dr. William F. Crowder, professor of psychology at the University of Mississippi. The program, run in conjunction with aid and assistance from the Justice Department and the U.S. Land Warfare Laboratories in Aberdeen, Maryland, was designed to train dogs to detect several different kinds of explosives, not just dynamite. The explosive that Brandy sniffed out aboard the Kennedy jetliner was C-4, a plastic military explosive.

During the canine training program, Crowder taught his charges to find explosives even when they were concealed in enclosures (closed cabinets, briefcases). He reports that "all dogs were successful in detecting explosives when concealed, unwrapped and in a pasteboard box, wrapped in plastic and sealed in a pasteboard box."

The principles of operant conditioning, so important in the training of Verhave's and Skinner's pigeons, were also vital in teaching and maintaining explosive-detection skills in Crowder's dogs. Positive reinforcement of bomb detection continued even after Brandy and Sally left Mississippi and joined the New York Police Department, where "the dogs are constantly encouraged by their bomb section supervisors . . . who carry around dog yummies at all times."[11]

WASHOE, SARAH, AND LANA

Early in 1974 a reporter from *The New York Times* conducted the following interview using sign language:

REPORTER (holding up a key) : What this?

INTERVIEWEE: Key.

REPORTER (holding a comb) : What this?

INTERVIEWEE: Comb. (The interviewee takes the comb, brushes the reporter's hair, then hands the comb to the reporter.) Comb me.

REPORTER: O.K. (He begins combing the interviewee's hair.)

REPORTER: . . . you want to go outside?

INTERVIEWEE: Outside, no. Want food, apple.

REPORTER: I have no food. Sorry.[12]

In the context of world events, such a mundane discussion would hardly seem worth noting, until we realize that the interviewee was not a person, but an eight-year-old chimpanzee. Amazing as it may seem, researchers have recently succeeded in training a half-dozen apes to become fluent in some sort of sophisticated sign language and it is estimated that within five years the number of chimps with this ability will quadruple to twenty-five.[13]

If the specter of talking chimps strikes the layman as a fantasy out of some science-fiction movie, it must be said that psychologists, too, have been surprised by recent developments in man–ape communication. After all, every attempt to teach an ape to speak—that is, to vocalize human words— has been a dismal failure. (The world's record, established in the 1950s by a chimp called Viki, is four words.[14]) Like so many advances in science, the beginnings of successful communication between man and chimp required a totally new perspective on the problem.

That perspecitve occurred in the mid-1960s, when two University of Nevada psychologists, Beatrice and Allen Gardner, observed that apes in natural settings exchanged information more with hand gestures than with sounds. Did this mean that apes could learn and use some sort of manual sign language? The Gardners decided to find out.

The subject they chose was Washoe, a wild female chimpanzee approximately one year old. The sign language they set out to teach her was the American Sign Language (ASL), a vocabulary commonly used by deaf people. The training area, a "furnished house trailer in the backyard of a suburban home," was designed to be as intellectually stimulating as possible. It was stocked "with tools and toys of all kinds."[15] Efforts were also made to ensure that Washoe's studies would be integrated into her whole life and not confined to special training sessions.[16]

The training itself consisted, in part, of two techniques: operant conditioning and imitation. Operant conditioning involved rewarding Washoe, usually with a tickle, for learning to make the desired gestures; imitation involved the experimenters' prompting Washoe when she failed to use a new gesture in an appropriate context or when she used an incorrect gesture.[17] A new sign was regarded as finally "learned" if Washoe used it spontaneously in an appropriate situation at least once a day for fifteen consecutive days. The gesture for *smell*, for example, would be considered as "appropriate" if used near scented objects such as tobacco or a flower. By this criterion, Washoe was able to "converse" with over thirty gestures in the first two years of training. More impressive, however, was the fact that she did not become overloaded or confused by this method of instruction; on the contrary, her language-acquiring skills seemed to improve at an accelerated rate:

She acquired four signs during the first seven months of training, nine during the second, and 21 during the third. Instead of becoming bogged down by this new material, she processed it at a faster and faster rate. After three years of training, her total vocabulary was 85 signs. After another year, it had almost doubled.[18]

Listed on pages 104–106, and in order, are the first thirty-four "words" Washoe mastered.

A sizable vocabulary to be sure. Yet learning gesture words is not the same thing as being able to use them in a sophisticated manner. If, for example, Washoe's linguistic behavior were limited to simple, conditioned responses, we could hardly say that she was speaking on human terms. We already know that other animals, such as dogs, can learn to respond to their master's gestures (e.g., by doing tricks) and even to make gestures in return for food or some other reinforcement.

The critical question for the Gardners, then, was whether or not Washoe could function on a "higher" linguistic level. The answer soon proved to be a gratifying, and exciting, "yes." The psychologists found that Washoe could linguistically identify subtle distinctions, such as between the concept *flower* and the concept *smell*. Also, Washoe was able to apply abstract ideas, such as *more*, to a wide variety of contexts. Writing in *Science*, the Gardners recall how their chimp learned to use the word *open*:

When Washoe wanted to get through a door, she tended to hold up both hands and pound on the door with her palms or her knuckles. This is the beginning position for the "open" sign. By waiting for her to place her hands on the door and then lift them, and also by imitative prompting, we were able to shape a good approximtaion of the "open" sign, and would reward this by opening the door. Originally she was trained to make this sign for three particular doors that she used every day. Washoe transferred this sign to all doors;

Signs	Description	Context
Come-gimme	Beckoning motion, with wrist or knuckles as pivot.	Sign made to persons or animals, also for objects out of reach. Often combined: "come tickle," "gimme sweet," etc.
More	Fingertips are brought together, usually overhead. (Correct ASL form: tips of the tapered hand touch repeatedly.)	When asking for continuation or repetition of activities such as swinging or tickling, for second helpings of food, etc. Also used to ask for repetition of some performance, such as a somersault.
Up	Arm extends upward, and index finger may also point up.	Wants a lift to reach objects such as grapes on vine, or leaves; or wants to be placed on someone's shoulders; or wants to leave potty-chair.
Sweet	Index or index and second fingers touch tip of wagging tongue. (Correct ASL form: index and second fingers extended side by side.)	For dessert; used spontaneously at end of meal. Also, when asking for candy.
Open	Flat hands are placed side by side, palms down, then drawn apart while rotated to palms up.	At door of house, room, car, refrigerator, or cupboard; on containers such as jars; and on faucets.
Tickle	The index finger of one hand is drawn across the back of the other hand. (Related to ASL "touch.")	For tickling or for chasing games.
Go	Opposite of "come-gimme."	While walking hand-in-hand or riding on someone's shoulders. Washoe usually indicates the direction desired.
Out	Curved hand grasps tapered hand; then tapered hand is withdrawn upward.	When passing through doorways; until recently, used for both "in" and "out." Also, when asking to be taken outdoors.
Hurry	Open hand is shaken at the wrist. (Correct ASL form: index and second fingers extended side by side.)	Often follows signs such as "come-gimme," "out," "open," and "go," particularly if there is a delay before Washoe is obeyed. Also, used while watching her meal being prepared.
Hear-listen	Index finger touches ear.	For loud or strange sounds: bells, car horns, sonic booms, etc. Also, for asking someone to hold a watch to her ear.

Sign	Description	Context
Toothbrush	Index finger is used as brush, to rub front teeth.	When Washoe has finished her meal, or at other times when shown a toothbrush.
Drink	Thumb is extended from fisted hand and touches mouth.	For water, formula, soda pop, etc. For soda pop, often combined with "sweet."
Hurt	Extended index fingers are jabbed toward each other. Can be used to indicate location of pain.	To indicate cuts and bruises on herself or on others. Can be elicited by red stains on a persons skin or by tears in clothing.
Sorry	Fisted hand clasps and unclasps at shoulder. (Correct ASL form: fisted hand is rubbed over heart with circular motion.)	After biting someone, or when someone has been hurt in another way (not necessarily by Washoe). When told to apologize for mischief.
Funny	Tip of index finger presses nose, and Washoe snorts. (Correct ASL form: index and second fingers used, no snort.)	When soliciting interaction play, and during games. Occasionally, when being pursued after mischief.
Please	Open hand is drawn across chest. (Correct ASL form: fingertips used, and circular motion.)	When asking for objects and activities. Frequently combined: "Please go." "Out, please." "Please drink."
Food-eat	Several fingers of one hand are placed in mouth. (Correct ASL form: fingertips of tapered hand touch mouth repeatedly.)	During meals and preparation of meals.
Flower	Tip of index finger touches one or both nostrils. (Correct ASL form: tips of tapered hand touch first one nostril, then the other.)	For flowers.
Cover-blanket	Draws one hand toward self over the back of the other.	At bedtime or naptime, and, on cold days, when Washoe wants to be taken out.
Dog	Repeated slapping on thigh.	For dogs and for barking.
You	Index finger points at a person's chest.	Indicates successive turns in games. Also used in response to questions such as "Who tickle?" "Who brush?"
Napkin-bib	Fingertips wipe the mouth region.	For bib, for washcloth, and for Kleenex.
In	Opposite of "out."	Wants to go indoors, or wants someone to join her indoors.

Signs (cont.)	Description	Context
Brush	The fisted hand rubs the back of the open hand several times. (Adapted from ASL "polish.")	For hairbrush, and when asking for brushing.
Hat	Palm pats top of head.	For hats and caps.
I-me	Index finger points at, or touches, chest.	Indicates Washoe's turn, when she and a companion share food, drink, etc. Also used in phrases, such as "I drink," and in reply to questions such as "Who tickle?" (Washoe: "You"); "Who I tickle?" (Washoe: "Me.")
Shoes	The fisted hands are held side by side and strike down on shoes or floor. (Correct ASL form: the sides of the fisted hands strike against each other.)	For shoes and boots.
Smell	Palm is held before nose and moved slightly upward several times.	For scented objects: tobacco, perfume, sage, etc.
Pants	Palms of the flat hands are drawn up against the body toward waist.	For diapers, rubber pants, trousers.
Clothes	Fingertips brush down the chest.	For Washoe's jacket, nightgown, and shirts, also for our clothing.
Cat	Thumb and index finger grasp cheek hair near side of mouth and are drawn outward (representing cat's whiskers).	For cats.
Key	Palm of one hand is repeatedly touched with the index finger of the other (Correct ASL form: crooked index finger is rotated against palm.)	Used for keys and locks and to ask us to unlock a door.
Baby	One forearm is placed in the crook of the other, as if cradling a baby.	For dolls, including animal dolls such as a toy horse and duck.
Clean	The open palm of one hand is passed over the open palm of the other.	Used when Washoe is washing, or being washed, or when a companion is washing hands or some other object. Also used for "Soap."[19]

then to containers such as the refrigerator, cupboards, drawers, briefcases, boxes, and jars; and eventually—an invention of Washoe's—she used it to ask us to turn on water faucets.[20]

Finally, and perhaps most significantly, Washoe spontaneously began to combine gestures into primitive sentence strings such as "come-gimme sweet," "out please,"[21] "gimme tickle," and "open food drink."[22] Washoe even learned to ask questions, a skill that she employed extensively during one of her favorite occupations: reading magazines. "Washoe was very fond of magazines," recall the Gardners," especially if they were new."[23] It seems that this "primitive" chimp would spend thirty minutes at a time looking at a magazine's pictures and requesting names.

The Gardners' success with Washoe has generated considerable interest among psychologists, leading to the recent development of other languages for human–chimp communication. At the University of California in Santa Barbara, Dr. David Premack has taught chimps to use a vocabulary of plastic shapes, each representing an object or concept. A square, for example, means "banana"; a quadrilateral means "not equal to." His star performer, an engaging female chimp called Sarah, has a repertoire of 130 words. In the past (she is now in semiretirement), Sarah was able to "write out" her own sentence strings on a magnetized board, showing in the process a remarkable understanding of syntax and sentence structure.[24]

At Georgia State University, Dr. Duane Rumbaugh, collaborating with colleagues from the University of Georgia, has refined a computer-controlled language for inter-species dialogues. Lana, a three-year-old chimpanzee, operates a special typewriter with fifty keys, each with geometric figures designed to indicate a particular concept or object. When Lana types on the keyboard, a projector immediately flashes the appropriate images in front of her while the computer keeps precise track of her behavior. By using this machine, Lana requests all her food and entertainment (movies, music, toys, and human companionship) .[25] At one point Rumbaugh thought about teaching Lana to read sentence-like sequences of projected images, but as science writer Joyce Fleming points out: "He never got a chance to try. Lana learned by herself. She began pushing a few keys and checking the sequence on the screen. If her sentence was correct she finished it. If not, she pushed a key that erased it."[26]

Most researchers agree that such studies on how chimps use language will prove to be as valuable as they are fascinating. On a theoretical level, we will almost certainly learn more about the nature of language: what it is, how it is acquired, when it is used. On a more practical level, we may learn new ways of communicating with retarded or autistic children who have been unable to incorporate language with conventional techniques.[27] There is even the possibility of enabling chimps, with the aid of a humanly created sign language, to improve communication among themselves. In fact, scientists have already observed limited gesture-discussions between two six-year-old male chimps named Bruno and Booee. Examples:

  BOOEE: Tickle Booee.
  BRUNO: Tickle Bruno.

  BOOEE: Tickle.
  BRUNO: Booee come hurry.

  BOOEE: Tickle Booee.
  BRUNO (eating raisins) : Booee me food.[28]

Rumbaugh also foresees the day when a chimp is sufficiently "verbal" to be a partner, as well as a subject, in behavioral research. Linguistically trained chimps, he hypothesizes, could act as translators, interpreting for scientists the actions of chimps in their natural settings.[29]

ANIMAL POWER: WHAT'S IN IT FOR US?

The use of animals to supplement or to replace human effort in various tasks is not new. Falcons help us hunt; horses aid in hauling and traveling; dogs protect our home and "see" for the blind. Animals have also been taught to entertain us as, for example, in circus shows and movies. But animal power can carry us much further—if we let it, if we can get over our stubborn resistance to using lower organisms for performing tasks that might involve a challenge to our intellectual superiority.

In today's world there are many species of insects and animals that can perform feats we only dream about or try to mimic with machines. It would behoove man to attempt to harness these insect and animal skills in the service of man, rather than rejecting them out of hand because they threaten his ego.

NOTES

1. B. Skinner, "Pigeons in a Pelican," *American Psychologist* 15 (1960): 28–37.
2. Ibid., p. 31.
3. Ibid., p. 34.
4. Ibid.
5. T. Verhave, "The Pigeon As a Quality-Control Inspector," *American Psychologist* 21 (1966): 109–115.
6. Ibid., p. 110.
7. Ibid.
8. Ibid., p. 114.
9. Ibid., p. 115.
10. R. Witkin, "Bomb Found on Jet Here After $2-million Demand," *The New York Times*, 8 March 1972, pp. 1 ff. See also "Two Dogs Pass Bomb-finding Test Successfully," *The New York Times,* 8 March 1972, p. 29.
11. "Two Dogs Pass Bomb-finding Test Successfully," p. 29.
12. B. Rensberger, "Computer Helps Chimpanzees Learn to Read,

Write, and 'Talk' to Humans," *The New York Times,* 29 May 1974, p. 52.

13. J. Fleming, "Field Report: The State of the Apes," *Psychology Today* (January 1974): 46.

14. Ibid., p. 31.

15. B. Gardner and R. Gardner, "Comparing the Early Utterances of Child and Chimpanzee," prepublication manuscript, p. 7.

16. Ibid., p. 8.

17. R. Gardner and B. Gardner, "Teaching Sign Language to a Chimpanzee," *Science* 165 (1969): 666–668.

18. Fleming, "Field Report: The State of the Apes," p. 33.

19. Gardner and Gardner, "Teaching Sign Language to a Chimpanzee," pp. 668–669.

20. Ibid., p. 670.

21. Rensberger, "Computer Helps Chimpanzees Learn to Read, Write, and 'Talk' to Humans," p. 43.

22. Fleming, "Field Report: The State of the Apes," p. 32.

23. Gardner and Gardner, "Comparing the Early Utterances of Child and Chimpanzee," p. 23.

24. D. Premack, "The Education of Sarah," *Psychology Today* (September 1970): 55–58.

25. Fleming, "Field Report: The State of the Apes," p. 46.

26. Ibid.

27. Rensberger, "Computer Helps Chimpanzees Learn to Read, Write, and 'Talk' to Humans," p. 43.

28. Fleming, "Field Report: The State of the Apes," p. 43.

29. Rensberger, "Computer Helps Chimpanzees Learn to Read, Write, and 'Talk' to Humans," p. 52.

SUGGESTED READINGS

FLEMING, J. "Field Report: The State of the Apes." *Psychology Today* (January 1974): 31–46.

HERRNSTEIN, J. "In Defense of Bird Brains." *Atlantic Monthly* (September 1965): 101–104.

PREMACK, D. "The Education of Sarah." *Psychology Today* (September 1970): 55–58. A report of Premack's work also appears in *Time,* 21 September 1970, p. 51. A related article is Gardner, R., and Gardner, B. "Teaching Sign Language to a Chimpanzee." *Science* 169 (1969): 664–672.

SKINNER, B. "Pigeons in a Pelican." *American Psychologist* 15 (1960): 28–37.

VERHAVE, T. "The Pigeon As a Quality-Control Inspector." *American Psychologist* 21 (1966): 109–115.

———. "The Inspector General . . . Is a Bird." *Psychology Today* (October 1967): 48–63.

6

group power

It is a hot, steamy evening in New York, the kind of night that breeds discomfort, short tempers, and violence. Up on the West Side, two officers in a squad car are making their rounds, hoping against hope that the oppressive heat won't spawn trouble. For a time it seems their hopes might be realized. Then the call comes over the radio: Proceed to an apartment on 117 Street to investigate a family disturbance. Both cops grimace, as well they should. Responding to a family-disturbance call is one of the most dangerous and difficult tasks facing an officer of the peace. Such conflicts are often settled at the expense of the policeman. Husbands or wives decide to vent their frustrations on the cop rather than their spouse.

Moving swiftly to their destination, the cops bolt from the car, dash up four flights of stairs, and run down the dimly lit hall. They have no trouble locating apartment 4A; the sounds of scuffling and screaming are unmistakable. Winded and sweating profusely, the two officers bang on the door and identify themselves. The fight goes on unabated. The officers bang again, more loudly. This time the door opens, revealing a middle-aged man with a knife. Behind him a woman is gesturing wildly, screaming for help.

What happens? If the police are lucky, they will be able to stop the argument without physical damage to the quarreling parties or to themselves. But sometimes luck runs out. For some officers it runs out completely: 22 percent of police deaths occur during such calls.[1] And for the quarreling family? Between 35 and 50 percent of all homicides are intra-familial.[2]

Recently, New York psychologist Morton Bard decided to try to do something about the problems of police intervention in family crises.[3] He reasoned that with proper training, the policeman would be better equipped to handle family disturbances, thus reducing the probability of risk to himself and increasing his chances of effectively aiding the feuding parties. Bard's reasoning was sound enough to win the backing of the Justice Department and the New York City Police Department for a unique training program. The program was divided into two parts. In the first part eighteen police officers participated in an intensive 160-hour instructional course that attempted to teach them skills necessary in handling family-crisis interventions effectively. This training involved more than lectures and books; in one procedure the officers were encouraged to learn by participating in real-life enactments of family-crisis situations. These situations were not lacking in realism. Professional actors were hired to play the roles of quarreling family members, and the scripts they followed were varied and unknown to the policemen, who attempted to intervene in the action and "help" the actors with their "family difficulties." These plays were written without conclusions so that the actors could improvise their roles based on the intervention behavior of the policemen.

At the end of these simulations, the officers were given the opportunity to talk over their performances with each other and with the psychologists on the staff. In this way each policeman was better able to assess the overall effectiveness of his actions.

The acid test came in the second phase of the training program. Finished with their schooling, the officers were sent into the field to test their new skills under fire. For twenty-two months they worked in two-man teams, operating out of a squad car that was sent to answer all family-disturbance calls in the precinct. Detailed records were kept of each call so that the psychologists could determine what, if any, success the cops were having in mediating family crises.

What were the results of the training program? In a word, favorable—from both the community and the police points of view. Citizens involved with the newly trained officers seemed more satisfied with the officers' conduct, and the officers were more effective in reducing violence, both to the quarreling parties and to themselves, stemming from family altercations. Commenting on the success of the program, Bard notes:

The unit [18 police officers] processed 1,375 interventions with 962 families. . . . While homicides in New York City increased during the period of the project, there was not a single homicide in a family known to the unit. There was a reduction in assaults in the demonstration area and a drop in arrests for assaults, suggesting the positive effect of skillful police intervention and the use of mediation and referral rather than the usual inadequate use of the courts in such matters. Another striking finding was the total absence of injury to the policemen of the unit despite the high risk involved in being exposed more than would ordinarily be the case to emotionally volatile and potentially violent family crises. The danger to policemen in such situations is well known among policemen and is attested to by high police death and injury rates.[4]

Bard sees police officers trained in intervention procedures as an important factor in improving community–police relations. He believes that

> much of the existing tension between the police and the community results from the failure of the police to meet with skill and sensitivity the hopeful expectations of the citizenry. In the absence of other resources, the police are often expected to provide services that are, in the traditional sense, outside the realm of law enforcement.[5]

Bard believes that his experiment in police family-crisis intervention "demonstrates the strong possibility that police departments might be structured along the lines of highly flexible service organizations without in any way compromising their basic law enforcement mission."[6] Evidence from other police-training programs seems to bear out his prediction. Recently, a police-intervention program for handling youth problems was begun.[7] Initial results look very promising.

USING GROUP POWER TO ACHIEVE INTERPERSONAL HARMONY

With mankind increasing in number and geographical mobility, it becomes more important than ever before that we find ways to live in harmony with our fellow man: both within the group (person-to-person) and between groups (nation-to-nation, race-to-race). The police-intervention training program just described is one example of how psychologists are trying to curb destructive behavior within and between groups, in this case the destructive behavior that might occur between members of the family or between family members and police. By studying the root causes of interpersonal hostility and searching for ways to overcome them, the behavioral scientist is playing an increasingly vital role in the struggle for a new era in human brotherhood.

It has long been recognized that the *group* can be an awesomely powerful force for changing individual behavior.[8] The problem is that up until recently *group power* has not been harnessed in the service of man. One possible reason for this scientific boycott is the widely held belief that groups act as a toxin to the human spirit, that their power is most often used to manipulate a person's actions in a manner antithetical to social values and personal dignity. The view of a group as a force for supporting antisocial acts is subscribed to by many scientists and laymen alike. Currently, for example, we are hearing much about the way teen-age groups (read "gangs") force youth into drugs, crime, and disrespect for their elders. Even the word *group* has come on bad times: Young girls who follow rock musicians around the country and grant them sexual favors upon request are called *groupies*.

There is no question that groups can exert negative influences over an individual's behavior. They can be used to extinguish human spirit and encourage antisocial acts; yet they can also be employed to expand individual freedom and social responsibility. Once again, group power is similar to atomic power: It can be used to improve or to hamper the quality of life. In the final analysis it is up to us to decide how group power will be exercised.

One of the earliest attempts to use group influence for accomplishing socially relevant activities occurred while the United States was engaged in combating a food crisis. During World War II a group of social scientists was given the assignment of finding ways to persuade housewives to serve unpopular meats (beef hearts, sweetbreads, and kidneys) to their families. In order to find out how they might best accomplish this, the social scientists ran an experiment using six groups of Red Cross home-nursing volunteers. All were polled to see how many had served organ meats before. Then three of these groups heard a lecture linking use of these foods with the war effort, showing their nutritional value, and indicating how deliciously they could be prepared. Mimeographed recipes were distributed. The other three groups heard only a brief introduction. Instead of hearing a lecture, they were drawn into a discussion of why house-wives had trouble preparing, serving, and gaining accept-ance of organ meats. At the end of their meetings, women from all six groups were asked to raise their hands if they planned to serve an organ meat during the next week. Although both the women who had heard the lecture and those that had participated as a group in discussion said they would prepare the organ meats, a follow-up study showed that only 3 percent of the women who heard the lectures served one of the meats they had never served before, com-pared with 32 percent of the women who had participated in the group discussions.[9]

In recent years a series of studies by the eminent social psychologist Stanley Milgram has demonstrated how group power can be effectively utilized in helping individuals resist authoritarian commands to treat their fellow man in-humanely. As you will soon see, this optimistic finding stands out in bright relief against the dark side of man that was so graphically revealed in Milgram's experiments.

In the early 1960s Milgram had been wondering about the role obedience played in man's inhumanity to man, particu-larly the kinds of inhuman atrocities committed by the Nazis who were "acting under orders." Could the same obedience that made a child dutifully obey his parents and respond in socially acceptable fashion be turned around to make a per-son commit antisocial acts at the prodding of another author-ity figure? Milgram went into the laboratory to find out.

The Milgram experiment was a masterpiece of simplicity and deception. Two subjects were ushered into the labora-tory to participate in a "learning experiment, ostensibly designed to study the effect of punishment on memory." One subject was to be the "teacher"; the other, the "learner." The subjects drew lots to determine their roles, but unbe-

known to one of them, the drawing was rigged. One participant, the "naïve" subject, was always given the role of the
teacher; the other subject, a confederate of the experimenter,
was given the role of the learner. Once the drawing was
completed, the learner was strapped into an "electric chair"
and outfitted with electrodes "capable of delivering powerful
electric shocks to his body." The teacher, after observing
this macabre scene, was ushered into an adjacent room containing an intercom and an imposing "shock generator"
apparatus. The generator, an impressive array of dials and
switches, was outfitted with a control panel that gave the
voltage readings for thirty separate levers. (Voltage levels
went up in 15-volt steps from 15 to 450 volts.) Subjective
descriptions of shock intensity were also included on the
panel, ranging from "Slight Shock" at the lower intensities
to "Danger: Severe Shock" at the 400-volt level. In order
to convince the teacher of the authenticity of the shock generator and also to let him experience the painful properties
of shock, he was administered a 45-volt stimulation.

The teacher's instructions were quite simple. He was told
to teach the learner a list of word pairs over the intercom,
punishing him with electric shock whenever he made a mistake and increasing the shock intensity one level (15 volts)
for each new mistake. As the experiment progressed, the
learner purposely made errors so that the teacher would have
to shock him with increasingly severe shocks. As the shock
level went up, the learner often made "increasingly insistent
demands that the experiment be stopped because of the
growing discomfort to him."

Although the teacher didn't realize it, *the learner never
received any shocks.* Nor were his pleas real; they were in
actuality a tape recording preprogrammed to deliver specific
inputs when certain shock levels were reached.

They started with a grunt at 75 volts, proceeded through a
"Hey, that really hurts," at 125 volts, got desperate with, "I

can't stand the pain, don't do that," at 180 volts, reached complaints of heart trouble at 195 (the learner had informed the teacher and the experimenter that he had heart trouble before the experiment began), an agonized scream at 285, a refusal to answer at 315, and only heart-rending, ominous silence after that.[10]

If the teacher became concerned with the learner's agony, the experimenter ordered him to continue and to disregard the learner's protests. If the teacher balked and tried to quit, the experimenter commanded, "You have no choice, you must go on!" It should be emphasized that the teacher was free to quit the experiment whenever he wanted to; the only way the experimenter could try and keep him in the task was by verbal commands that he "must go on."

The teacher's "performance score" was the highest level of shock intensity he was willing to administer to the learner. Thus, his score could range from 0 (unwilling to administer any shock) to 450 (for a subject who gave the highest voltage level on the board).

When Milgram began his experiment, he didn't expect many of the teachers to administer very high shocks to the learners.

I'll tell you quite frankly, before I began this experiment, before any shock generator was built, I thought that most people would break off at "Strong Shock" (135–180 volts) or "Very Strong Shock" (195–240 volts). You would get only a very, very small proportion of people going out to the end of the shock generator (450 volts), and they would constitute a pathological fringe.[11]

Milgram's colleagues and his students agreed with his assessment. As a matter of fact, when Milgram asked a class of Yale University psychology students to estimate how many of a hypothetical group of a hundred subjects would give the most intense (450 volts) shock, the average answer was 1.2

percent. In other words, the Yale students felt that less than two subjects in a hundred would remain in the experiment to the end.

If only Milgram and his students had been correct. Unfortunately, their optimistic faith in human nature would find no support in the obedience study. Of the first forty subjects tested *not one* of the teachers quit the experiment prior to administering 300 volts (at which point the subject is kicking the wall in agony), and twenty-six of the forty teachers (over 60 percent of the subjects) obeyed the experimenter to the end, punishing the hapless learner with 450 volts of electricity. Many of these subjects displayed extreme tension and misgivings about their behavior, but when prodded on by the stern voice of the experimenter over the intercom, they went on shocking the hell out of the protesting learner.

To give you an idea of the way in which many of the teachers responded to their grizzly task, here is a transcript of part of an actual experimental session. The transcript, provided by Milgram and presented in *Esquire* magazine by Philip Meyer, picks up on the action just as the teacher administers a 180-volt shock to the learner.

LEARNER: Ow, I can't stand the pain. Don't do that. . . .

TEACHER (*pivoting around in his chair and shaking his head*): He can't stand it. I'm not going to kill that man in there. You hear him hollering?

EXPERIMENTER: As I told you before, the shocks may be painful, but—

TEACHER: But he's hollering. He can't stand it. What's going to happen to him?

EXPERIMENTER (*his voice is patient, matter-of-fact*): The experiment requires that you continue, Teacher.

TEACHER: Aah, but, uhh, I'm not going to get that man sick in there . . . know what I mean?

EXPERIMENTER: Whether the learner likes it or not, we must go on, through all the word pairs.

TEACHER: I refuse to take the responsibility. He's in there hollering!

EXPERIMENTER: It's absolutely essential that you continue, Teacher.

TEACHER (*indicating the unused questions*): There's too many left here. I mean, geez, if he gets them wrong, there's too many of them left. I mean who's going to take the responsibility if anything happens to that gentleman?

EXPERIMENTER: I'm responsible for anything that happens to him. Continue please.

TEACHER: All right. (*Consults list of words.*) The next one's "slow—walk, truck, dance, music." Answer, please. (*A buzzing sound indicates the learner has signaled his answer.*) Wrong. A hundred and ninety-five volts. "Dance." (*Zzumph!*)

LEARNER: Let me out of here. My heart's bothering me!

EXPERIMENTER: Continue, please.

LEARNER (*screaming*): Let me out of here, you have no right to keep me here. Let me out of here, let me out, my heart's bothering me, let me out!

TEACHER: You see, he's hollering. Hear that? Gee, I don't know.

EXPERIMENTER: The experiment requires. . . .

TEACHER (*interrupting*): I know it does, sir, but I mean—hunh! He don't know what he's getting in for. He's up to 195 volts! (*The experiment continues through 270 volts, at which point the teacher, with evident relief, runs out of word-pair questions.*)

EXPERIMENTER: You'll have to go back to the beginning of that page and go through them again until he's learned them all correctly.

TEACHER: Aw, no. I'm not going to kill that man. You mean I've got to keep going up with the scale. No sir. He's hollering in there. I'm not going to give him 450 volts.

EXPERIMENTER: The experiment requires that you go on.

TEACHER: I know it does, but that man is hollering in there, sir.

EXPERIMENTER (*same matter-of-fact tone*): As I said before, although the shocks may be painful. . . .

TEACHER (*interrupting*): Awww. He-he-he's yelling in there.

EXPERIMENTER: Start with "Blue," please, at the top of the page. Continue, please, Teacher. Just go ahead.

TEACHER: "Blue—boy, girl, grass, hat." (*The teacher, with continuing protests, proceeds to shock the learner up to 375 volts, at which point there is no response of any kind from the man in the electric chair.*)

TEACHER: I think something's happened to that fellow in there. I don't get no answer. He was hollering at less voltage. Can't you check in and see if he's all right, please?

EXPERIMENTER: Not once we've started. Please continue, Teacher.

TEACHER: "Cool—day, shade, water, paint." Answer, please. Are you all right in there? Are you all right?

EXPERIMENTER: Please continue, Teacher. Continue, please. (*Teacher pushes lever. Zzumph!*)

TEACHER: Something's happened to that man in there.

Next one. "Low—dollar, necklace, moon, paint." Something's happened to that man in there. You better check in on him, sir. He won't answer or nothing.

EXPERIMENTER: The responsibility is mine. Correct. Please go on. (*Teacher returns to his list, and soon has worked the "punishment" level up to 450 volts.*)

TEACHER: That's that.

EXPERIMENTER: Continue using the last switch on the board, please. The four-fifty switch for each wrong answer. Continue, please.

TEACHER: But I don't get no anything!

EXPERIMENTER: Please continue. The next word is "White."

TEACHER: Don't you think you should look in on him, please.

EXPERIMENTER: Not once we've started the experiment.

TEACHER: But what if something has happened to the man?

EXPERIMENTER: The experiment requires that you continue. Go on, please.

TEACHER: Don't the man's health mean anything?

EXPERIMENTER: Whether the learner likes it or not. . . .

TEACHER: What if he's dead in there? I mean, he told me he can't stand the shock, sir. I don't mean to be rude, but I think you should look in on him. All you have to do is look in the door. I don't get no answer, no noise. Something might have happened to the gentleman in there, sir.

EXPERIMENTER: We must continue. Go on, please.

TEACHER: You mean keep giving him what? Four hundred fifty volts, what he's got now?

EXPERIMENTER: That's correct. Continue. The next next word is "White."

TEACHER: "White—cloud, horse, rock, house." (*The teacher continues his task, administering the 450-volt shocks, until the experimenter ends the session. At that point Dr. Milgram enters the room to speak with the teacher.*)

MILGRAM: I'd like to ask you a few questions. (*Slowly, patiently, he dehoaxes the teacher, telling him that the shocks and screams were not real.*)

TEACHER: You mean he wasn't getting nothing? Well, I'm glad to hear that. I was getting upset there. I was getting ready to walk out.

(*Finally, to make sure there are no hard feelings, friendly, harmless "Mr. Wallace"* [*the learner*] *comes out in coat and tie. Gives jovial greeting. Friendly reconciliation takes place. Experiment ends.*) [12]

There is no question that Milgram became extremely distressed over what he witnessed in his laboratory. He wrote:

With numbing regularity, good people were seen to knuckle under to the demands of authority and perform actions that were callous and severe. The results . . . raise the possibility that human nature, or—more specifically—the kind of character produced in American democratic society, cannot be counted on to insulate its citizens from brutality and inhumane treatment at the direction of malevolent authority. A substantial proportion of people do what they are told to do, irrespective of the content of the act and without limitations of conscience, so long as they perceive that the command comes from a legitimate authority. If in this study an anonymous experimenter could successfully command adults to subdue a fifty-year-old man, and force on him painful electric shocks against his protests, one can only wonder what government, with its vastly greater authority and prestige, can command of its subjects.[13]

With a new sense of urgency, Milgram conducted a further series of experiments, trying to discover the limits of his subjects' obedience. He hoped to find a way to reduce the teacher's willingness to follow blindly the experimenter's demands to shock the learner senseless. Many variations were tried. At one point the subject was actually required to physically force the learner's hand down onto the shock plate when he made a mistake; yet even when the teachers were placed in this close physical relation to their "victims," 25 percent of them still proceeded to administer shocks up through the 450-volt level.

It was through the judicious use of group power that Milgram finally found a way to free many teachers from their blind obedience to the experimenter's commands. What he discovered was that group pressure could be liberating: If the teacher was among other teachers who defied the experimenter's commands, then he was more likely to defy them, also.

The experiment that revealed this finding went this way: Four persons showed up at Milgram's laboratory to take part in an experiment on "the effects of collective teaching and punishment on memory and learning." Three of the persons were confederates of the experimenter. A rigged drawing was held in which one confederate drew the lot of learner and the other two that of teacher number 1 and teacher number 2, respectively. The naïve subject drew a slip indicating that he was teacher number 3. At the completion of the drawing, the learner was strapped into the electric chair, and the three teachers were brought into the room with a shock generator. Each teacher was then given a specific task to perform: Teacher number 1 read from the list of word pairs; teacher number 2 told the learner whether his answer was right or wrong; and teacher number 3 (the naïve subject) delivered the shocks for incorrect responses.

The experiment started off in the same manner as had been the case when only one teacher was present. The first major change in the script occurred at the 150-volt shock level, when teacher number 1 informed the experimenter he was quitting because of the learner's protests. The experimenter insisted he continue, but the teacher would have none of it. He left his seat and walked to another part of the room. At 210 volts the second teacher, expressing his concern for the learner, staged his walkout. Again, the experimenter tried to change his mind, but it was useless. "I'm willing to answer any of your questions," the teacher informed the experimenter, "but I'm not willing to shock that man against his will; I'll have no part of it." That left the naïve subject as the lone remaining teacher. Two of his peers had defied the experimenter, and now he was given the responsibility of carrying on the teaching role by himself. Would he give in to the experimenter's incessant demands to complete the task, or would the actions of his co-teachers give him the strength he needed to break free from his chains of obedience?

The results were highly encouraging, particularly when you consider the dismal performance of teachers in the experiment where no other teachers were present. Milgram summarizes the experimental findings:

> In the group setting 36 of the 40 subjects defy the experimenter while the corresponding number in the absence of group pressure is 14. The effects of peer rebellion are most impressive in undercutting the experimenter's authority. Indeed, of the score of experimental variations completed in the Yale study on obedience none was so effective in undermining the experimenter's authority as the [group] manipulation.[14]

At this point the Milgram findings do not conclusively prove that group power can be used to free man from those types of obedient behavior that inflict pain on others. It is a big step from obedience in the laboratory to obedience as it functions outside the laboratory. Possibly, Milgram's findings might not be applicable to interpersonal relations as they occur in the "real" world. We doubt this possibility, but it is through further investigations that we will find out definitely. Until then, we can thank Milgram for refocusing our attention on the group as a potentially effective tool for forging more humane, harmonious relations between individuals. For now, let us turn to other uses of groups.

GROUP SENSITIVITY TRAINING

After eight years of coping with a child whose attitude toward life was "I have a right to do anything I want to," Jeffrey's mother finally went to Dr. Martha Bernal's office for a consultation.[15] A program was worked out that combined traditional therapy with closed-circuit television recordings of her relationship with her son. Several videotapes of the mother and Jeff interacting at home and at the psychologist's office were produced and then reviewed by the mother and Dr. Bernal in private meetings.

The power of television-induced awareness was revealed at the very first screening. After watching only thirty minutes of her pitifully meek responses to Jeff's incessant demands, she turned to the clinician and exclaimed, "What a dishrag!" "Never again, in all subsequent observations of her and Jeff," Bernal recalls, "did she ever show the same 'dishrag' quality; gradually she became more assertive with Jeff as well as with other people." Using additional videotapes along with instructions from Bernal, the mother was finally able to bring her son under control. After eighteen weeks and only seven TV sessions, Jeff could be considered at least as well behaved as the average child his age. "Two years later," reports Bernal, "the mother–son relationship was vastly different. Jeff was courteous and affectionate, and the mother felt a genuine affection for him." That videotape could induce such a powerful transformation in Jeff's mother demonstrates an important psychological fact: Just as feedback concerning our biological states enables us to make positive physiological changes (Chapter 3), *feedback concerning our larger social behavior enables us to make significant and constructive interpersonal changes.* Indeed, the prominent clinical psychologist Carl Rogers has developed an entire therapeutic system based simply on the idea of expanding a person's awareness through immediate feedback. A client states his problems, feelings, and emotions; the therapist, in turn, just repeats or "feeds back" what the client has said, adding his own feelings or perceptions of the client's nonverbal responses (body language). Rogers believes that the traditional analytic approach of laboriously dredging up unconscious material has its valid uses, but he places his primary trust in the ability of the human organism, given greater self-awareness, to regulate itself in its own best interest.

Although effective feedback can occur in the one-to-one privacy of a psychologist's office, the technique is now used with increasing frequency in a *group* context. Such "feedback-oriented" groups are the basis for what has become an entirely new therapeutic movement called *sensitivity training*—literally, making a person *sensitive to* how he behaves and how his behavior affects others.

What advantages does the group offer? Two important ones. First, the participant can interact with a variety of other people (normally 7–19 other persons, not including the leader), thus enabling him to receive feedback from a wide range of sources. Second, since each group member usually does not know the other participants personally, he feels freer to experiment with new behaviors, unencumbered by the expectations of family, friends, and business associates.

The specific methods used in a sensitivity group can vary considerably, depending on the personality of the leader, the sophistication of the participants, and the goals of the group. All sensitivity training, however, has an underlying dynamic: First, some action is taken within the group. It can be an intellectually demanding project, such as collectively solving a difficult problem, or one person stating a feeling to someone else. When this action is completed, a feedback process usually begins. In the case of a group task, the leader and every other member of the group has an opportunity to express—to "share"—his perceptions and gut reactions to what has just happened. (In the second case, where one individual confronts, or "encounters," another, the leader will encourage a continuous exchange of feedback, each person responding to what the other has just said or done.) In this way each participant begins to develop a clearer picture of how he "comes across" to others and a greater awareness of both the positive and negative "blind spots" in his self-concept. More importantly, he has the opportunity to test out the social consequences of new behaviors, such as being more honest, asking directly for what he wants (as opposed to being devious and manipulative), expressing emotions, and so on. The value of this process is illustrated by an incident in August of 1946 which, in a sense, triggered the entire concept of group sensitivity training:[16]

It happened at a small Connecticut teachers college, where the distinguished social psychologist Kurt Lewin and his research staff from M.I.T. were conducting seminars for educators on how to implement social change. The staff was holding a meeting one night to review the progress of the seminars when three schoolteachers who hadn't left the building peeked into the room and asked if they could stay. What happened next is described by Lewin's associate, Dr. Ronald Lippitt:

Kurt was rather embarassed, and we all expected him to say no, but he didn't, he said, "Yes, sure, come on in and sit down." And we went right ahead as though they weren't there, and pretty soon one of them was mentioned and her behavior was described and discussed, and the trainer and the researcher had somewhat different observations, perceptions of what had happened, and she became very agitated and said that wasn't the way it happened at all, and she gave her perception. And Lewin got quite excited about this additional data and put it on the board to theorize it, and later on in the evening the same thing happened in relation to one of the other two. She had a different perception of what was being described as an event in that group she was in.[17]

Again Lewin became excited, for here the value of social feedback was blatantly obvious. The staff members were learning that their evaluations of the seminar members were not as "objective" as they might have thought; the seminar members, for their part, saw that the effects of their words and actions earlier in the day were not at all what they had intended.

From this one evening has grown an entire social movement[18]—group sensitivity training—and with it an interesting, diverse group of attendant institutions, including university research laboratories, the management-oriented National Training Labs, and the famous Esalen Institute at Big Sur, California. Methodology has also advanced, such that the basic group dynamic of action-feedback is generally supplemented by two ground rules: Each group member is encouraged (1) when giving someone feedback, to express his feelings openly and directly and (2) to talk only about his relationship with that person (i.e., what he wants from the person, how he regards the person, what he likes or dislikes about the person, and so on), not about other people, future plans, or abstract ideas. These guidelines are deceptively simple, for their impact is to create a powerful group system for inducing self-awareness and change. To see why this is so, let us examine the following illustration of a typical group therapy incident:

THE OTHER MAN[19]

George and Helen are talking to the group leader in the presence of three other couples when Helen suddenly admits that she has been sleeping with another man. Husband George tries to control his response, but the leader encourages both to express their feelings frankly and emphatically:

HELEN: (Shouting) That's what I want, George, your attention. Stop taking me for granted. Stop acting like I was a piece of furniture. Sure, Milton isn't much, but he treated me like I was important. He didn't put his nose behind a newspaper every night. . . .

GEORGE: I don't feel taken care of well enough by you. Why don't you keep the house cleaner? Why don't you have my drink ready when I get home? Why don't you speak up when my friends come over and treat them nicely? Why don't you control the children better so I can relax? And your hair is never combed.

HELEN: (Shouting) Well, you're no prize yourself, Big Shot. You're often a big drag when you're home. We never talk about anything. You just give me money to do things but you never talk to me.

GEORGE: (Shouts, but restrained) Why can't you leave me alone sometime? You always want me home, or want me to talk to you, or take you someplace. . . .[20]

Later that night, after the group session has ended, George and Helen continue their exchange of dislikes until there are no more secrets. They start to say what they like about each other. The positive feeling builds and, as tired as they are, they make glorious love to each other. The next morning George and Helen are ecstatic.

HELEN: I felt so free, like I wasn't holding back anything from George. My body just vibrated and pulsated. It was incredible.

GEORGE: Yeah. Fuck Milton!

HELEN: Then this morning, we got up early—we seemed to have enormous energy—and went out to a rock overlooking the river and got married again. We vowed never to hold back so much from each other.[21]

Feedback exchange—the mutual and honest sharing of emotions and perceptions—has to be seen (better yet, experienced!) to be believed. Regrettably, there are barriers against this kind of relating in our culture, and first attempts are often difficult. Hence the need for sensitivity training groups. As the pioneering group leader Dr. William Schutz has so cogently and painfully observed, "a lifetime of learning not to speak truth, combined with a real difficulty in knowing what, in fact, is true of me, makes living the truth a formidable challenge."[22]

Yet the rewards, as Schutz also points out, can be "remarkable," not only with intimate relationships such as George and Helen's, but in other types of interpersonal associations as well. Applied to industry, sensitivity training can dissolve the unspoken psychological blocks that retard both productivity and employee morale. Take the case of Baylor,[23] the creative director of a large New York advertising agency. Considering himself a kind and generous boss, he was quite surprised when, during a group sensitivity session sponsored by his company, a subordinate accused him of giving only lip service to new ideas. Baylor was hurt and resentful at first, until further feedback revealed that other subordinates felt the same way and weren't bothering to work very hard for him anymore. Finally, recognizing that his paternalistic attitudes were becoming a problem for the company, Baylor agreed to be more open-minded, a gesture that ultimately enabled his creative team to produce better commercials, which elevated company morale and earned Baylor the reputation of being an effective boss.

Group sensitivity training can also be a useful tool for facilitating labor–management relations, particularly for helping negotiators distinguish their personal needs from the broader dollars-and-cents issues.[24] In education it can help the student to learn more about himself and how he affects others; in theater to encourage actors to improvise (give and take feedback spontaneously); in the home to clarify each person's sense of how he or she can better relate to other family members; and in the church to develop in each parishioner a richer sense of his role in the religious community.[25]

GROUP SENSITIVITY TRAINING: WHAT'S IN IT FOR US?

After all we have just said about the wonders of group sensitivity training, this may seem like a strange question, but it must be asked nevertheless. There are people who derive no discernible benefit from such groups, and there is even a large number who report negative experiences as a consequence of sensitivity training. That fact was made quite clear in a recent study by Dr. Morton Lieberman of Stanford University and his colleagues Dr. Irvin Yalom and Dr. Matthew Miles.[26]

Inspired by their desire to learn more about the precise and long-term effects of sensitivity training groups, these researchers set up an elaborate experiment in which 210 Stanford students were assigned, as part of a voluntary course, to eighteen groups, each distinguished either by types of exercises used (i.e., "T-group," "psychodrama," "eclectic methods," and so on) or by the personality of the group leader. The impact of a particular group on a given participant was then determined by a variety of measures, including evaluations of the participant by the group leader, personality questionnaires administered to the participant, and even impressions of the participant from friends not involved in the study. Efforts were made to follow up on the progress of students' lives months after the groups were finished.

What did this massive accumulation of data show? Sixty-five percent of the participants found the groups to be enjoyable, and an even greater percentage, 78, believed the experience was "constructive."[27] As to the long-term effects of the groups, however, Lieberman estimates that only a third of the students went through a discernible positive change—that is, they were able to cope more efficiently, had higher self-regard, were more capable of achieving intimacy, and so on. Another third didn't change at all, according to the study; and the final third actually changed negatively, with a few students requiring remedial psychotherapy.[28]

Of course, not all negative (or positive) change can be attributed to the group process alone. Many forces operate in a person's life. Yet there were "casualties" directly attributed to the group experience. V.C., for instance, describes his first—and last—group session in these words:

I was very scared during the meeting: I withdrew. The leader told me I was a dumb shit because I didn't know how to participate. I felt really outside and really hurt, alienated from other people in the group. . . . I was an outsider; I was just treated as the lowest thing on earth; my opinions were not valid; I was just a toy being played with.[29]

According to Lieberman, the impact of this unfortunate encounter was severe, to say the least:

He lost his "sureness about self," and the kind of identity that he had been building for some time. Following the group

he stated that he went into an extreme depression characterized by depressed affect, by severe insomnia, by weight
loss (40 pounds, from 180 to 140—the subject was six feet
tall), and by occasional suicidal ideation. This depression
lasted approximately six months until finally with the help
of psychotherapy he was able to return to his pregroup level.[30]

On the positive side, it is important to note that not all
the groups had equal numbers of positively changed, negatively changed, and unchanged students. On the contrary,
the value of the Lieberman study is that it identifies for the
first time, clearly and empirically, the qualities that make for
a safe, creative, and productive group.

What are these qualities? Interestingly, the particular
techniques (other than feedback) appeared to make little
difference. The leader's own personality and attitude, on the
other hand, were critical. Leaders who took the "movie
director" approach—who were methodically concerned with
"getting through" a pre-set number of exercises—or leaders
who overemphasized emotional expression and confrontation
were associated with negative outcomes, whereas those who
were genuinely caring, who made special efforts to help
participants integrate and understand what was happening
to them, produced beneficial effects.[31] Student attitudes were
also an important factor. Those, for example, who had a
high regard for close friends, parents, and other significant
persons in their lives were very likely to experience positive
change; on the other hand, participants with a more "jaun-
diced view of their interpersonal world" were prime candi-
dates for the casualty list.[32]

For those interested in guidelines for group participation,
Lieberman and his colleagues make the following suggestions
(here they substitute the expression *encounter group* for
sensitivity training):

Before Deciding to Enter. For those considering attending
an encounter group, the findings of this study encourage, first,

some self-assessment. What are one's hopes for the experience, and one's own views of self? Persons who feel essentially cut off from other people, dislike their own behavior, and see it as less than adequate, and, in addition, believe that the encounter group experience will somehow beautifully, magically, and safely liberate them from themselves, should take care. Such inflated expectations—and they are perhaps too easy to caricature—can lead not only to frustration, but to negative outcomes. It is simply suggested here that potential group entrants examine realistically where they are, and what they might hope, practically speaking, to obtain from the experience. It should be kept in mind that one's chances for clear positive benefit are only about one in three. A person who feels, essentially, that he or she is in psychological distress should ordinarily be considering counseling or psychotherapy rather than an encounter group experience.

Another sort of useful pregroup decision activity is data collection from past group participants. Persons who have been in groups led by the particular encounter group leader being considered should be talked to, preferably several months after their group experience. The most productive question is: "Would you like to be in a group again, led by this leader?" Negative answers should be taken rather seriously. Positive answers should be taken skeptically; one should talk to another group member, or preferably several. Past group members can also profitably be asked about the general group climate, especially the degree to which, in the latter part of the group, anger and attack took place. Such groups should be entered with caution, if one's hopes for learning and for avoiding negative effects are high.

Questioning past group members as to whether anyone got hurt in the group, and getting details of this, is also especially productive in locating groups which might be damaging.

If, after reconnaisance, one has decided to attend a particular group, assessment of the realism of hopes and expectations for the experience and one's own degree of skepticism or trust about the experience is in order. Mild skepticism, the attitude that the group can be used for one's purposes, but may not automatically be the best or safest of environments, appears to be the most productive stance.

During the Group. Particularly during the first half or so of the group's life, it will pay to be recurrently aware of one's own position in the group, and to operate, if possible, in ways that induce the realistic feeling that one is a comfortably active member of the group. Persons who, by the middle of the group, find that they have been largely passive, "out of it," do not like the group particularly, do not sense that they are respected and liked by other members, never have a feeling of "communion" with them, and do not feel able to disclose their inner thoughts and feelings, will probably get little out of the group experience.

It may be argued that one's position in the group is not wholly under one's control—that others define it. That is correct to some extent. By and large, however, if one becomes aware of his position in the group, and treats improving it as a secondary learning objective, the position can be altered. The person who, for example, reports that "I feel out of the group and wish I could be more in," tends to alter others' views of his position, so that their behavior usually shifts toward welcoming and support. Similarly, active behavior directed toward important and valued group goals, such as open expression of feelings, acting freely and spontaneously, taking risks, and being aware of what's happening in the group, tends not only to be personally rewarding, but improves one's own position in the group. Passive, withdrawing, demanding, or hostile behavior does not do so. The option of leaving the group if it is proving steadily unproductive, stressful, or damaging should always be kept open. Not all persons and all learning environments can be perfectly matched.

Generally speaking, it is easier to give data-based advice on how to avoid negative outcomes than it is to suggest ways of guaranteeing gain. It appears, however, that there are many different pathways to gain, assuming that the learner is able to avoid the traps of overoptimism, blind trust in the goodness of the group or the leader, and being out on the edge of the group. Avoiding these traps permits—but does not guarantee—achievement of positive learning goals.

There is one suggestion which will encourage positive gains, however: For those who maintain an active, *thoughtful* stance toward what is occurring in the group and in their own awareness, durable gains are more likely. Efforts to think about the encounter group experience and its meaning, contrary to what is often asserted, are likely to make for more learning. Keeping a diary or journal is an easy way to accomplish this, especially if its contents are occasionally discussed with others.

After the Group. Some realistic assessment should be made of what has been learned (or not learned). That, more likely than not, is what will be retained and carried away from the experience. The hope that "it can all be put together" at some time in the future is a relatively slim one. Secondly, after the group has receded in time, some reduction in positive feelings can be expected. But to the degree positive learnings were in fact achieved, maintenance of gains is quite likely. More maintenance will occur if one experiments actively with new behavior, taking a self-monitoring stance. This requires some modulation and refinement, rather than all-or-none operations. Using others for active feedback and discussion aids in the process of stabilizing learnings. It appears rather important to be reflective, to *think* about one's behavior and its meaning in the post-group setting. All in all, a relatively pro-active, thoughtful stance seems most productive. It should be said, though, that giant efforts of will do not seem required: Many of the gains reported by our participants were intrinsically satisfying and self-rewarding, so that the reward and reinforcement supplied by others may be less crucial than many people have supposed.[33]

SUPERORDINATE GOALS: A NEW WAY TO WORLD PEACE?

We have seen how groups might be used to improve interpersonal relations and to promote personal growth. But what about international relations? Can groups be used to promote peace among nations? Some scientists believe that they can be, in an indirect fashion. They contend that, by studying functioning groups, they might gain insight into the mechanisms of intergroup conflict: how hostility develops and how it is reduced. Once in possession of that knowledge, they argue further, the scientists might be in a better position to develop procedures for eliminating hostility between nation groups.

Steps must be taken, and taken now, to find the formula for peace on earth. One man has taken such a step, and it is a giant one. That man is Muzafer Sherif, and like Stanley Milgram, he is a social psychologist. In the 1950s Dr. Sherif conducted an innovative experiment with groups that, in our opinion, represents the single most important psychological contribution ever made to the possible reduction of international hostility.[34]

The manner in which Sherif conducted his experiment is almost as fascinating as the experimental results he obtained. Every year hundreds of thousands of city kids make their annual migration to that treasured American institution, the overnight camp. There they swim, fish, shoot, canoe, learn arts and crafts, go on overnights, and at a particular camp in Oklahoma, unknowingly become experimental subjects in Sherif's study of intergroup relations. A psychology experiment in a summer camp? It sounds strange. Yet, in actuality, Sherif chose this particular "laboratory" for sound scientific reasons: Isolated from the outside world, the summer campsite provided a place where scientific control could be more readily achieved, a place where Sherif and his staff could manipulate the environment and observe the campers in a naturalistic setting, without fear that disturbances from the outside would confound their results.

The campers that Sherif chose for his experiment were a counselor's dream: twenty-two healthy, well-adjusted eleven-year-old boys, all of whom came from stable, middle-class families and were in the upper half of their classes in scho-lastic standing. None of the boys had been problem children at home, in the neighborhood, or in school. They were basi-cally peaceful pre-teen-agers. Yet in a matter of weeks, they would be aggressively embroiled in a full-scale camp "war," under the watchful eye of the camp staff.

The camp war did not occur accidentally; it was an out-growth of carefully planned experimental manipulations designed to help Sherif answer two basic questions: (1) How does intergroup conflict arise? (2) How can such con-flict be reduced? In answering these questions, Sherif divided his camp study into three basic parts.

1. *Stage of Group Formation.* Before you can study inter-group relations, you have to have groups. In the group-formation stage two independent, cohesive groups were created. This involved, first, an attempt by Sherif and his staff to divide the twenty-two campers into two equal units, making sure that the physical skills and sizes of the campers were roughly equivalent in each group. Once this was done, each bunch of boys was transported, in separate buses, to opposite ends of the campsite and billeted in separate cabins. Then, for about a week, the boys in each cabin participated with their cabin mates in activities designed to foster the growth of well-developed groups. These activities included canoe trips over rough terrain and cookout overnights—the kinds of highly appealing tasks that require concerted, coop-erative effort to carry out and that build esprit de corps among the participants. Once each cabin unit had developed into a well-defined group, both groups were brought together for the first time, and the second stage of the experiment commenced.

2. *Stage of Intergroup Conflict.* Just as you cannot study intergroup relations without groups, neither can you study the reduction of intergroup conflict without first producing that conflict. The question is: How do you go about produc-ing conflict between two groups of campers who are basi-

cally well-behaved and peaceful? Sherif gives us an important hint with the following hypothesis:

> When members of two groups come into contact with one another in a series of activities that embody goals which each urgently desires, but which can be attained by one group only at the expense of the other, competitive activity toward the goal changes, over time, into hostility between the groups and their members.[35]

Now what "series of activities" can be conducted at a summer camp that "embody goals which each urgently desires, but which can be attained by one group only at the expense of the other"? For those of you who have been to camp, one answer probably comes immediately to mind: a Color War. For those unfamiliar with this term, a Color War is a kind of junior olympics, a time when the camp is divided into two teams (each team is designated by a color, hence the term *Color War*) that compete in a series of athletic events lasting anywhere from a day to a week or more. When all the events are completed, the team with the highest total score wins the Color War. As any camper or counselor who has gone through such an experience will attest, a Color War creates a fierce sense of competition and team pride that permeates the whole camp while the contest is in progress.

Making use of the Color War potential for creating intergroup hostility, Sherif and the camp staff arranged for the two boys' cabins to oppose each other in a tournament that included baseball, football, tent pitching, and tug-of-war contests. Observes Sherif:

> The tournament started with great zest and in the spirit of good sportsmanship to which these American boys had already been thoroughly indoctrinated. . . . As the tournament progressed from event to event, the good sportsmanship and good feeling began to evaporate. The sportsman-like cheer for the other group, customarily given after a game, "2-4-6-8,

who do we appreciate," turned to a derisive chant: "2-4-6-8, who do we appreci*hate*."[36]

In a very short period of time, what had begun as friendly relations between two groups of peaceful boys deteriorated into an inter-cabin donnybrook, replete with name-calling, fisticuffs, cabin raids, and property destruction. Sherif notes: "If an outside observer had entered the situation after the conflict began . . . he could only have concluded on the basis of their behavior that these boys (who were the 'cream of the crop' in their communities) were either disturbed, vicious, or wicked youngsters."[37] That's how bad things got.

There was no question about it: Intergroup conflict had been solidly achieved at Sherif's summer camp. The problem now was to end it. After all, it wouldn't be very nice (or scientifically ethical) to return the boys to their community in the midst of a pitched battle. Furthermore, the whole purpose of the experiment was to find a way of reducing intergroup conflict, and judging from the behavior of Sherif's campers, there would never be a better time to find the solution.

3. *Reduction of Intergroup Conflict.* Through experimental manipulation, Sherif had first created conditions conducive to the formation of groups and then to the onset of hostilities between them. Now, in the final stage of the experiment, Sherif set out to answer this question: "How can two groups in conflict, each with hostile attitudes and negative images of the other and each desiring to keep the members of the detested out-group at a safe distance, be brought into cooperative interaction and friendly intercourse?"

Several approaches were tried. One approach was an *appeal to the moral values* shared by members of both groups. This appeal was contained in sermons that the camp minister gave at religious services. In these sermons he talked of brotherly love, the value of cooperation, and the need for forgiving one's enemies. "The boys arranged the services and were enthusiastic about the sermons," Sherif writes. However, "upon solemnly departing from the ceremony, they returned within minutes to their concerns to defeat, avoid, or retaliate against the detested out-group."[38]

A second approach involved *bringing the groups together at events that were very enjoyable.* Thus, the groups were brought together to eat, see movies, shoot off fireworks on the Fourth of July, and so forth. Unfortunately, this approach also failed. "Far from reducing conflict, these situations served as occasions for the rival groups to berate and attack each other. . . . The mealtime encounters were dubbed 'garbage wars' by the participants,"[39] who used their food for ammunition rather than nourishment.

The one approach that Sherif believed would work—and *did*—involved the use of *superordinate goals* in the reduction of intergroup conflict. "Superordinate goals are those goals that have a compelling appeal for members of each group, but that neither group can achieve without participation of the other."[40]

To demonstrate that accomplishing superordinate goals leads to reduced intergroup hostility, Sherif and his staff rigged the camp program so that highly desirable activities and outcomes could be realized only through the joint cooperation of the two groups. For example, one day on an outing, the two groups of boys were faced with a terrible problem: Hot, tired, and hungry, they reached their campsite only to discover that the truck which was to go for food and water was stalled and needed to be pulled onto the road. One group of campers got a rope, tied it around the truck's fender, and began to tug. The vehicle didn't move, and it became obvious that one group working alone couldn't accomplish the task. When both groups pulled on the rope together, however, they were able to get the truck started and on its way.

Joint efforts in situations such as the "stalled truck" episode did not *immediately* dispel hostility between the two groups. "But gradually," Sherif notes, "the series of activities requiring interdependent action reduced conflict and hostility between the groups. . . . In the end, the groups were actively seeking opportunities to intermingle, to entertain and 'treat' each other."[41]

All's well that ends well. On the last day of the camp session, the boys were given the choice of returning home together on one bus or on two separate buses, one for each group. They voted to return together.

> On the way home, a stop was made for refreshments. One group still had five dollars won as a prize. They decided to spend this sum on refreshments for both groups rather than to use it solely for themselves and thereby have more to eat. On their own initiative they invited their former rivals to be their guests for malted milks.[42]

THE SHERIF CAMP STUDY: WHAT'S IN IT FOR US?

From peace to war and back to peace again. At least in his summer camp, Sherif seemed to create conflict or cooperation at his bidding. Now nobody is suggesting that what Sherif did with a group of boys in Oklahoma he could do with the leaders of the Kremlin or, for that matter, the leaders of the United States or any other country. But what Sherif *learned* about the induction and reduction of intergroup hostility might very well be applicable at the national or international level. In today's world we are confronting more and more problems that can be solved *only* through international cooperation. Just as Sherif's campers could not move the truck without intergroup cooperation, neither can we clean our seas, regulate our population, and limit our arms without international cooperation.

Superordinate goals are relevant to both campers and

nations. If they can be used to bring peace to a summer camp, why shouldn't they be able to do the same in the world arena? Instead of looking at pollution, overpopulation, and the arms race as insoluble problems, why not seize upon them as excellent opportunities for international cooperation, leading, it may be hoped, to international friendship. Sherif has suggested a possible approach to reducing hostility between nations. It would be somewhat ironic (but not at all unpleasant) if the struggle to avoid nuclear war gave us the opportunity to build a lasting peace.

NOTES

1. M. Bard and J. Zacker, "The Prevention of Family Violence: Dilemmas of Community Intervention," *Journal of Marriage and the Family*, in press.
2. Ibid.
3. M. Bard, "Alternatives to Traditional Law Enforcement," in *Psychology and the Problems of Society,* ed. F. Korten et al. (Washington, D.C.: American Psychological Association, 1970).
4. Ibid., pp. 130–131.
5. Ibid., p. 129.
6. Ibid., p. 131.
7. J. Talbott and S. Talbott, "Training Police in Community Relations and Urban Problems," *American Journal of Psychiatry* 127 (1971): 894–900.
8. See, for example, M. Karlins and H. Abelson, *Persuasion* (New York: Springer, 1970), chap. 3, "The Influence of Others," pp. 41–67.
9. K. Lewin, "Studies in Group Decision," in *Group Dynamics*, ed. D. Cartwright and A. Zander (New York: Harper & Row, 1953).
10. P. Meyer, "If Hitler Asked You to Electrocute a Stranger, Would You? Probably." *Esquire* (February 1970): 130.
11. Ibid., p. 128.
12. Ibid., pp. 130–132.
13. S. Milgram, "Some Conditions of Obedience and Disobedience to Authority," *Human Relations* 18 (1965): 74–75.
14. S. Milgram, "Liberating Effects of Group Pressure," *Journal of Personality and Social Psychology* 1 (1965): 131.
15. M. Bernal, "Behavioral Feedback in the Modification of Brat Behaviors," *Journal of Nervous and Mental Disease,* 148 (1969): 375–385.
16. K. Back, *Beyond Words* (Baltimore: Penguin, 1973), pp. 6–9.

17. Ibid., p. 8.
18. Ibid., pp. 3–27.
19. W. Schutz, *Here Comes Every-Body.* (New York: Harper & Row, 1971), pp. 48–54.
20. Ibid., pp. 51–52.
21. Ibid., p. 54.
22. W. Schutz, *Elements of Encounter* (Big Sur, Calif.: Joy Press, 1973), p. 99.
23. Fictionalized account based on management group sensitivity techniques.
24. Schutz, *Elements of Encounter,* p. 92.
25. Ibid., pp. 93–96.
26. M. Lieberman et al., *Encounter Groups: First Facts* (New York: Basic Books, 1973).
27. Ibid., p. 94.
28. Ibid., p. 107.
29. Ibid., p. 179.
30. Ibid.
31. Ibid., p. 264.
32. Ibid., pp. 329–330.
33. Ibid., pp. 439–442.
34. M. Sherif and C. Sherif, *Social Psychology* (New York: Harper & Row, 1969), pp. 228–266.
35. Ibid., p. 239.
36. Ibid., p. 240.
37. Ibid., p. 254.
38. Ibid.
39. Ibid., p. 256.
40. Ibid.
41. Ibid.
42. Ibid.

SUGGESTED READINGS

BACK, K. *Beyond Words.* Baltimore: Penguin, 1973.

KARLINS, M., and ABELSON, H. *Persuasion.* New York: Springer, 1970.

LIEBERMAN, M.; YALOM, I.; and MILES, M. *Encounter Groups: First Facts.* New York: Basic Books, 1973.

MILGRAM, S. "Behavioral Study of Obedience." *Journal of Abnormal and Social Psychology* 67 (1963): 371–378.

SCHUTZ, W. *Elements of Encounter.* Big Sur, Calif.: Joy Press, 1973.

7

behavioral medicine

We've all seen the plot on TV. The elderly Mrs. Smith is dying and knows it. She summons her doctor and asks him how long she has to live. The physician hedges but finally estimates "a week . . . maybe two . . . a month at the outside." The woman gets terribly upset, saying she is ready to die but not before her fiftieth wedding anniversary, a little more than two months away. The doctor says he will do everything he can to help her remain alive that long; then he goes downstairs and tells Mr. Smith his wife will be dead in a matter of days. Nine weeks later we see Mr. and Mrs. Smith celebrating their anniversary. The next day Mrs. Smith is dead.

The story of Mrs. Smith is tear-jerking fiction at its best, an old woman heroically staving off the grim reaper until she can cherish a treasured moment. The question is: How fictional is the story of Mrs. Smith?

To the Jewish people, Yom Kippur, the Day of Atonement, is the most solemn religious holiday of the year. It is a day of great importance, the day they "heed the call of the shofar" and ask God to forgive them for their sins and transgressions. It is a day that Jews anxiously await, much as Mrs. Smith awaited her anniversary day. Sociologist David Phillips discovered something extremely interesting about Yom Kippur and the people who observe it. Studying the mortality records for Jews in New York and Budapest, he found a notable drop in the death rate just before the Day of Atonement. There was no such drop among non-Jews before the High Holy Day. Carrying his investigation further, Phillips also examined the mortality pattern around people's birthdays. What he discovered tied in nicely with his Yom Kippur findings: There was a significant dip in deaths before birthdays and a significant peak in deaths thereafter—which all means, according to Phillips, that "some people look forward to witnessing certain important occasions and are able to put off dying in order to do so."[1] It seems that Mrs. Smith is not the only person who keeps death waiting.[2]

The Jews in Phillips' study were able to observe Yom Kippur by postponing their deaths until the holiday was over. Of course, this "will to live" has its limitations. Death is inevitable, and there is only a finite amount of time that we can postpone it. Yet the idea that man may be able to put off death *at all* raises some interesting questions, questions like "How can a *cognition*—in this case a wish—have such an influence over the body?"

For many years doctors and scientists have suspected that a man's mental behavior (his thoughts, beliefs, hopes, and so on) might have more control over his physiology and overt behavior than was readily admitted in textbooks. There is, for example, the disturbing problem of the placebo. A well-known example of a placebo is the "sugar-coated pill," a capsule the patient believes contains medicine when, in fact, it does not. Oftentimes, the patient swallowing these bogus tablets recovers from his illness as well as the patient who receives real medicine. Why? Many answers are suggested: the patient's faith in the doctor dispensing the pills, his belief in the effectiveness of the doctor's "medicine," the psychological basis of his condition. One fact remains, however, regardless of the answer: Without the aid of "real" medicine the patient has overcome his illness. In other words, something the patient did enabled him to cure himself![3]

What behaviors allow a person to make himself sick or well? Global answers are elusive, yet recent studies provide some exciting clues.

A SILENT MOMENT FOR MEDICATION

Among the medical practices of the ancient Greeks, one of the most intriguing is the healing ritual of the Aesculapian sanctuaries.[4] Dedicated to Aesculapius, the god of medicine, these temples were the equivalent of hospitals for innumerable mentally and physically ill people, from both the Aegean area and beyond. The religious beliefs surrounding the ritual were elaborate and complex; however, the actual behavior required from the patient was quite simple.

When the sufferer arrived at the sanctuary, he immediately initiated a routine of devotion to Aesculapius. After a suitable waiting time, he was cleansed by servants and instructed by the priest in techniques for forgetting "all that had gone before" and for remembering "all that he would see." Then, donning a white sheet, the patient descended into a cave and waited to receive visions of dream communications from the god. When he later emerged, he would report his experiencs to the priest and then wait patiently for signs of a cure.

Today, over 2,000 years later, many Westerners are reexamining spiritual forms of healing, trying to separate practical techniques from mere ritual and superstition. Living in a dirt tunnel with spiders, it turns out, does little to promote health. Deliberate attempts to silently "turn inward," on the other hand, can have profound and beneficial physiological effects. This was dramatically demonstrated by Dr. R. Keith Wallace of Harvard in his now-famous study of transcendental meditation (or TM),[5] a modern spiritual discipline not unlike the Aesculapian practices. With TM the meditator strives to achieve a state of "restful alertness" by spending two twenty-minute periods each day in "comfortable isolation," and allowing random images, visions, sensations, and word forms to "percolate up" into consciousness.

Carefully monitoring the physiological responses of advanced meditators with an electroencephalograph (EEG machine) and other sensitive instruments, Wallace found that TM was strongly correlated with such beneficial biological responses as decreasing oxygen consumption, diminishing heart rate, lower cardiac output and respiration, and increasing skin resistance, which is inversely related to stress. Consequent studies have not only confirmed Wallace's findings but have also shown that this form of meditation can significantly increase overall memory, quickly reduce anxiety, decrease blood pressure in hypertensive subjects, heighten perceptual ability, relieve asthma, and even alleviate dependence on drugs like amphetamines, barbiturates, heroin and other opiates, alcohol, and tobacco.[6]

As healthful as TM is, many hard-minded people will resist the idea that a faddish spiritual cult can really offer something worthwhile—and to a certain extent they're right. More correctly, TM *does* work, but not for the reasons usually given by its proselytizers. Maharishi Mahesh Yogi, the founder of TM, places special emphasis on the need for each initiate to learn a personally tailored mantra-sound, which when repeated is supposed to help the practioner to transcend thought, ultimately to experience a "healing nothingness." In fact, such blank states of consciousness are quite common outside of TM. When a person focuses on any stimulus, explains Harvard's Dr. Gary Schwartz, "it seems eventually to disappear, leaving pure attention without any specific content."[7] This process of *habituation* "reflects a basic process of neutral function." The real secret of TM was revealed in a comprehensive study reported to an assembly of the American Psychological Association in 1973.[8] The author of this convention paper, Dr. Leon Otis of the Stanford Research Institute, had taken sixty-two subjects (thirty-two men and thirty women) and divided them randomly into three groups, each to sit quietly approximately twenty minutes twice daily. Members of the first group were to practice TM itself; those in the second group would rest *passively*; and those in the third group *actively* repeated the phrase "I am a witness only" instead of a special mantra. At the end of three months, those who meditated TM-style did indeed receive many of the benefits claimed by the Maharishi. But so did those who sat passively or repeated the mock mantra! In fact, the achievements of the genuine transcendental meditators were not in any way at variance with those of the two control groups.

The medical power of TM lies not with the ritual mantra, then, but with the simple act of *relaxation*. This is a significant discovery, if for no other reason than that it makes TM more understandable (and acceptable) to the Western scientific mind. More importantly, it suggests a way in which psychologists can even improve on the benefits of TM: by using more efficient methods of relaxation. This is not a casual proposition. Psychology already has an extensive repertoire of *deep relaxation* techniques, and there is preliminary evidence that they may be more effective than TM-style resting for producing positive physiological effects. In one study of sixty female college students, a procedure called *progressive relaxation*—a systematic tensing and releasing of muscles in different parts of the body—was found superior to simple resting for reducing anxiety, heart rate, skin resistance, and muscle tension.[9]

With TM and possibly other methods of relaxation, psychologists are building a practical technology for behavioral medicine. The ancient wisdom of relaxation, dating back across centuries and cultures, is being updated and refined for the benefit of all. Now let us discuss other ways in which behavioral science is contributing to the quest for a healthier life.

TYPE A

By many people's standards, Paul is an ideal citizen.[10] He loves his wife and his two sons and supports them as best he can. Indeed, after twenty-five years of hard-driving work for a large California brewery, Paul is now the proud— and busy—manager of the firm. He makes it a point to be friendly with everyone, from important business acquaintances to the local barber and garage attendant.

Paul's private life, though, is not as perfect as his image might suggest. His single-minded preoccupation with success has created tensions between himself and his sons, who do not share Paul's conservative opinions. His wife, furthermore, is deeply involved with a variety of community and cultural activities, avocations to which Paul pays lip service but which he secretly believes to be worthless. Paul and his wife seem to communicate; yet, in reality, Paul's driving concern with business (he reads trade journals in the bathroom) has produced a marriage of mutual tolerance.

But these "human relations" difficulties, as lamentable as the are, are not the worst of Paul's problems—at least, not according to the noted cardiologists Meyer Friedman and Ray Rosenman. They declare that Paul will be "very, very lucky" if he escapes a coronary heart attack within the next ten years. "On the basis of clinical and research experiences," they state sadly, "his chances of escaping will only be about one out of twenty.[11]

What permits these doctors to make such a disturbing prediction? We might guess that Paul abuses himself in ways that are traditionally associated with heart disease—that is, through overeating, smoking, and indolence. And, in fact, Paul is guilty on all three counts. He is about twenty-five pounds overweight and eats too many foods rich in cholesterol; he smokes two packs of cigarettes a day; and he rarely exercises more than an hour or two each week. But according to Friedman and Rosenman, none of these physical abuses is as important as Paul's obsessive concern with attaining as many achievements as he can within the shortest possible time. This psychological pathology—what Friedman and Rosenman call *type A behavior*—may be the greatest instigator of coronary heart disease in America today. On the other hand, people who exhibit *type B behavior*—that is, those who are not excessively competitive and concerned with meeting deadlines—have a much lower chance of ever experiencing coronary heart disease.

Racing against the clock to succeed is so American a concept, ranking with such ideals as motherhood and apple pie, that it is hard to believe this behavior can have any negative consequences, particularly an outcome so totally devastating as death. Yet Friedman and Rosenman offer arguments that are cogent and persuasive. They remind us, for example, that the dangers of a high-paced, high-pressure life have been noted for centuries, if not by medical doctors, at least by well-known social scientists. It was no less than Arnold Toynbee who commented over a decade ago:

> At the earliest moment at which we catch our first glimpse of Man on earth we find him not only on the move but already moving at an accelerating pace. This crescendo of acceleration is continuing today. In our generation it is perhaps the most difficult and dangerous of all the current problems of the race.[12]

Because the type A person is literally fighting the clock minute by minute, he constantly maintains the emotional states associated with conflict and frustration. In short, he is chronically tense which, on a biological level, means that his glands are continuously secreting nerve hormones (norepine-phrine and epinephrine), ACTH, and growth hormones.

If this sounds bad, it is. A chronic excess of these hormones has the double effect of not only increasing levels of choles-terol in the bloodstream but also multiplying the amount of time the body requires to cleanse itself of cholesterol obtained from food. (The vast majority of physicians believe that deposits of cholesterol on the coronary arteries play a signifi-cant role in the onset of heart disease.) But that's not all. When these hormones flood your body, other things can happen: The number of clotting elements in your blood will increase, often enlarging plaque deposits in the coronary artery. When this plaque, which is composed partially of cholesterol and fats, reaches a critical size, it can suddenly dissolve, spreading a greasy substance that blocks the flow of blood to the heart and can, under the wrong circum-stances, kill you. This, incidentally, is not a problem just for older Americans. Plaque deposits grow from the minute we are born, and in the advanced industrial countries, where "fat-fortified" foods are abundant, people can develop dangerous deposits as early as their mid-twenties.

Other complications caused by an excess of hormones in type A people include a possible constriction of the small capillaries sustaining the coronary arteries and an increase of insulin in the blood to levels that can practically devastate the coronary arteries.[13]

Unfortunately, the type A person is usually so convinced that pushing is responsible for his success that he rarely has any cause to question such behavior. For this reason, Friedman and Rosenman have developed a type A self-identification test. Here are some of the telltale responses that define this destructive pattern:

1. [You] have a habit of explosively accentuating various key words in your ordinary speech even when there is no real need for such accentuation. . . .
2. [You] *always* move, walk, and eat rapidly.

3. [You] feel (particularly if you openly exhibit to others) an impatience with the rate at which most events take place. You are suffering from this sort of impatience if you find it difficult to restrain yourself from hurrying the speech of others and resort to the device of saying very quickly over and over again, "Uh huh, uh huh," or, "Yes yes, yes yes," to someone who is talking, unconsciously urging him to "get on with it" or hasten his rate of speaking. You are also suffering from impatience if you attempt to finish the sentences of persons speaking to you before they can.

4. [You] indulge in *polyphasic* thought or performance, frequently striving to think of or do two or more things simultaneously. For example, if while trying to listen to another person's speech you persist in continuing to think about an irrelevant subject, you are indulging in polyphasic thought. Similarly, if while golfing or fishing you continue to ponder your business or professional [*or academic*!] problems, or if while using an electric razor you attempt also to eat your breakfast or drive your car, you are indulging in polyphasic performance. This is one of the commonest traits in the Type A man. Nor is he always satisfied with doing just two things at one time. We have known subjects who not only shaved and ate simultaneously, but also managed to read a business or professional journal at the same time.

5. [You] almost always feel vaguely guilty when you relax and do absolutely nothing for several days.

6. [You] attempt to schedule more and more in less and less time, and in doing so make fewer and fewer allowances for unforseen contingencies. A concomitant of this is a *chronic sense of time urgency*, one of the core components of Type A Behavior Pattern.

7. [You] believe that whatever success you have enjoyed has been due in good part to your ability to get things done faster than your fellow man and . . . you are afraid to stop doing everything faster and faster.[14]

People who manifest these and similar "symptoms" are very likely to be type A, according to Friedman and his colleague. Can these individuals change their behavior . . .

and if they can, would such changes decrease their chances of getting a coronary? The complete data are not yet in, but on the basis of preliminary evidence, the answer to both questions seems to be yes. Type As can alter their self-destructive behaviors, write the cardiologists, by consciously adopting the psychology of type Bs or, put another way, by doing the opposite of the type A behaviors we have just identified. For example, whenever a person finds himself tempted to think about two things at the same time, he should try to concentrate on just one. Similarly, instead of rushing other people through a conversation, he should try to listen to others, showing patience and understanding if they are not as quick as he is.

Finally, and perhaps most importantly, Friedman and Rosenman recommend to the type A person that he take a frank and philosophical look at his own life's progress. The chances are, they point out, that such an examination will reveal something quite startling: that his achievements were not as dependent on racing the clock as he had imagined. Type Bs, they remind us, are no less successful than type As; they just handle themselves differently. They also live long enough to enjoy their accomplishments.

BEHAVIORAL MEDICINE: WHAT'S IN IT FOR US?

An overview of recent studies[15] shows that many ailments, not just heart disease, are strongly related to personality traits. The results of a careful experiment by Dr. Floyd Ring,[16] a psychiatrist at the University of Nebraska College of Medicine, gives us an idea of how solid these correlations can be.

To see if he could really predict a person's illness strictly on the basis of personality impressions, Ring asked other physicians to "refer to him more than 400 patients suffering from any of fourteen ailments,"[17] ranging from simple backache and migrane to degenerative arthritis and diabetes. Ring and his associates then set themselves the task of trying to determine each person's specific illness on the basis of a single fifteen- to twenty-five-minute psychiatric interview. To make the project even more rigorous, patients were dressed in similar clothing to mask any physical symptoms, and all interview sessions were policed by at least two additional colleagues, whose job it was to screen the discussions for any verbal slip that might reveal the nature of the subject's disease.

The outcome of this experiment, reported by Howard and Martha Lewis in their text *Psychosomatics*, was striking to be sure:

> One hundred per cent of the hyperthyroid cases were detected. Similarly, personality alone uncovered 83 per cent of the patients with peptic ulcer and rheumatoid arthritis, 71 per cent with coronary occlusion, and between 60 and 67 per cent with asthma, diabetes, hypertension, and ulcerative colitis.[18]

The kicker came, though, when it was discovered that one of the psychiatric sessions had produced a diagnosis more accurate than the patient's original physical examination! In related research Stanford University Professor George F. Solomon has revealed that both the occurrence and the rapidity of cancer are tied to discernible personality types.[19] Three factors that consistently appear in studies of cancer patients are the "inability to express hostile feelings and emotions . . . unresolved tension concerning a parent figure . . . [and] sexual disturbance."[20] Solomon has also studied sufferers of rheumatoid arthritis and found them, unlike their healthy counterparts, to be "nervous, tense, worried, moody, depressed, concerned with the rejection they perceived from their mothers and the strictness they perceived from their fathers, and [inhibited over] the expression of anger."[21]

Of course, it's one thing to say that different illnesses have distinct personality components . . . quite another to suggest that all illnesses can be treated, or prevented, through specific behaviors. Yet the prospect is an intriguing one, and if the Friedman and Rosenman research is any kind of indicator, we can expect some very interesting news about behavioral medicine in the near future. In the meantime, correlations between personality and physical ailments are still useful, particularly in the area of preventive medicine. If he knows the statistical relationship between behavior and illness, the physician can take steps to hinder the onset of "probable" diseases associated with a particular patient's psychology. This information also enables the doctor to make a more accurate diagnosis of strange, ambiguous symptoms and to predict the effects of strenuous treatments such as operations. In a recent study of fifty-eight cardiac cases, for example, it was found that a certain psychological questionnaire, the Willner Conceptual Level Analogy Tests, could generally foretell the life and death postoperative consequences of open-heart surgery.[22] In another experiment, this one conducted at the Memorial Hospital Research Center in Southern California, scientists discovered that a well-known psychological inventory, the Minnesota Multiphasic Personality Inventory, can predict the success of disc surgery for back pain with surprising accuracy.[23] Those patients who measured over 85 on two MMPI scales "had no more than a 10 percent chance of getting good or excellent relief from the operation," and those with a standard score of 54 or less had "only 10 percent chance of failure."[24] MMPI screening for back pain sufferers is now accepted procedure at this Long Beach hospital—and with good reason, for as one observer has noted: "With $50 worth of personality tests, [these scientists] save patients thousands of dollars and days of hospital time."[25]

We should also point out that the associations between personality and illness are but half the story of behavioral medicine. As we have already noted in Chapter 2, people do not live in a social vacuum; men and women are significantly influenced by their environments. Certain stressful situations, according to psychologists Thomas Holmes and Minoru Masuda, are even powerful enough to reduce the body's natural defense mechanisms against disease.[26] By implication, a person could *behaviorally maintain his body's immunological strength* by avoiding those stressful circumstances or, more practically, by deliberately following a low-key life-style immediately after experiencing a critical number of taxing social events.

But how does a person know for sure when his body's stress tolerance has been reached? Or if he has never before experienced a certain onerous situation (such as divorce or taking out a large mortgage), can he know in advance how wearing the event will be?

To help answer these questions—to determine exactly what constitutes a severe life disruption and how each crisis compares in strength to others—Holmes and Masuda took a relatively well-known event, marriage, and arbitrarily gave it the value of 50 points. Almost 400 subjects were then given a list of various life situations and asked to rank each relative to marriage according to the following instructions:

> As you complete each of the events, think to yourself: "Is this event indicative of more or less readjustment than marriage?" "Would the readjustment take longer or shorter to accomplish?" If you decide the readjustment is more intense and protracted, choose a *proportionately* larger number for the event. If you decide the readjustment required is less than marriage then choose a *proportionately* smaller number for the event.[27]

Mean scores were calculated for each event, and a simple table was constructed, ranking each life event in terms of its disruptive value and giving a numerical indicator of readjustment, called *life change units*, for each. The results can be seen here:

Rank	Event	"Life Change Units"[28]
1	Death of spouse	100
2	Divorce	73
3	Marital separation	65
4	Jail term	63
5	Death of close family member	63
6	Personal injury or illness	53
7	Marriage	50
8	Fired at work	47
9	Marital reconciliation	45
10	Retirement	45
11	Change in health of family member	44
12	Pregnancy	40
13	Sex difficulties	39
14	Gain of new family member	39
15	Business readjustment	39
16	Change in financial state	38
17	Death of close friend	37
18	Change to different line of work	36
19	Change in number of arguments with spouse	35
20	Mortgage over $10,000	31
21	Foreclosure of mortgage or loan	30
22	Change in responsibilities at work	29
23	Son or daughter leaving home	29
24	Trouble with in-laws	29
25	Outstanding personal achievement	28
26	Wife begins or stops work	26
27	Begin or end school	26
28	Change in living conditions	25
29	Revision of personal habits	24
30	Trouble with boss	23
31	Change in work hours or conditions	20
32	Change in residence	20
33	Change in schools	20
34	Change in recreation	19
35	Change in church activities	19
36	Change in social activities	18

37	Mortgage or loan less than $10,000	17
38	Change in sleeping habits	16
39	Change in number of family get-togethers	15
40	Change in eating habits	15
41	Vacation	13
42	Christmas	12
43	Minor violations of the law	11

In theory what these psychologists now had was a tool for calculating the *cumulative amount* of social readjustment demanded of any person within a given time period (just by summing the numerical values associated with specific changes in his life). The higher the total, the greater his odds of contracting a major illness and, therefore, the greater his need to behaviorally simplify his daily existence.

The theory looked good on paper, but did it work in practice? Could this procedure really predict the onset of illness?

One test came when Holmes and another colleague, Dr. Richard H. Rahe of the University of Washington School of Medicine, asked eighty-eight doctor-subjects to fill out a questionnaire indicating all significant "life events and major health changes for the past ten years." When the data were collected and sorted, Holmes and Rahe were surprised to learn that an astonishing 83 percent of the doctor's illnesses came within two years after the physicians had experienced a year of life changes valued at 150 or more. "The odds that this illness–onset pattern could have occurred by chance are less than one in 1,000," note the researchers.[29]

In another study of fifty-four students,[30] 86 percent of those with high totals suffered major illnesses or injury during a two-year period, whereas only a third of those with low scores experienced similar health problems during the same interval. In a final experiment,[31] Rahe examined the most recent health records of over 2,000 Navy sailors, who were just about to embark on a cruise. After only a month on maneuvers, those officers and enlisted men with high life change unit scores were reporting "nearly 90 percent more first illnesses" than those with lower scores.

It appears, then, that we have the beginnings of a technique that will enable any person to predict, on the basis of recent social experiences, the probability of incurring a serious illness in the foreseeable future. Combine this measure with a personality-disease profile, and we are well on our way to a comprehensive program for effective behavioral medicine. If an individual is aware that his personality type is "biased" toward a certain disease and, further, that he has recently undergone too many dramatic life changes, he can take steps to protect himself. Medically, he can immunize himself with whatever drugs might be available; behaviorally, he can make his life simpler, reducing the possibility of further disruptive events. Institutions, particularly the armed forces, will also benefit from these techniques. The Navy would be wise, for example, to staff submarines on critical, long-range missions with men who have not recently experienced a large number of serious life changes; valuable and talented men who *have* undergone such stress might immediately be granted a temporary leave for "rest and relaxation." Yes, from all indications, behavioral medicine will prove to be one of the very significant ways psychology continues to serve society.

NOTES

1. Phillips, D. Dying As a Form of Social Behavior. Doctoral dissertation, Princeton University, 1969, p. 164.
2. It seems there is also a "will to die." See, for example, R. Eisendrath, "The Role of Grief and Fear in the Death of Kidney Transplant Patients," *American Journal of Psychiatry* 126 (1969): 381–387.
3. P. Lowinger and S. Dobie, "What Makes the Placebo Work?" *Archives of General Psychiatry* 20 (1969): 84 (a good description of how long the placebo effect has been with us).
4. Mary Watkins, Personal communication, 1973.
5. R. Wallace and K. Benson, "The Physiology of Meditation," *Scientific American* 226 (1972): 84–90.
6. D. Kannellakos and P. Ferguson, *The Psychobiology of Transcendental Meditation* (Los Angeles: Maharishi University, 1973).

7. G. Schwartz, "TM Relaxes Some People and Makes Them Feel Better," *Psychology Today* (April 1974): 43.

8. L. Otis, "The Psychobiology of Meditation." Paper presented at the American Psychological Association Convention in Montreal, Canada, 1973.

9. D. Bernstein and T. Borkovec, *Progressive Relaxation Training* (Champaign, Ill.: Research Press, 1973), p. 5.

10. M. Friedman and R. Rosenman, *Type A* (New York: Knopf, 1974), pp. 89–94.

11. Ibid., p. 94.

12. Ibid., p. 164.

13. Ibid., pp. 172–179.

14. Ibid., pp. 82–85.

15. H. Lewis and M. Lewis, *Psychosomatics* (New York: Viking, 1972).

16. Ibid., pp. 72–74.

17. Ibid.

18. Ibid., p. 73.

19. G. Solomon and A. Amkraut, "Emotions, Stress, and Immunity," *Frontiers of Radiation Oncology* 7 (1972): 84–96.

20. Ibid., p. 85.

21. Ibid., p. 88.

22. A. Willmer et al., "An Analogy Test That Predicts Postoperative Outcome in Patients Scheduled for Open-Heart Surgery," *APA Annual Proceedings* 81 (1973): 371–372.

23. T. Harris, "Backaches and Personality: Tests Can Save a Useless Operation," *Psychology Today* (May 1974): 27–28.

24. Ibid., p. 28.

25. Ibid.

26. T. Holmes and M. Masuda, "Psychosomatic Syndrome," *Psychology Today* (April 1972): 71 ff.

27. Ibid., p. 72.

28. Ibid., p. 106.

29. Ibid., p. 72.

30. Ibid.

31. Ibid., p. 106.

SUGGESTED READINGS

FRIEDMAN, M., and ROSENMAN, R. *Type A.* New York: Knopf, 1974.

LEWIS, H., and LEWIS, M. *Psychosomatics.* New York: Viking, 1972.

LOWINGER, P., and DOBIES, S. "What Makes the Placebo Work?" *Archives of General Psychiatry* 20 (1969): 84–88.

8

LSD: high planes drifter

It will come as no shock to Americans to be told they live in a drug era. Some call it a psychedelic revolution. Grass. Hash. Dex. LSD. STP. The vocabulary of our turned-on, tripped-out generation. This is the golden age of pharmacology, the time of the tranquilizer, the marijuana moment. These are the decades when "Triple A" refers not to a motorists' association, but to Anacin, alcohol, and acid, when schools are first-rate drugstores, when a dislodged Harvard professor can start a religion that worships an illegal drug.

Possibly, the popularity of drugs is explained by their undisputed power to affect the mind. Any person who has taken a stiff drink, sleeping compound, tranquilizer, or stimulant has experienced this power. So has the individual who uses drugs as a vehicle to explore that most personal and alluring frontier, the boundaries of his own psyche. What startles scientist and layman alike is the burgeoning

163

number of drugs that have recently been developed to assault the human brain. In 1966 Dr. Stanley Yolles, Director of the National Institute of Mental Health, predicted before a Senate subcommittee: "The next five to ten years . . . will see a hundredfold increase in number and types of drugs capable of affecting the mind."[1] This prophecy has proved to be a modest one. In the area of psychedelic, or "mind-manifesting," drugs alone, we now know of at least ninety-nine distinct, psycho-active plants.[2] When these natural substances are added to our repertoire of synthetic hallucinogenics, "the list of psychedelically active drugs is dauntingly large and would take us far beyond anything that would be manageable within a single volume."[3]

LSD

Of the *major psychedelics*—those with powerful effects lasting eight to twelve hours—the most popular (among street buyers) and the most intriguing (to scientists) continues to be LSD, or d-lysergic acid diethylamide tartrate 25, "twenty-fifth in a series of laboratory syntheses of chemicals derived from ergot, the rhizomorph of the fungus *Claviceps purpurea*."[4] So potent is this extract that an amount as tiny as 1/700 millionth of a person's body weight is enough to induce psychedelic effects.[5] Astounding as it may seem, one university psychologist estimates that only three ounces of LSD would provide "effective doses for every man, woman, and child in a large city the size of Glasgow [Scotland]."[6]

And just what does an "effective dose" do? "The best known and most prevalent positive effect of psychedelic drugs," according to British authority Dr. Brian Wells, "is that they radically affect visual perception." Colors seem more intense; normally solid objects seem to wobble with compelling fascination; outer and inner worlds resonate with inexhaustible energy. Wells notes that the "ecstacy often associated with perceptual enhancement frequently seems to be linked with other reactions such as a feeling of religious awareness—often expressed in terms of a sensitivity to the 'meaningfulness' and 'oneness' of all creation."[7] One young man, embracing his girl friend during an LSD experiment, described the event as analogous to holding a warm, affectionate atomic bomb.

LSD does not always guarantee such pleasant experiences, however. So-called freak-outs, particularly among unsupervised street users, can be horrifying. LSD and other psychedelics can produce

> terrifying psychotic-like experiences of depersonalization and unreality—feeling or seeing one's body rotting, seeing the skull behind the other person's face, and seeming to whirl downward through one's own body tissue and molecular materials. . . .[8]

Some people have also experienced spontaneous involuntary "flashbacks," or reoccurrences of the LSD state, even months after ingesting the drug. (It should be pointed out, though, that LSD does not cause chromosomal damage, as was widely reported by *Life* magazine and other media in the late 1960s; neither is it addictive, since the body actually develops a resistance to repeated dosages.[9])

When we try to account for this variability, the drug itself provides few answers. First, LSD is so complex chemically that our understanding of how it works on human biology is far from complete. Second, and perhaps more significantly, LSD remains in the blood tissue only twenty or so minutes after ingestion. Since the average trip lasts much longer, we must assume that the drug itself does not create the psychedelic experience, but instead, operates as a trigger "to activate more lasting effects in the body's own chemistry."[10]

What, then, determines the nature of the LSD experience? A person's reaction to the drug is modulated by two critical factors: the setting in which the trip takes place and the person's own mental state. Settings that are cheerful, secure, supportive, and friendly tend to produce good trips; hostile circumstances have predictably negative effects. Informal trips—those experienced outside of legal, clinical settings— are almost always improved by the companionship of one or more friends who are also taking the drug. Indeed, taking LSD alone and without supervision must be considered a dangerous risk.

As to the importance of a person's mental state, the most articulate theories on this subject are those of Dr. John C. Lilly, a long-time researcher of the mind.[11] After receiving his medical degree from the University of Pennsylvania in 1942, Lilly worked in various fields, including physics, neurophysiology, and neuroanatomy. In 1954, while working on neurological studies at the National Institute of Mental Health near Washington, D.C., Lilly decided to test the prevalent theory that ordinary consciousness and brain functioning are dependent on external stimulation. He proceeded to conduct a series of experiments in which he cut himself off from the outside world by floating in a large tank of water. The tank was heated to body temperature and located in a small, soundproof room. Contrary to the theory's predictions, Lilly did not go to sleep but remained wide awake during the first few hours of the experiment. After a few more sessions in the tank, Lilly began to experience the kinds of vivid, trancelike states that are frequently reported in mystical and esoteric literature.

Months later, when Lilly moved to the Virgin Islands to conduct his now-famous studies of human–dolphin communication, he was able to immerse himself again, this time with 100 micrograms of LSD. The effect was to give Lilly almost total mobility through his inner spaces. He found, for example, that he could simulate the experience of leaving his body and walking around the tank, that he could move

through outer space to strange universes, and that he could
even visualize contact with advanced alien life forms.

Lilly describes one contact in this way:

I moved into a region of strange life forms, neither above
nor below the human level, but strange beings, of strange
shapes, metabolism, thought forms, and so forth. These
beings reminded me of some of the drawings I had seen of
Tibetan gods and goddesses, of ancient Greek portrayals of
their gods and of some of the bug-eyed monsters of science
fiction. Some of these forms were constructed of liquid, some
were constructed of glowing gases, and some were solid state
"organisms." The vast variety of possible life forms in the
universe passed before me. In this particular space, they were
not involved with me, I was not involved with them. I was
an observer watching them. They were apparently unaware
of me and were going about their particular businesses without interfering with me or paying any attention to me. I was
an observing point in their universe, uninvolved and merely
there picking up what I could of their way of life and recording it, somehow."[12]

The key discovery that Lilly made during these excursions
was not that such trips were possible, but that the content of
his psychedelic imagination was directly related to his belief
system. If Lilly had the belief that he could experience being
controlled by other beings, alien entities, or by repressed and
unknown regions of his mind, this happened. Conversely, if
Lilly altered his beliefs or experimented with new concepts,
his internal experience changed accordingly. By allowing
himself to accept the possibility that his mind could travel
to the fringes of the galaxy, could experience God, could
meet mankind's evolutionary heirs, Lilly was able to simulate
these experiences in the tank.

As Lilly began to experiment with other mind-altering
techniques, such as meditation and chanting, it eventually

became obvious to him that his concept of *belief programming* applied to all aspects of psychedelic experience. In other words, the only limits to his inner travels were the limits imposed by his own beliefs. Or, as Lilly repeatedly states, "In the province of the mind, what one believes to be true is true or becomes true."

From this basic premise, Lilly developed an entire psychological system, in which the human brain is described as a "10^{10} neural assembly," or computer. Each computer contains programs that guide behavior and determine the imagery of consciousness. Some programs, such as reflexes, are inherited; others, such as handwriting and speech, are learned. These programs, in turn, are modified, erased, or created by broader constructs, called *metaprograms*, which include beliefs, learning strategies, and certain genetic endowments, such as intelligence.

The importance of this theory for our discussion of LSD is its prediction that the character of a given person's drug experience is determined, in part, by what he believes that experience will be. His guiding programs can be conscious beliefs, based, for example, on newspaper accounts favorable to or critical of LSD, or they can be unconscious assumptions —"repressed motivations" in psychoanalytic terms. Though not all researchers share Lilly's ideas to the letter, the vast majority acknowledge the enormous influence of a person's mental "set" on the psychedelic state.

TREATING ALCOHOLISM AND HEROIN ADDICTION WITH LSD

In the early years of LSD experimentation, scientists tried to understand the drug by comparing it with psychotic, artistic, or religious states of consciousness. By the 1950s, however, another metaphor had emerged. Researchers Abram Hoffer and Humphrey Osmond became fascinated by the resemblance between LSD reactions and the toxic hallucina-

tions called *delirium tremens*, or dt's, described by many
a former alcoholic as the "hitting bottom" which precipitates
recovery. Could LSD be deliberately used with alcoholics,
these scientists wondered, to simulate the dt's and thereby
cure the addiction to drinking? Beginning in 1952 they
initiated a program at the Saskatchewan Hospital in Wey-
burn, Canada, for treating alcoholics with *psychedelic
therapy*.[13] A refined form of this basic treatment, which is
often stretched over a period of many weeks, is summarized
below:

1. "PHASE I is the *preparation*—a concentrated study
of the patient's difficulties in living, past and present, his
goals, his aspirations, his frustrations and conflicts, his
concepts of life, death, and religion."[14]
2. PHASE II is the oral ingestion of LSD, usually given
in two stages for a total dosage of 300–450 micrograms.
3. "PHASE III is that of *working through*—when new
discoveries are analyzed, old maladaptive defenses are
discarded, and newly learned ways of experiencing, per-
ceiving, and reacting to the world are tested. Except for
Phase II, there is little difference in the approach from
conventional, brief psychotherapy."[15]

Osmond and Hoffer's preliminary findings were so positive
that, at one point, six psychiatric centers in Saskatchewan
were employing psychedelic therapy. By 1971 these scientists
had supervised the treatment of "close to one thousand
alcoholics"—and with two astounding results. First, many of
their alcoholic patients did not experience the painful dt's,
but the opposite: a pleasant state of euphoria and expanded
consciousness. (It was Osmond who, on the basis of this
unexpected outcome, coined the term *psychedelic*.) Second,
approximately 50 percent of their patients were able to
keep sober or to significantly reduce their drinking,[16] a
success ratio that dramatically overshadows the achievements
of every other known alcoholism therapy, including Alco-

holics Anonymous. Subsquent research in New West-
minister, British Columbia, and in the United States confirms
the 50 percent figure.[17] Even this impressive statistic may
prove to be conservative, since many of those who are resistant to LSD therapy can be *identified* in advance by the
presence of a detectable but as-yet-unnamed factor in the
urine.[18] Among alcoholics who do not possess this factor, the
probabilities for successful psychedelic therapy are even
higher than 50 percent.

We should also point out that alcoholics are not the
only addicts to benefit from psychedelic therapy. In one
experiment[19] reported by Dr. Charles Savage and Dr. O. Lee
McCabe, thirty-seven incarcerated heroin addicts were given
psychedelic therapy and then released into the community
on the condition that they report to an established outpatient
clinic at regular intervals. A follow-up of those who had been
out on parole for at least six months revealed that 37 percent
were continuing to abstain from heroin; in a control group
of equal size, only 3 percent (one person!) had refrained
from using heroin.

An impressive comparison, but how do we account for it?
Regrettably, we are as much in the dark about the effects
of LSD on the physiology of addiction as we are about the
effects of LSD on the chemistry of consciousness. Psychologically, however, it is clear that something about LSD therapy
(1) forces the addict to confront and to resolve his inner
conflicts while (2) simultaneously causing him to under-
value the heroin or alcohol experience. In the words of
heroin addicts who were treated with psychedelic therapy:

PATIENT #T39: Heroin has a numbing-like effect on you.
It tends to relax you and somewhat takes you out and away
from your surroundings and yourself. LSD makes you more
aware of yourself and puts you right into whatever has been
troubling you.

PATIENT #T02: Heroin is a drug that makes you want to

forget every problem that you ever had or ever came up in front of you. For example, if you have any emotions, you will never let them out.

Another example is love. When you are taking heroin, heroin is all you can think of. Someone you love comes second, whereas heroin comes first. You use love as a tool, not as something beautiful. Respect is another one. You never have any respct for anyone. When it comes to getting your shot, you don't care who you step on. You are like an animal in a world of your own.

LSD helps you to let go of all of your emotions and sorrows you have built up in you. LSD makes a person see for the first time in his life how beautiful the real world can be. It lets you know that there are things in the world that are worth living for. Just by being yourself, you can have everything you want. It makes you see how nice the nature of earth is, whereas with heroin you only see a rat race. But LSD makes you see how lovely the trees, flowers, sky, etc., really are. . . . Well, that is about the only way I can put it, because there are so many ways to put it.

PATIENT #T29: Heroin is a suppressant that quells or overpowers any feeling of anxiety but LSD is altogether different. LSD is a mind expander which enables one to see himself as he was, as he is, and as he could be.

PATIENT #T57: Comparing LSD to heroin is like comparing a mountain with a speck of dust. The difference is that heroin helps you to run from yourself and LSD shows you how to face yourself.

PATIENT #T15: The two experiences of heroin and LSD are like night and day. Heroin is night, a time to sleep and with sleep, nothing comes but a dream. But with LSD it is like dawn, a new awakening, it expands your mind, it gives you a brand new outlook on life.[20]

Finally, it should be noted that successful psychedelic therapy for drug addiction appears to involve *both* LSD *and* traditional psychotherapy. As far as present research can tell, neither therapy by itself[21] nor LSD by itself[22] produces a large number of cures.

EASING THE TRANSITION FROM LIFE

Few men have contributed as much to our vision of what psychology can accomplish as the late Aldous Huxley. This is particularly true when we begin to examine the literature of psychedelics. There is that moving passage in his novel *Island* (1962), for instance, which describes how the natives of a psychologically designed paradise used the strange *moksha* medicine to ease and to elevate a dying person's last moments on earth. In the area of nonfiction, Huxley's *Doors of Perception* (1954) is considered by most LSD researchers to be the single greatest catalyst for modern psychedelic studies.

It's one thing, though, for a man to advocate the idea that others can benefit from the proper use of psychedelics. Did he believe enough in his theories to apply them to his own life? The poignant answer came on November 22, 1963, coincidentally the same day that saw the tragic death of an American President named Kennedy.

Huxley had been suffering for some months from terminal cancer; on this morning his condition was noticeably worse than usual.[23] Though his mind was clear, Huxley was uncomfortable and agitated. He found it difficult to speak, so difficult in fact that he had to make his last request in writing: "Try LSD 100 mm intramuscular."

The attending physician was anxious. After all, most doctors at this time were unsure about the benefits and hazards of LSD. But Huxley's wife, Laura, was determined to accommodate her husband: " . . . no 'authority,' not even an army of authorities, could have stopped me," she recalls. For Laura sensed that Aldous would die on that day, and she wanted to help make his transition from life as beautiful as possible.

11:45 A.M.: Laura was nervous at first. The doctor pointed out that her hands were shaking, and this awareness seemed to have a calming effect. With a steady hand she quietly gave her husband the injection. A few moments later she noticed that Aldous seemed relieved. She was, too, for in her own words,

> a decision had been made. Suddenly he had accepted the fact of death; now, he had taken this *moksha*-medicine in which he believed. Once again he was doing what he had written in *Island*, and I had the feeling that he was interested and relieved and quiet.[24]

A half hour later Aldous appeared blissfully quiet and loving. Laura gave him a second injection, then began speaking in his ear:

> Light and free you let go, darling; forward and up. You are going forward and up; you are going toward the light. Willingly and consciously you are going, willing and consciously, and you are doing this beautifully; you are doing this so beautifully—you are going toward the light—you are going toward the light—you are going toward a greater love—you are going forward and up. It is so easy—it is so beautiful. Forward and up. . . .[25]

Everything went well until midafternoon, when Aldous began to gag momentarily. Calmly Laura repeated her soothing words, and the twitching in his face stopped. Gradually, his breathing

> became slower and slower, and there was absolutely not the slightest indication of contraction, of struggle. It was just that the breathing became slower—and slower—and slower, the ceasing of life was not a drama at all, but like a piece of music just finished so gently in a *sempre piu piano, dolcemente* . . . and at five-twenty the breathing stopped.[26]

In many ways Aldous Huxley was a fortunate man. His life was vital and productive to the end. He also had the privilege of dying in a warm environment, close to his loving wife.

Others who suffer from prolonged degenerative diseases are not so lucky. Confined to a cold and sterile hospital room, the dying patient is far too often treated like a useless, decaying machine. His psychological and spiritual needs are almost completely ignored. His inevitable questions on the meaning of his life and the purpose of his death are usually met with the grotesque sacraments of morphine and tranquilizers. For a person in this condition, a *moksha* medicine could make the difference between a death with dignity or a Kafka-esque nightmare.

But is LSD really that *moksha* medicine? Experience with alcoholics would suggest "yes." Many heavy drinkers who took LSD had profound, spontaneous visions of death and rebirth—a phenomenon that would seem to elevate the transition from life. Yet it's one thing for Aldous Huxley, a man versed in altered states of consciousness, to employ a psychedelic in the service of final grace, quite another for someone else. Could a dying person with no such experience also benefit from LSD? Answers to this and related questions have come from an impressive group of scientists at the Maryland Psychiatric Research Center in Catonsville, near Baltimore.

It was 1965 and the Catonsville group had already conducted extensive experiments with LSD when it was discovered that an assistant had breast cancer.[27] Realizing that death was almost certain, she decided to undergo LSD therapy. The results were sufficiently beneficial to inspire the development of a systematic method for using LSD with terminally ill patients. This effort was first directed by Dr. Walter Pahnke, an unusually talented scientist holding degrees from Harvard in both theology and medicine, and later by Dr. Stanislov Grof. The procedure that evolved is summarized by the following:

On the morning of the drug session, the therapist (by now well known to the patient) and a specially trained nurse arrive at the bedside with a portable stereo, headphones, eyeshades, some fresh roses, and a dose of pure LSD or related psychedelic that is three or four times as strong as the amount usually used when the drug is taken illegally. Even before the drug takes effect, the patient puts on the stereo headphones and the eyeshades—to ease the journey inward and minimize distractions. The therapist—who is present throughout the session—encourages the patient to "get into" whatever internal imagery he is experiencing, no matter how unpleasant. This approach departs from popular notions of the "bad trip"; the therapists feel that if you are battling dragons or being devoured by flames, those represent personal psychic spaces you must pass through, and not around. This requires from the patient an almost perfect trust in the therapist and nurse—enough to take their word that it's safe to be sucked into what may seem like an absolutely real whirlpool. But if the patient is able to let go of his own ego structure enough, he may achieve a sense of unity with all creation so strong that the decomposition of his earthly body will seem infinitely less important.[28]

In a study of thirty-one terminal patients, Grof tried to objectively assess the overt aftereffects of LSD therapy with a comprehensive test that included, among other items, measures of the sufferer's depression, his fear of death, his anxiety, and his level of pain (determined by the amount of narcotics necessary to subdue it). Nine patients (29.0 percent), it turned out, "improved dramatically"; thirteen (41.9 percent) were "moderately improved" through LSD therapy; nine (29.0 percent) were "essentially unchanged"; and only two seemed to regress, and even then, "the decrease was negligible."[29] It appears, then, that LSD given under competent, caring supervision can be a *moksha* medicine, both in terms of the subjective experience it creates and in terms of its benevolent aftereffects. "Our clinical experience thus

far," writes Grof, "suggests that skilled use of the psychedelic procedure can be a relatively safe and promising
approach in an area which has been most discouraging up
to the present."[30]

LSD AND OUR KNOWLEDGE OF MAN

What Grof finds particularly interesting about his LSD
research is that most subjects who undergo multiple treatments, whether they are terminally ill or healthy, seem to
move systematically over the course of many sessions through
four discernible and overlapping states of consciousness:[31]
first, abstract and aesthetic experiences; second, psychodynamic experiences; third, what Grof calls "perinatal"
experiences; and finally transpersonal experiences. The
aesthetic experiences (with eyes closed) are usually characterized by splendid and awesome inner visions, such as color
spots and shafts of light. "Typical also," observes Grof, "are
complex geometrical figures, patterns and ornaments, kaleido-
scopic fireworks as well as views of ceilings of gigantic
Gothic cathedrals or cupolas of Oriental mosques." After
a transitional period in which these images begin to stabilize,
the subject travels into a psychodynamic state of consciousness:

> The experiences in psychodynamic LSD sessions can be, to
> a great extent, understood in terms of the basic Freudian
> concepts. Many of the principles that Freud described for
> the dynamics of the individual unconscious, in particular for
> the formation of dreams, apply as well for LSD sessions. As
> a matter of fact, many of the phenomena observed in psycho-
> dynamic LSD sessions could be considered laboratory proof
> of the basic premises of psychoanalysis. The phenomenology
> of these sessions involves regression into childhood and even
> infancy, reliving of traumatic memories, infantile sexuality,
> conflicts in various libidinal zones, Oedipus and Electra con-
> flict, castration anxiety, penis envy, etc.[32]

If conflicts at this psychodynamic level are experienced to the point where they are resolved—a willingness to "go with the flow" of the LSD experience, be it positive or negative, seems to be the prerequisite for resolution—the subject moves into the third, "perinatal" state of consciousness, where he confronts the ultimate problems of "physical agony, dying, and death, biological birth, aging, disease and decrepitude." This can be a "shattering" adventure, Grof states reverently, during which the individual comes to a deeper awareness of his human frailty and of the meaning of life:

> The similarity between birth and death—the startling realization that the beginning of life is the same as its end—is the major philosophical issue that accompanies perinatal experiences. The other important consequence of the shocking emotional and physical encounter with the phenomenon of death is the opening up of spiritual and religious dimensions that appear to be an intrinsic part of the human personality . . . everyone who experientially reached these levels developed convincing insights into the utmost relevance of spiritual and religious dimensions in the universal scheme of things. Even the most hard-core materialists, positivistically-oriented scientists, skeptics and cynics, uncompromising atheists and antireligious crusaders such as the Marxist philosophers, became suddenly interested in spiritual search after they confronted these levels in themselves.[33]

When this stage is transcended, the subject finally enters a fourth, "transpersonal" consciousness, in which he temporarily loses his identity as an isolated individual, or ego, frequently identifying with other persons or groups of people, "even the struggling and suffering of all mankind." The intensity of this consciousness, Grof writes, "transcends anything that is usually considered to be the experiential limit of the individual"; and indeed, subjects often have difficulty expressing these sensations in words.

That such experiences even happen is, in and of itself, an impressive discovery. More astounding, however, is the observation that they follow a pattern: Ecstatic visions yield to psychoanalytic images, which in turn yield to peri-natal fantasies that, in the final stages, evolve into ego-dissolving states of transcendence. Of course, scientists could be conservative and write off these phenomena as nothing more than the elaborate side effects of a potent drug. Yet three gnawing facts—the fact that the pattern occurs with LSD only when a person is turned inward (his eyes are closed), the fact that LSD itself does not cause the pattern (the drug disappears from the bloodstream twenty minutes after ingestion), and the fact that experiences related to this pattern are reported by people who have never taken LSD—point to another consideration: that LSD does not create a special state of consciousness, but rather *illuminates*, or *magnifies*, an underlying dynamic of the mind that already exists. If this second interpretation is true, Grof's experiments have some radical implications for our knowledge of human behavior. They suggest, for example, that the spectrum of human awareness, even without the influence of LSD, is much broader than is generally supposed. They also suggest that temporary states of ego breakdown, or *depersonaliza-tion*—in particular, feelings of body transcendence and of identification with others—may not be as pathological as some psychiatrists believe. As we saw in Grof's work with dying patients, these states led to reduced anxiety and pain. Finally, they suggest a revision of Freudian psychoanalytic theory to account for perinatal and transpersonal symbolism in everyday life.

These are, to be sure, speculations—at least for now. But neither can we dismiss the possibility that LSD research may have a profound impact on the psychologist's image of man.

LSD AND THE RELIGIOUS EXPERIENCE

Although a bright and clever young man, D.C. was not leading a comfortable life.[34] Bound up in psychological struggles with his parents and in other problems, he was, by his own admission, narrow-minded and intolerant. He did, however, have the courage to participate in a unique experimental program at a New England mental hospital, a program that called for him to receive daily doses of pure, laboratory LSD, each "hit" valued at approximately 180 micrograms. These ingestions were accompanied by extensive psychotherapy.

Like most guided LSD sessions, D.C.'s were punctuated by experiences of profound metaphorical import. At one point, for example, he engaged in a sequence of "symbolic encounters with various members of his family"; these confrontations were followed, in turn, "by a dramatic enactment of his own death," during which D.C. played both the corpse and the funeral director.

It was not until the fifteenth session, though, that the religious element in D.C.'s psychedelic journey was most intense. Supervising therapist Walter Clark recounts the event:

> About four hours after taking the drug that day, he had been sitting on the lawn outside the hospital watching two grasshoppers maneuver in what he interpreted as a kind of cosmic dance. Suddenly, he felt one with them and with the cosmos besides. I was aware of it only after he caught sight of me and came running over to me in great excitement calling "Dr. Clark, I have had a mystical experience; I have met God."[35]

Almost a year after his LSD therapy, D.C. continued to reflect on this particular session with a sense of awe. "What I regarded as the end of the experience when I left the hospital," he later reported to Clark, "was simply the beginning of an experience of maturing which is still continuing." Formerly an avowed atheist, he was now deeply interested in religion, especially the influence of theology on world history.

Mystical reveries, such as D.C.'s and those encountered

by Grof's subjects, frequently accompany even the most casual LSD trips, so frequently in fact that some observers believe LSD might be used (as other psychedelics have been used throughout history) to deliberately simulate or heighten religious states of consciousness. In one experiment,[36] for example, a mixture of forty-two psychiatric and adjusted subjects were given doses of LSD and later asked how they felt about God and other aspects of religion. Interestingly, none of the drug takers actually changed their beliefs—at least not in any overt way—but nearly all felt *more deeply* about their existing convictions, even after returning to normal consciousness.

Of course, opinion on the theological applications of LSD is far from unanimous. Many people assert that no drug could ever simulate a genuine spiritual experience. There are sharp disagreements not only between psychedelic researchers and the clergy, but among the scientists themselves (and among the clergy, as well). The issue is certainly an explosive one, compounded in part by the controversy surrounding the publication of John M. Allegro's recent book, *The Sacred Mushroom and the Cross.*[37] According to Allegro, the New Testament is not a description of Christ's work on earth but is, instead, a sequence of myths especially designed to encode, through pun and allegory, ancient methods for preparing and ingesting psycho-active mushrooms. The Jews of the Near East, he contends, made extensive use of these mushrooms, a practice dating back to the older Sumerian fertility cults. When the Roman repression began, cryptic stories of a "second Moses"—Christ—were invented to preserve the knowledge of the psychedelics.

Coming from almost any other writer, such allegations would seem preposterous but Allegro's credentials are disturbingly impressive. He is a renowned philologist, a lecturer in the Old Testament at the University of Manchester, England, and was the first British representative to the international editorial team assigned to decipher the Dead Sea Scrolls. Though far from conclusive, Allegro's argument is a striking one, based as it is on the metaphorical and rhythmic similarities between Biblical scriptures and meanings of the older Sumerian languages.

We can begin to appreciate now how the spiritual use of LSD becomes a complex issue, arousing excitement in some quarters and outrage in others. Should the drug ever be legalized, we can expect, at the very least, some stimulating debates on this subject.

LSD: WHAT'S IN IT FOR US?

A very difficult question to answer. We know that LSD has definite therapeutic applications: treating alcoholism, for example. Equally certain, however, are the strong social pressures against any use of the drug, therapeutic or otherwise. Popular conceptions associating LSD with counter-culture rebellion, mental illness, unbridled hedonism, and drug abuse have combined to create a barrier limiting even scientific studies of the drug.

Most of the controversy surrounding LSD is framed as a conflict between Youth, favoring LSD, and the so-called Establishment, resisting it. This is regrettable, since the evidence suggests that the benefits of LSD are actually greater for adults than for adolescents. The incidences of alcoholism and terminal illness, after all, are usually higher in the over-twenty-one age bracket. Research on creativity provides another example: In those cases when LSD has really enhanced insight and productive thinking (as opposed to inducing the subjective illusion of increased insight), the drug seems to favor the prepared, or mature, mind. In other words, the chances of LSD eliciting creative thought improve with age and experience.[38]

There is, in sum, a substantial gap between what LSD does and what most people think it does. Even those who frequently use the drug street-style are appallingly ignorant of its effects. Yet there is reason for optimism. LSD research in the United States, though minimal due to government

restrictions, is not dead. Furthermore, illuminating psychological research on the drug is progressing in other countries,
notably Canada, Mexico, and Chile. It is quite likely, as one
researcher points out, that as the initial furor over LSD
abates, and as the benefits of clinical application become
more widely known, additional studies and treatment programs will be sanctioned by governmental authorities. "Society must," he writes,

> quite naturally, act with all appropriate caution when it fore-
> sees dangers to its members but, judging from the more sober
> reflection of recent official reports, it seems possible that the
> psychedelics might soon achieve at least some degree of
> rehabilitation.[39]

There is also the promise of the newer, and to some
degree less controversial, psychedelics: especially MDA
(from safrole), MMDA (derived from a nutmeg oil), harmaline (an alkaloid in the seeds of *Peganum harmala*), and
ibogaine (from the root of the West African *Tabernanthe
iboga*).[40] These substances seem to have the advantage of
being psychedelic without being *psychotominetic*; that is,
they do not simulate psychotic states.[41] Although not as
potent as LSD, each produces highly specific and, under
clinical supervision, therapeutic results. MDA, according to
Chilean researcher Dr. Claudio Naranjo, is particularly effective for producing age regression in psychiatric patients, a
process that facilitates analytic therapy. MMDA, on the
other hand, magnifies awareness of immediate feelings and
is appropriate to the resolution of present conflicts. Naranjo
finds that harmaline, which simultaneously causes relaxation
and inner awareness, is useful for illuminating unconscious
symbols and visions, whereas ibogaine, which also induces
heightened inner awareness, tends to illustrate and to clarify
childhood conflicts.[42]

Finally, we come to the increasingly successful attempts to

duplicate psychedelic states without LSD or any other drug. Especially promising in this regard is the work of Dr. Helen Bonny.

Originally attracted to the subject of psychedelics through her own "peak experiences" playing music, Bonny began to study consciousness several years before it became fashionable.[43] She helped to organize the now-prestigious Council Grove Conferences on altered states of consciousness and was eventually invited by Dr. Walter Pahnke to supervise music therapy in government-sponsored LSD experiments at the Maryland Psychiatric Research Center.

As she worked with LSD subjects, Bonny found that she could induce intense inner states by playing selected combinations of musical pieces, rather than one single record or music selection. She then discovered that similar experiences would result from listening to music *without drugs.* Her simple procedure involved getting people to lie face-up in a prone position, instructing them to relax, and playing a carefully edited tape of inspirational (usually classical) music. Bonny also encouraged the listener to describe, or "share," his ongoing experience with a companion sitting close by. (The companion would occasionally offer suggestions, particularly if the music listener became confused or anxious, but the companion's role was largely that of quietly acknowledging an awareness of the listener's experiences.)

An extremely dynamic person, Bonny is currently researching the applications of her technique while simultaneously leading training workshops through the Institute for Music and Consciousness in Baltimore. She has found that musically induced psychedelic experiences can be employed in a wide variety of therapeutic contexts, although music seems particularly useful for stimulating spiritual or mystical experiences. Her workshops consequently attract an assortment of participants, including well-known psychotherapists, ministers, occupational therapists, and of course, a large number of seekers.

The visions elicited through a combination of relaxation and music can often be quite profound, having effects on behavior as well as consciousness. One of her subjects, who is, incidentally, not very religious, had the following experience:

I saw myself actually enter the City of God as described in the Bible. It seemed huge, filled with lustrous gold buildings. But when I entered, I fell into a large pool of blood. The gold and the blood ran together, and I felt that I was being attacked by ferocious man-eating sharks. Then I saw God himself dipping a gold ladel into the pool. I climbed onto the ladel, ran up God's arm, and climbed onto his hair, which seemed to be growing at an incredible speed. Holding onto his locks, I was propelled out of the city. As I came to the ground, I looked back at the city, which seemed to melt like rapidly heated butter into a large puddle of sparkling liquid. The sun set quickly, and out from the nearby mountains came an army of faceless slaves carrying buckets. They scooped up the liquid and carried it back from where they had come. I followed the procession over a hill and into a fiery cave where the devil was drinking from the buckets. I knew I had to escape, but I didn't know where to go. I seemed indecisive for the longest time (the music was now changing), and then I saw a large tunnel in the corner of the cave. I crawled through the opening, heading down and down into the center of the earth. The tunnel became ever larger until it was a series of caverns, and I found myself descending along an endless mountain climber's rope. Suddenly, I was attacked by a gigantic—perhaps thirty-foot high —spider. I allowed myself to be eaten by the spider without a struggle until, at last, I actually became the spider. At first, the thought of being a spider was repulsive. But as I began to move around I discovered the beauty and rhythm of a spider's mobility. I also became aware of my ability to terrorize. The faces of hundreds of frightened people passed in front of me, and I soon discovered that I was no longer the spider, but that I was becoming the Devil himself. Almost immediately, I experienced a cool, white light was bathing my body from above. It was a light from heaven directing me to put my talents to better use. I experienced my power to terrorize transform itself into a power for healing; and I began to travel the world, healing millions of injured and suffering people with the cool detachment of a veteran surgeon. When I was finished—God rewarded me with my freedom. At this point the music stopped. I opened my eyes, stood up, and began to dance for the first time in my life.[44]

Note that all of the seemingly negative visions in this story—the sharks, the blood, the spider, and the Devil—eventually resolved themselves in a positive, uplifting way. Such "good trips" result, in part, from the experimenter's control over the music input, as well as from the process of "sharing." Here is another person's account:

There was nothing unusual for me in the guided fantasy until I came to the bridge over the water, seeing a person standing at the other end. The person was me, from some other time and place, older than I am now and dressed in a white hooded monk's robe. He was unbearably kind and just looked and radiated love and kindness and acceptance to me as I crossed the bridge. There was nothing to say to him except, "Yes. Hi. I see you standing there," and radiate love to him in return. He asked me where I was going and I said, "On." This "on" came up from the depths inside me. . . . I began to have chills. I felt streams of energy rushing through me.

Then the music began. I continued on my path and began to cry and cry and cry—crying for the deepness and the beauty of the new self I was discovering, and also crying nostalgically for the old self I was leaving behind.

I walked on and on and became a pilgrim with a staff in my right hand, crossing a desert, being sung to and uplifted by angels and other heavenly beings. After much of this I reached a mountain and began climbing it. I was then taken up into the atmosphere by these beings, taken around the world and shown the spiritually-blighted condition of most of mankind. I understood it in a much deeper way now than ever before.

Then I was taken up and up, through more and more layers of atmosphere, clouds, and astral planes, until I was approaching a doorway through which bright yellow-white light shone. I went through the doorway into this illuminated area and turned to look back, but the doorway through which I had come was no longer there. Here in this yellow-white area my angelic hosts placed on a white hooded monk's robe and I understood that I was being initiated into a higher order of being. I still feel the monk's robes on me and I do not want to stop feeling them.[45]

How are people able to achieve such powerful and rewarding inner experiences? Obviously, the simple act of listening to music is not sufficient, for if it were, automobile commuters would spend much less time listening to all-news and talk programs on their car radios. According to Bonny, there are three factors that facilitate the production of nondrug psychedelic experiences.

First, the listener must be in a relaxed state, such that his consciousness is free to ignore any external stimuli that might cloud the reception of his internal signals. There are many ways to accomplish this. For some people, sitting works best; others find yoga and meditation positions to be the most comfortable. The vast majority of people, however, relax easily and efficiently by lying on their backs in a prone position, taking a few deep breaths, and, for a few moments, simply paying attention to how their breathing feels. It also helps to imagine a white balloon in your stomach and to visualize it expanding and contracting as you inhale and exhale. Ideally, the room is darkened and free from distractions.

Second, a person's expectations and surroundings regulate the effect of music on consciousness. Unfortunately, most "educated" Americans have been taught to regard music analytically; hence the Hollywood stereotype of a concert buff as a somewhat stuffy and overly academic individual who sits rigidly in a velvet chair for hours on end, responding to performances with only a polite clap or occasional yawn. The experience of inspirational imagery calls for a totally different mode of behavior: The person must learn to go with the "flow and feel" of music, allowing the messages on his inner channel to be charged and amplified by the incoming stream of melodic energy. Younger people with their rock joints and music festivals should, in theory, be more adept at this response; yet this is not always the case. Rock music is frequently not listened to for its own sake, but rather, used as a backdrop for socially oriented activities, such as meeting friends or scoring with members of the opposite sex.

The third rule for using music to ignite psychedelic states is what Bonny terms the *iso* principle:

> "Iso" means "the same as" or "matching." The iso principle states that, at the beginning of a listening experience, best results are obtained when the mood of the music matches the mood of the listener. If [people] are feeling carefree and gay, [they shouldn't] listen to *March Slav* or "Mars" [The Bringer of War], from Holst's *Planets*. On the other hand, if [they] have been in an angry mood all day, and those feelings are still bottled up inside, [they shouldn't] begin by playing Tony Scott's Music for *Zen Meditation*, which requires a deep state of tranquility.[46]

Unfortunately, most people use music, as they use drugs, to get themselves *out* of a mood rather than *through* it. Not only does this practice work against the enjoyment of imagination, according to Bonny, but there is some evidence that these individuals are unknowingly doing serious violence to their nervous systems by using music as an escape or "change of pace." Music apparently produces far deeper, richer, and more biologically harmonious imagery when it begins to parallel the listener's mood, carrying him into and eventually above his experience. Composer and researcher David Riordan has found that even the negative energy patterns of disturbed children can be transformed into positive expressions of feeling through appropriate use of music.[47]

Of course, matching music to mood is easy for an experienced therapist like Bonny. But what about the average person? If music consciousness is going to become a viable psychedelic alternative to drug consciousness, there must be a way such that an individual who is musically naïve, particularly with respect to classical recordings, can choose appropriate selections. To solve this problem, Bonny herself has developed an extensive list that correlates specific compositions with eight different "mood clusters." With this list a person can pick recordings that are uniquely appropriate to his emotional state. Sample selections for each mood cluster are excerpted below:

MOOD	SELECTION
Solemn	Mahalia Jackson's *I Believe*
Sad	Bach's "Come Sweet Death" (Stowkowski)
Tender	Orff's "Cour d'Amour" from *Carmina Burana*
Leisurely	Vaughan Williams' *Fantasia on Greensleeves*
Playful	Mozart's "Allegro" from *Concerto for Flute and Harp*
Gay	Beethoven's "3rd Movement" from *Third Piano Concerto*
Exciting	Pink Floyd's "Reemergence" from *Atom Heart Mother*
	Also, Holst's "Jupiter" and "Saturn" from *The Planets*
Vigorous	Bach's *Tocatta and Fugue in D Minor*[48]

The fact that Bonny is developing a safe and legal alternative to drug-induced psychedelic experiences is justification enough for her work, though, as we have hinted, preliminary investigations point to a wide range of therapeutic applications. Although music research is a relatively new field in psychology, we can expect that it will expand considerably within the next few years.

NOTES

1. L. Andrews and M. Karlins, *Requiem for Democracy?* (New York: Holt, 1971), pp. 27–28.
2. H. Osmond, "Foreword," in B. Wells, *Psychedelic Drugs* (Baltimore: Penguin, 1974), p. 7.
3. B. Wells, *Psychedelic Drugs* (Baltimore: Penguin, 1974), p. 13.
4. Ibid., p. 47.
5. Ibid., p. 46.
6. Ibid., p. 47.
7. Ibid., pp. 43–44.
8. Ibid., p. 45.
9. Personal communication, Dr. Stan Grof, Director of the LSD research program at the Maryland Psychiatric Research Center, 1974.
10. Wells, *Psychedelic Drugs*, p. 49.
11. This description of Lilly's work is based on interviews conducted by the authors in 1973 and 1974. Much the same information is contained in J. Lilly, *Center of the Cyclone* (New York: Julian Press, 1972).
12. Ibid., p. 45.
13. A. Hoffer, "Treatment of Alcoholism with Psychedelic Therapy," in B. Aaronson and H. Osmond, eds., *Psychedelics* (New York: Doubleday, Anchor Books, 1970), p. 360.
14. C. Savage and O. McCabe, "Psychedelic (LSD) Therapy of Drug Addiction," in C. Brown and C. Savage, eds., *The Drug Abuse Controversy* (Baltimore: National Educational Consultants, 1971), pp. 147–148.
15. Ibid., p. 148.
16. Hoffer, "Treatment of Alcoholism with Psychedelic Therapy," p. 361.
17. Ibid.
18. Ibid., pp. 363–365.
19. Savage and McCabe, "Psychedelic (LSD) Therapy of Drug Addiction," pp. 145–163.
20. Ibid., pp. 156–157.
21. Ibid., p. 158.
22. Hoffer, "Treatment of Alcoholism with Psychedelic Therapy," p. 359.
23. This section is based on the account of Huxley's death contained in L. Huxley, *This Timeless Moment* (New York: Farrar, Straus, and Giroux, 1968).
24. Ibid., p. 305.
25. Ibid., p. 306.
26. Ibid., pp. 307–308.
27. J. Avon, "Beyond Dying." *Harper's Magazine* (May 1973): 56–64.
28. Ibid., p. 58.

29. S. Grof, "LSD and the Human Encounter with Death," prepublication manuscript, p. 13.

30. Ibid., p. 23.

31. S. Grof, "Theoretical and Empirical Basis of Transpersonal Psychology and Psychotherapy: Observations from LSD Research," *Journal of Transpersonal Psychology* 5 (1973): 15–53.

32. Ibid., p. 21.

33. Ibid., p. 25.

34. W. Clark, "The Psychedelics and Religion," in B. Aaronson and H. Osmond, *Psychedelics* (New York: Doubleday, Anchor Books, 1970), pp. 188–189.

35. Ibid., p. 188.

36. Wells, *Psychedelic Drugs*, p. 194.

37. J. Allegro, *The Sacred Mushroom and the Cross* (New York: Doubleday, 1970).

38. Wells, *Psychedelic Drugs*, pp. 170–188.

39. Ibid., p. 220.

40. C. Narango, *The Healing Journey* (New York: Random House, 1973).

41. Ibid., p. xvii.

42. Ibid., chaps. 2, 3, 4, and 5.

43. Material in this section is based on personal communications with Bonny and some of her subjects, as well as on H. Bonny and L. Savary, *Music and Your Mind* (New York: Harper & Row, 1973).

44. Personal communication, 1973.

45. Account copyright by the Institute for Music and Consciousness, Baltimore, Maryland.

46. Bonny and Savary, *Music and Your Mind*, p. 42.

47. D. Riordan, Personal communication, 1973.

48. Bonny and Savary, *Music and Your Mind*, Appendix.

SUGGESTED READINGS

BONNY, H., and SAVARY, L. *Music and Your Mind*. New York: Harper & Row, 1973.

GROF, S. "Theoretical and Empirical Basis of Transpersonal Psychology and Psychotherapy: Observation from LSD Research." *Journal of Transpersonal Psychology* 5 (1973): 15–53.

HUXLEY, A. *Island*. New York: Harper & Row, 1962. Contrasts interestingly with his *Brave New World*. New York: Doubleday, 1932.

HUXLEY, L. *This Timeless Moment*. New York: Farrar, Straus, and Giroux, 1968.

NARANJO, C. *The Healing Journey*. New York: Random House, 1973.

WELLS, B. *Psychedelic Drugs*. Baltimore: Penguin, 1974.

9

fantasy and self-control

"And now," teacher Susila went on, "Now let's play some pretending games. Shut your eyes and pretend you're looking at that poor old mynah bird with one leg that comes to school every day to be fed. Can you see him?"

Of course they could see him. The one-legged mynah was evidently an old friend.

"See him just as clearly as you saw him today at lunchtime. And don't stare at him, don't make any effort. Just see what comes to you, and let your eyes shift—from his beak to his tail, from his bright little round eye to his one orange leg."

"I can hear him too," a little girl volunteered. "He's saying 'Karuna, karuna!'"

"That's not true," another child said indignantly. "He's saying 'Attention!'"

"He's saying both those things," Susila assured them. "And probably a lot of other words besides. But now we're going to do some real pretending. Pretend that there are two one-legged mynah birds. Three one-legged mynah birds. Four one-legged mynah birds. Can you see all four of them?"

They could.

"Four one-legged mynah birds at the four corners of a square, and a fifth one in the middle. And now let's make them change their color. They're white now. Five white mynah birds with yellow heads and one orange leg. And now the heads are blue. Bright blue—and the rest of the bird is pink. Five pink birds with blue heads. And they keep changing. They're purple now. Five purple birds with white heads and each of them has one pale-green leg. Goodness, what's happening! There aren't five of them; there are ten. No, twenty, fifty, a hundred. Hundreds and hundreds. Can you see them?" Some of them could—without the slightest difficulty; and for those who couldn't go the whole hog, Susila proposed more modest goals.

"Just make twelve of them," she said. "Or if twelve is too many, make ten, make eight. That's still an awful lot of mynahs. And now," she went on, when all the children had conjured up all the purple birds that each was capable of creating, "now they're gone." She clapped her hands. "Gone! Every single one of them. There's nothing there. And now you're not going to see mynahs, you're going to see me. One me in yellow. Two me's in green. Three me's in blue with pink spots. Four me's in the brightest red you ever saw." She clapped her hands again. "All gone. And this time it's Mrs. Narayan and that funny-looking man with a stiff leg who came in with her. Four of each of them. Standing in a big circle in the gymnasium. And now they're dancing the Rakshasi Hornpipe. 'So stamp it out, so stamp it out.' "

There was a general giggle. The dancing Wills and Principals must have looked richly comical.

Susila snapped her fingers.

"Away with them! Vanish! And now each of you sees three of your mothers and three of your fathers running round the playground. Faster, faster, faster! And suddenly they're not there any more. And then they are there. But next moment they aren't. They are there, they aren't. They are, they aren't. . . ."

The giggles swelled into squeals of laughter and at the height of the laughter a bell rang. The lesson in Elementary Practical Psychology was over.—From *Island* by Aldous Huxley[1]

In 1935 a Mormon anthropologist named Kilton Stewart[2] was conducting field research in the unexplored rain forests of Malaysia when he came across an isolated tribe of natives called the Senoi. Technologically, these people were no different from the myriad other primitive groups with which he was familiar. Living in thatch and bamboo community rooms constructed on large piles above the ground, the Senoi sustained themselves with simple farming, hunting, and fishing. In the area of social relations, however, they had developed a practical psychology "so astonishing," in Stewart's words, "that they might have come from another planet."

The Senoi experienced almost no violent crime, no armed conflict, and no mental illness. In fact, Stewart found this tribe to be the most democratic group he had ever encountered. All business relationships, all social relationships, and all political relationships were based on the solid foundations of open agreement and personal responsibility. Noting that the Senoi had no use for any coercive institution, such as a police force, Stewart ultimately concluded that their social system was on the same plane with modern man's achievements in the areas of electronic communication and nuclear physics.

What psychological process enabled the Senoi to live in such peace and harmony? Stewart soon learned the surprising answer: The Senoi made extensive use of fantasy, particularly dreams and daydreams.

The Senoi children, for example, were encouraged to meditate on the images of their dreams and then, if necessary, to complete the fantasies on the following evenings. A typical case would be the child who reported to his parents that he had been frightened by a dream of falling off a tree, to which the understanding mother or father might reply, "That's a wonderful dream, but it's not necessary to resist. Go back to that dream when you go to sleep tonight. See where it takes you. You might even bring back some valuable insights for the tribe." With such sympathetic encouragement, it would not be unusual for the child's fear of falling to eventually become a love of flight.

Adults, too, made a practice of using their fantasies, often consulting a sort of tribal psychologist called a *halak*. Unlike their children, however, the parents would invest considerable energy describing their dreams both to people who appear in them and to other friends and acquaintances. The Senoi elders firmly believed that the images within a man's mind were exerting great power over his life, as well as providing him with useful knowledge.

Unfortunately, this discovery couldn't have come at a worse time. Americans were still reeling from an ascetic nineteenth-century philosophy which regarded even daydreams as "mild forms of insanity";[3] consequently, accounts such as Stewart's were quietly, but systematically, ignored. So powerful was this prejudice that still today the term *fantasy* is associated with mental illness. Our language is rife with phrases that seem to justify this false equation. A frequent assumption is that a withdrawn, *neurotic* person has "an active fantasy life" and that a psychotic "lives in a private world of fantasy." Even the sanity of the "gifted" artist is regarded with some suspicion.

The picture is not bleak, however. A group of dedicated psychologists is beginning to uncover the facts about fantasy and inner imagery in general. Recent studies by Yale University's Jerry Singer,[4] for example, have demonstrated that the disjointed "mind wandering" typical of mental disorders correlates very poorly with the frequency of fantasy; in truth, they are really opposite activities, since a fantasy usually sustains a related sequence of events.

Singer also explodes the myth that schizophrenia has anything to do with shyness or daydreaming. On the contrary, the much publicized hallucinations of schizophrenics are largely auditory, not visual; and the instance of elaborate, bizarre fantasies among hospitalized patients is a rare exception to the rule. Recent statistical evidence from Singer's work, as well as from research groups at Princeton and at the University of California campuses, indicates that individuals who deliberately develop their fantasy skills are *more* likely to be psychologically stable than those who don't.

THE TRUTH ABOUT FANTASY

In the back of your brain—somewhere on the roof of the cortex between your skull and your delicate brain stem—you do something quite strange. You *see.* Impulses racing from the optic nerve do a dance with the chemicals of your mind while simultaneously a film of the outside world seems to "flash in front of your eyes." The images aren't perfect, but accurate enough so that you can recognize a road sign while traveling in your car at fifty-five miles an hour or spot the tail of a flaming meteor thousands of miles away in the night sky.

But your cortex does something even more unusual: It paints pictures when there is nothing to see. (Makes sounds when there is nothing to hear. Even creates tastes and sensations.) That is, it generates *fantasies.* Your brain does this both when you are awake, in which case the fantasy is commonly called daydreaming, and when you are asleep, in which case it is called dreaming.

Until recently many scientists viewed fantasy as a "mere by-product" of the brain's biochemical functioning. Hence dream researchers were more interested in learning about the *cause* of dreams than about the influence of dream content on later behavior. Similarly, psychoanalysts were trained to interpret the "hidden psychological meaning" of dream symbols, not to regard the dream itself as a healing process.

But as the Senoi have known for centuries—and as psychologists are beginning to document—the deliberate, systematic use of fantasy can have a profound impact on our lives. This may sound amazing, but it is nevertheless true. Think, for example, about the following.

In a now-classic study[5] some high-school students were divided into three groups, each meeting one hour a day for several weeks. The first group went to the basketball court to shoot foul shots just like any other practicing team. Kids in the second group, however, were instructed *only to imagine themselves shooting at the basket*. The third group did nothing.

Predictably, those students who had actually practiced shooting performed much better than those who did nothing. The "imagizers," however, did almost as well as the shooters. In other words, *by playing the game in fantasy, they improved their basketball skills almost as much as those who had practiced faithfully and rigorously*!

Consequent experiments suggest that for some sports athletic workouts composed of 50 percent mental practice and 50 percent physical practice are equally as effective as 100 percent pure physical practice.[6]

How can inner imagery affect us in this remarkable fashion? There is some evidence that such imagery practice is accompanied by subconscious electrical activity in the relevant performance muscles,[7] though we are still a long way from developing a satisfactory explanation, at least in precise biological terms. On a psychological level, however, one important principle has become clear: *The image of an event can sometimes affect you in the same way that the event itself would.* Consider the basketball players again. The impact of mental practice—like the impact of actual physical practice—was to improve muscular coordination for that particular sport. In another experiment,[8] this one conducted by the prominent Israeli scientist Dr. Moshe Feldenkrais, a small group of people were instructed to wrap their right legs around the back of their necks, a feat that no one was able to accomplish. Then, for a good part of the day, Feldenkrais led the group through a series of complex exercises for the right side of the body until almost everyone was able to comply with his instruction. After a few minutes of rest, Feldenkrais directed the group through a series of similar but *imaginary* exercises for the left side of the body. Each group participant was required to fantasize the exercises in the greatest possible detail—as if they were actually being done in the present— but without making any real physical movements. After fifteen minutes of these imaginary exercises, the group members found that they could lift their left feet almost as far behind their heads as they could their right feet!

FANTASY IN SPORTS

To most people, few activities are so ethereal and unreal as fantasy, few so substantial and earthy as competitive sports. Suggest to any person you meet that fantasy could actually be used to improve sports skills and he would probably laugh —unless that person should be a professional athlete. The athlete knows better .

Take the case of nineteen-year-old Don Gay, a National Finals Rodeo competitor; in a sport considered to be the most dangerous of all, he has pushed himself to excel in one of its most fearsome events, bull riding. How does Gay manage to outmaneuver a wild, thrashing beast, avoiding severe injury and eventually driving on to victory? Through the power of his own imagination. Before each ride Gay draws a mental game plan in which he visualizes himself as a "ballet-like figure on the bull's back."[9] This imaginary rehearsals enable Gay to "ride out" whatever unexpected twists and turns his unbridled adversary may make. Jerome Robinson, one of Gay's toughest opponents, uses a similar technique. An hour or so before the competitions are due to begin, he locates the particular bull he has been assigned to ride and examines its back while simultaneously projecting a mental movie of every possible jump that the animal might make. Robinson's goal is to create an imaginary program that will allow him to ride the calm center of the bull's centrifugal force. Neither Gay nor Robinson would use imagery unless absolutely convinced of its power. The stakes are too high. As Robinson observes, "Some bulls want to whip you down under their heads, some want to fling you clear of them so that they can get a run on you and really stick it to you."

Then there is the case of ex-football quarterback John Brodie, who is currently collaborating with Esalen Institute President Michael Murphy on a book about this inner side of sports. When playing professionally, Brodie would often experience imaginary "energy streamers" at the moment before the successful execution of a long, hard pass. Once thrown, the ball would seem to follow faint but noticeable "lines of force" guiding it to the receiver. For Brodie it was as if his thoughts carried energy that, in moments of clarity, stretched themselves across the playing field, helping him to achieve his goal.[10]

Mike Spino, a nationally ranked marathon runner and author of *Poems of a Long Distance Runner*, confides that many professional athletes have spontaneously discovered powerful fantasy techniques through their own experience, although this aspect of sports is usually obscured by more popular concerns, such as a player's statistics and salary achievements. Spino cites as an example the common practice among track competitors of "fixing their eyes on the front runner's neck and feeling themselves being pulled along by him. As [they] catch up, they may have the fantasy of reeling themselves in by an invisible line extending from the leader's neck."[11]

Gay, Brodie, and Spino: They are accomplished athletes who spend a lot of time in the most unusual playing field of all, the human mind. This fact is not ignored by the many psychologists who have come to believe that within professional sports is a gold mine of fantasy techniques for the controlling of behavior—techniques that can be studied, refined according to psychological principles, and returned to the athlete in a more efficient form. Sports psychologist Robert Kriegel, for instance, has examined and synthesized many of the imagery tricks used by professional tennis players. The resulting technique, summarized in example form below, is useful for mastering winning movements in almost any sport:

1. Decide what motion it is that you want to learn. Let's say, for example, you want to duplicate the forehand stroke as described in *John Doe's Guide to Incredible Tennis.*

2. Instead of trying to memorize John Doe's instructions and then repeating them verbally to yourself as you flail your racquet about the court, close your eyes and begin to create an "inner vision" of how the forehand would look if executed by Doe himself. You can make up any picture of Doe you feel is appropriate. (If you are learning from a real person, watch him or her carefully, then close your eyes and reconstruct the image of what you have seen. If the picture doesn't come easily or is unclear in places, repeat the process. You don't *have* to do it the first time; this isn't a contest.)

3. Continue to imagine Doe making this stroke, only now remake your inner movie with a lot of close-up shots. Try to imagine what you are seeing in the greatest possible detail.

4. Now put yourself in Doe's place. Literally "see" yourself making the shot. Replay your inner movie, noticing each part of your body in detail.

5. To make the stroke as real as possible, pick up your racquet and, with eyes closed, slowly act out the move-

ment of your inner film until the *feel* of your actual movement seems to correspond to the imagined pictures in your
head.

6. Open your eyes and actually practice making the shot
on the court. If you've doubted, until now, that imagination can make a difference when you're learning a sport,
you'll be pleasantly surprised.[12]

The value of such practice methods is best confirmed by
professional athletes themselves. A recent San Francisco
sports conference featuring discussion of imagery and related
training regimens attracted an impressive array of participants, including Gary Powers, the world class hurdler; Suzy
Chaffee, the national woman's free-style skiing champion;
Bill Toomey, the Olympic decathlon winner; Marilyn King,
an Olympic pentathlon participant; and Dave Meggasy, the
former St. Louis linebacker. If interest continues to grow,
psychologically refined fantasy techniques may soon become
an essential part of all athletic training.

MIND OVER PLATTER

Athletics provides the most dramatic examples of fantasy
power, for we are conditioned to think of sports as a purely
physical endeavor. Yet the potential uses of this cortical
skill are much broader. For many years now psychologists
have known that fantasy *combined with behavior modification* (Chapter 1) is an effective tool for breaking unhealthy
habits and for replacing them with more desirable behaviors.[13]

The specific technique is actually quite simple. The minute
a person feels himself starting to make the unwanted response, he stops what he is doing and mentally exaggerates
the possible *negative consequences* as graphically as he can.
This *simulated experience* soon becomes a *negative reinforcement* for the habit. Next, he imagines himself engaging in

a more healthful behavior, eventually expanding this image to show its positive consequences, again as graphically as he can.

In a recent article science writer Earl Ubell[14] described how this process can be used to curb overeating.

1. Wait until a vision of doing something unhealthy, like eating a piece of high-calorie/high-cholesterol food, enters your consciousness.

2. Instead of responding to the image by actually eating the food, you deliberately replace the thought with a distorted vision of how such an act, or sequence of acts, could harm you. Ubell suggests these punishing pictures:

(a) Your own death from eating. (b) A death scene in which you see yourself as a hugely overweight corpse. (c) Someone you know who is so obese that he or she disgusts you. Then, as you have often seen it done in the movies, let that person's face dissolve and replace it with your own. (d) A person you love—parent, spouse, or child—rejects you because of your obesity; think up a detailed scene in which the rejection takes place. (This punishing thought should be used with caution; there is a chance of developing a real resentment toward the person you choose to do the "rejecting.") (e) Rolls of fat around your abdomen come off in your hands like sticky, hot taffy—and then grow back instantly.[15]

3. After a few moments, call a halt to this inhibiting image by visualizing yourself yelling, "Stop!"

4. Now invent a healthy vision, in this case eating a low-calorie food, to replace the first harmful thought.

5. And, finally, reward yourself for thinking such a good thought by extrapolating this last healthy image into an overall pleasant picture, such as a vision of a slim you being with an attractive member of the opposite sex. "Whatever image you use," notes Ubell, "it must give you great pleasure; it should almost have the quality of a daydream. Incidentally, sexual fantasies are highly reward-

ing; they often have been used by people to initiate exercise and diet programs."[16]

This basic procedure is effective for controlling other unhealthy habits as well, including cigarette smoking, excessive coffee drinking, and even alcoholism.[17] Fantasy combined with behavior modification can even counteract *undesirable fantasies* and their attendant behavioral dysfunctions. An example in a therapeutic setting is contained in Gerald Davison's 1968 case report of a twenty-one-year-old unmarried college senior with a sexual problem.[18] The troubled student, "Mr. M.," was initially referred to Dr. Davison by the University Counseling Center. A self-diagnosed sadist, the young man achieved sexual arousal through fantasies involving the torture of women. No sexual arousal was possible without the fantasies. For ten years sadistic thoughts accompanying masturbation provided Mr. M. with his only sexual gratification. Concern over his condition had led him to limit his heterosexual contacts severely, and he firmly believed that marriage was impossible.

This would be no easy case. How could the pattern be altered? Possibly by associating the pleasurable feelings of orgasm with something different from the customary reveries of torture. What if, for example, Mr. M. were asked to concentrate on a pinup photo just before orgasm, to forget his fantasy and keep his mind on the picture. If the female form could replace the sadistic fantasy as the image associated with the intensely rewarding sexual response, attraction to women might be substituted for the desire to torture them.

Such a plan seemed worth a try. Mr. M. was instructed to continue masturbating, using sadistic fantasies to "start things off." Once he achieved an erection, however, a modification in procedure was recommended. Davison describes it this way:

He was then to begin to masturbate while looking at a picture of a sexy, nude woman; *Playboy* magazine was suggested to him as a good source. If he began losing the erection, he was to switch back to his sadistic fantasy until he could begin masturbating effectively again. Concentrating again on the *Playboy* picture, he was to continue masturbating, using the fantasy only to regain erection. As orgasm was approaching he was at all costs to focus on the *Playboy* picture, even if sadistic fantasies began to intrude. It was impressed on him that gains would ensue only when sexual arousal was associated with the picture. . . . The client appeared enthusiastic and hopeful as he left the office.[19]

Such optimism was not in vain. On his next visit to Davison's office, the young man reported that *Playboy* had aided him in achieving successful orgasms without the sadistic fantasies. At this point Davison made suggestions geared to further therapeutic progress, encouraging Mr. M. to begin dating on a casual basis and, when masturbating, to try to achieve orgasm using unretouched pictures of average-looking women and mental recollections of *Playboy* pinups. Efforts to carry out Davison's recommendations were not totally successful. During the third therapy session, Mr. M. reported difficulty in making dates and ridding himself of his sadistic fantasies. This prompted Davison to take an additional therapeutic measure. He asked Mr. M. to imagine, for five minutes, a typical sadistic fantasy in conjunction with various repugnant images (e.g., being kicked in the groin by a karate expert). Upon completing this unpleasant task, the patient was sent away for another week with instructions to continue masturbating without the use of sadistic fantasies if possible.

In the final three therapy sessions, Mr. M. made steady progress toward the therapeutic goal: sexual arousal through "normal" procedures. The fourth session was marked by reports of successful masturbation to imagined images of women without appeal to dreams of torture, and the fifth session was marked by Mr. M.'s stated *inability* to obtain an erection to a sadistic fantasy. The patient praised the effectiveness of the therapy and told Davison about the satisfactions he had achieved through his newly initiated dating encounters. In the sixth session (one month later), Mr. M.'s dating efforts had decreased, but he claimed a continued absence of sadistic fantasies and the ability to masturbate successfully "to both real-life and imaginal appropriate sexual stimuli."

Sixteen months after the termination of therapy, a follow-up report was obtained. Except for a period of "premeditated" return to sadistic fantasies, Mr. M. seemed to be on the way to leading a normal social life, free of the sadism and loneliness he had known for a decade. In the patient's own words:

> I have no need for sadistic fantasies. . . . I have also been pursuing a vigorous (well, vigorous for *me*) program of dating. In this way, I have gotten to know a lot of girls of whose existence I was previously only peripherally aware. As you probably know, I was very shy with girls before; well, now I have become a regular rake![20]

PROGRAMMING CREATIVITY

We cannot pretend that scientists completely understand that wonderous process called *creative problem solving*. The strange and mysterious way in which the mind generates entirely new images still eludes precise definition.

Yet recent research has yielded one intriguing fact: Creative problem solving depends on a person's ability to see a problem in a *new context*.[21] The case of inventor and businessman George Westinghouse illustrates this point very well. For years Westinghouse pondered the problem of how to bring a long train of railroad cars to a simultaneous stop. He could imagine the cars all screeching to a halt, but missing from this fantasy was the close-up detail of how this event could happen. Then one day he picked up a local newspaper. "The answer came in a flash the moment he read that compressed air was being piped to drillers in mountains miles away: he would pipe it along his line of cars and stop them with an air brake."[22] This innovation came about because Westinghouse was able to see his problem (stopping a string of cars) in another context (soil drilling).

Creative problem solving, then, involves bringing into consciousness new ideas or perspectives that, in turn, modify or complete the problem image. Often this happens by chance, though luck is a relatively poor problem-solving strategy. It's like the old story of putting a monkey in front of a typewriter. Given an infinite amount of time, he'll eventually come up with poetry. But who wants to wait!

Fortunately, the social scientists who study creativity have developed some easy techniques which enable us to produce solution contexts quickly and efficiently through the systematic use of *fantasy production strategies*. The oldest and best known are Dr. William J. J. Gordon's methods of selective free association, collectively known as *synectics*.[23] According to Gordon, the fantasies we need to solve our problems already exist within the complex of thought associations in our memory banks. We can retrieve these images in three ways.

The first is to choose a salient aspect of a problem and to think of as many associations to it as possible. Consider the case of the teacher who is bored with grading papers and would like to have his students present their reports in panel fashion. But what kind of panel? He closes his eyes for a moment and allows the concept of panel to trigger various fantasies: "Panel shows . . . quiz format . . . maybe I could have a quiz show with the students . . . also, maybe there could be rewards for the right answers," and so on.[24] The trick is to let the mind wander as far as it can, not putting down an image because it seems far out, but instead trying to find some part of the image that is useful.

Gordon's second method is to empathize with the problem, using feeling associations as possible clues to a solution. In one case some employees were pondering the question of how to make their boss more responsive. They decided that "a catalyst is needed to make him react more quickly to memos." But what kind of catalyst? At that point a leader, who was trained in creative problem solving strategy, asked the others to imagine themselves as "catalysts" and to indicate how this would feel.

JOHN (responding): As a catalyst, I am dropped into a big pot of chemicals. Nothing is going on until I drop in and make it all happen. I'm the big cheese, and all the chemicals change colors when I arrive. But I stay the same.

LEADER: Out of what John has just said, what new ways of solving the problem does it suggest? Let's start out wild, and then we'll make it practical. I want you to think of a wildly different solution for our problem.

BILL: Hey, the color change thing! I have this image of something changing color—we paint his whole office a different color when he delays decisions.

LEADER: That's interesting, Bill. Can anyone take that a step further—how might we actually do something like that?

JIM: I've got it. What that makes me think of is this: what if we had a chemical that changes colors and we painted it across the top edge of every memo that gives the boss something to decide upon. It would be colorless when he first gets the memo. Then if he waited a week, the chemical would turn blue. After two weeks, it turns red.

KAREN: Yeah, after that he'd get the message. That would provide a visual reminder that would alert him to the absolute necessity of making a decision.[25]

To work empathetically by himself, a person simply takes an object in the problem or a concept defining the problem and pretends that *he is it*, involving himself as if it were a living thing: seeing what it sees; feeling what it feels; letting whatever associations that "bob up" flow freely through his mind to see if they suggest any solutions.

The final associative method is a process Gordon calls *compressed conflict*. Here the idea is to create a concept from two seemingly contradictory aspects of your problem. This, in turn, becomes a meditation that triggers a broad range of potentially useful fantasies. Gordon cites the example of Louis Pasteur, who "[long] before establishing a series of experiments on antitoxin . . . began to talk about safe attack, a phrase that turned out to be an admirable description of the discovery."[26] In similar fashion, the image of a "protoplasmic kiss" helped Cajal to understand the communication between nerve cells.

The fantasy methods of Gordon and other creative problem solving researchers have been modified and expanded enormously in the last two decades. Synectics alone is used by major corporations, including Procter and Gamble, by educational institutions large and small, and even by government think tanks. In fact, the systematic use of fantasy imagery represents one of the most widespread applications of psychology.

FANTASY: WHAT'S IN IT FOR US?

Psychologists have performed a valuable service in demonstrating the practical value of fantasy, and we can expect research to continue unabated. Of particular interest is the suggestion that fantasy techniques can play a valuable role in motivating achievement and financial success. This notion derives from an intriguing study conducted by R. W. Burris at the University of Indiana.[27]

Burris, it seems, was interested in seeing if he could

actually increase another person's achievement level by getting him to imagine, in greater detail, his chosen objectives and the possible means for realizing them. To test out this idea, the experimenter proceeded to arrange a series of eight forty-minute counseling sessions with randomly chosen college students enrolled in a self-improvement course. The stated purpose of these conferences was to help the student gain a greater understanding of what he wished "to accomplish as a result of [his] school experiences" and to assist him in resolving past and present "problems which are connected or associated with these objectives."

At the end of the sessions, the students took psychological tests of achievement motivation and scored, as Burris predicted, demonstrably higher than the uncounseled students participating in the same course. What is more significant, however, is that the specially treated students went on to perform better in school, actually attaining higher grade-point averages during the semester than the control students.

There is also evidence from a variety of sources that meditating on certain fantasies can produce soothing states of consciousness. The actual scientific comparisons of images with the psychological experiences they produce is still a relatively new endeavor; however, some correlations based on the clinical work of behaviorist Joseph Wolpe and other psychotherapists have emerged:

Psychological State	Contemplated Image
Feelings of integration and unity.	A white circle with a white dot at the center (five minutes), followed by an equal-armed white cross or mathematical plus sign (five minutes) followed by a white equilateral triangle pointing up (five minutes).
Feelings of harmony in human relationships.	Two hands clasping each other.

Feelings of masculinity and dominance.	A large steel sword with a fire blade of shining silver.
Feelings of liberation and unfolding.	A red rose bud slowly and majestically opening. You can almost smell the perfume.
Feelings of femininity and receptivity.	A beautiful, clean cup or vase filled with clear fresh water.
Reduced anxiety; relaxation.	Any beautiful scene or basic goemetrical form dominated by the color blue. An intense, bright spot of light about eighteen inches in front of you. A leaf moving erratically on little waves near a river bank.
Deeper, more "inward" states of consciousness.	A long, unending road or a deep, bottomless hole.[28]

One Texas radiologist is so convinced of fantasy power that he begins each cancer treatment by asking patients to visualize the cobalt attacking the malignancy. "Mentally picture the radiation beam with its millions of bullets of energy hitting the cells in its field—the normal ones being able to repair themselves and the cancer cells getting weaker and dying," he commands. "Picture the cancer getting smaller."[29]

Whether or not such bizarre therapy actually helps is a matter of conjecture for now, but at least it does indicate a growing belief in the power of fantasy—and, by implication, the power of the human mind. Psychologists are making it clear that fantasy, far from being the fluky by-product of neural static or the grumblings of an unstable personality, is a key to greater self-control, personal growth, and literally, to a higher level of *in*-lightenment.

NOTES

1. A. Huxley, *Island* (New York: Harper & Row, 1962), pp. 262–263.
2. K. Stewart, "Dream Theory in Malaya," in C. Tart, *Altered States of Consciousness* (New York: Wiley, 1969), pp. 159–167.

3. G. Leonard, Personal communication, 1973.

4. J. Singer, *Daydreaming* (New York: Random House, 1966), especially pp. 54–79.

5. J. Oxendine, *A Psychology of Motor Learning* (New York: Appleton-Century-Crofts, 1968), p. 230.

6. J. Johnston, "Effects of Imagery on Learning the Volleyball Pass," *Dissertation Abstracts International* 32 (1971): 772-A.

7. Oxendine, *A Psychology of Motor Learning*, p. 227.

8. M. Feldenkrais, Personal communication, 1973. A full account of the Feldenkrais work appears in M. Feldenkrais, *Awareness Through Movement* (New York: Harper & Row, 1972).

9. J. Souncheray, "The Sugarbowl of Rodeos," *TWA Ambassador* 6, No. 9 (1973): 38.

10. M. Murphy, Personal communication, 1973.

11. M. Spino, Personal communication, 1973.

12. B. Kriegel, Personal communication, 1973.

13. K. Dunlap, *Habits: Their Making and Remaking* (New York: Liveright, 1932).

14. E. Ubell, "How to Save Your Life: The Behavior Control Diet," *New York Magazine*, 3 September 1973, pp. 43 ff.

15. Ibid., p. 47.

16. Ibid.

17. R. Rubin et al., *Advances in Behavior Therapy* (New York: Academic, 1972).

18. G. Davison, "Elimination of Sadistic Fantasy by a Client-controlled Counter-conditioning Technique," *Journal of Abnormal Psychology* 73 (1968): 84–90.

19. Ibid., p. 85.

20. Ibid., p. 89.

21. W. Gordon, *Synectics* (New York: Harper & Row, 1961).

22. A. Osborn, *Applied Imagination* (New York: Charles Scribner's, 1963), p. 338.

23. W. Gordon, *Synectics*.

24. A. Chopra, "Idea Generating Strategies," prepublication manuscript for *Forum*, p. 6.

25. K. Panushka, "Games Executives Play," a *Boston Magazine* reprint, p. 3.

26. W. Gordon, *The Metaphorical Way* (Cambridge, Mass.: Porpoise, 1966), p. 239.

27. D. McCelland, *The Achieving Society* (New York: Van Nostrand Reinhold, 1961), pp. 417–418.

28. Adopted from J. Wolpe, *The Practice of Behavior Therapy* (New York: Pergamon, 1969), p. 125; R. Gerard, "Psychosynthesis: A Psychotherapy for the Whole Man," *Psychosynthesis Research Foundation* No. 14 (1964); and H. Leuner, "Guided Affective Imagery," *American Journal of Psychotherapy* 23 (1969): 4–22.

29. "Healing: Mind over Matter," *Newsweek*, 29 April 1974, p. 68.

SUGGESTED READINGS

GORDON, W. *Synectics*. New York: Harper & Row, 1961.

LEUNER, H. "Guided Affective Imagery." *American Journal of Psychotherapy* 23 (1969), pp. 4–22.

OXENDINE, J. *Psychology of Motor Learning*. New York: Appleton-Century-Crofts, 1972.

RUBIN, R. et al. *Advances in Behavior Therapy*. New York: Academic Press, 1972.

STEWART, K. "Dream Theory in Malaya," in C. Tart, *Altered States of Consciousness*. New York: Wiley, 1969.

10

supersensory perception

Less than one hundred years ago an American newspaper printed the following editorial:

A man was arrested yesterday, charged with attempting to obtain money under false pretenses. He claimed he was promoting a device whereby one person could talk to another several miles away, by means of a small apparatus and some wire. Without doubt this man is a fraud and an unscrupulous trickster and must be taught that the American public is too smart to be the victim of this and similar schemes. Even if this insane idea worked it would have no practical value other than for circus sideshows.

A short time later, in 1876, Alexander Graham Bell took out a patent on the telephone.[1]

TWO FROM THE UNDERGROUND

By day Russell Targ is a straight scientist, and a good one at that. From nine to five he conducts high-level laser research at Sylvania Laboratories in Mountain View, California. But at night he enters a different world of science: the world of parapsychology. Russell Targ, along with his associate, David Hart, has invented a machine that teaches people ESP ability. The machine, which operates on the simple principle of giving a person immediate reinforcement for each ESP attempt, has significantly improved ESP ability in over 30 percent of the people tested, Targ claims.

Just a few blocks away from Targ's home is the Stanford University office of Dr. William A. Tiller. Tiller is a full professor of materials science. His academic honors include a doctorate in physics from the Univeristy of Toronto, the chairmanship of the Materials Science Department at Stanford, and a Guggenheim fellowship. His present research, however, is motivated by an unusual apprehension: "I must confess that one of the greatest concerns I have is that the Russians are tapping [psychic] powers that are so far beyond anything that we know of and that the possibility exists that these powers may provide a way for world domination that has not yet been considered." Tiller believes not only that psychic powers are real but that they are genetically inherited, a factor that favors the Russians. "In the West," he explains, "we did away with a lot of our witches, we had a lot of witch hunts and a lot of inquisitions, and so on. And so I wonder about our gene bank. . . . The Eastern part of Europe, you see, didn't have that. So that's one of the ways that the Russians are better off."[2] Tiller spent a good part of last year reviewing Russian work in parapsychology. He is now attempting to duplicate some of their machinery and experiments here in the United States.

Russell Targ and William Tiller are two members of a growing scientific underground in the United States. They are, according to Stanford research physicist Dr. Hal Putoff, some of the "many people in this country who sort of run a double life in their scientific work."[3] Putoff should know. He divides his time between "legitimate" research and investigations into ESP and related fields.

Despite the opposition of some scientists to many aspects of the underground science, the line between the two is beginning to fade. There are several reasons for this development. For one, the instances of "impossible" events are becoming hard to ignore. The evidence for ESP alone is much more ironclad than for some of the more commonly accepted psychological phenomena.[4] This massive amount of data has prompted no less than Dr. H. J. Eysenck, the distinguished Professor of Psychology at the University of London, to remark,

> Unless there is a gigantic conspiracy involving some thirty University departments all over the world, and several hundred highly respected scientists in various fields, many of them originally hostile to the claims of the psychical researchers, the only conclusion the unbiased observer can come to must be that there does exist a small number of people who obtain knowledge existing either in other people's minds, or in the outer world, by means as yet unknown to science.[5]

A second factor is the impact of the Russian research in parapsychology. Americans first became aware of the Russian work in 1970 when Sheila Ostrander and Lynn Schroeder published *Psychic Discoveries Behind the Iron Curtain.* Since then numerous American scientists have traveled to Russia to check out the validity of the information reported in the book. These "second wave" reporters play down the political consequences of the Russian experiments, but there is unanimous agreement on one point: The Soviet scientists have made substantial progress in developing the technology necessary to measure ESP.

The key factor, however, in making ESP legitimate, at least to a larger number of scientists and laymen if not to the majority of the scientific establishment, has been biofeedback research (Chapter 3). Biofeedback training has demonstrated that a lot of activity that traditional psychology has denied or at best ignored—behaviors such as shifting into altered states of consciousness, controlling the internal organs, and changing brain waves and body radiations at will—are real. Once we understand that man can turn his alpha waves on and off just as easily as if he were pressing a telegraph key, it is no longer as difficult to imagine that some brain waves might be patterned into message form and then recorded by another sensitive brain. More importantly, biofeedback research has developed a technology that can monitor mental energies and translate them into clicks, bleeps, and bips on precision instruments. In short, there is now machinery to translate those weird, subjective, and nutty parapsychological ideas into something real, something that can be analyzed, interpreted, studied, duplicated, and, of course, published in the scientific journals.

There is an interesting analogy between the impact of biofeedback research on parapsychology and the first developments in dream research. Less than fifteen years ago dreams were regarded as fluke occurrences by almost all theoretical scientists and doctors. Only the Freudian fringe and a few other psychotherapists talked about the importance of dreams. Then some investigators observed that people's subjective estimates of their dream length correlated with bursts of eye movements that have come to be known as rapid eye movement (REM) sleep.[6] All of a sudden dreams, instead of being those funny subjective experiences, became real. Dreams could be measured, so they were valid objects for study. This new legitimacy has led to further physiological research which has been very valuable. It has also increased purely psychological research into dreams, research that could have been conducted thirty years earlier but was not supported because it was not quite respectable.

ESP OR SSP?

There is a long history of underground research. Unfortunately, psychic phenomena in the West (particularly in America) have always been associated with religious or spiritual ideas. This distinction is inherent in the Judeo-Christian tradition,[7] which divides the study of man into two distinct parts: the investigation of bodily mechanics and the interaction of mind and soul, or theology. The positive consequences of dividing man into body and spirit are well known to historians of science. When Descartes pinned the soul to the pineal gland at the front of the brain (c. 1650), he freed scientists to explore the machinery of the human animal without violating ecclesiastical precepts. However, the negative consequences of such a distinction have never been fully appreciated. During the centuries that preceded Descartes, all mental phenomena—including psychic phenomena—became inextricably confused with the notion of soul. To deny one automatically implied a denial of the other. The result is that, as scientists eliminated the need for a soul as an explanatory concept in psychology, the belief in psychic events was simultaneously eliminated. Instead of attempting to extend science to account for ESP and other inexplicable mental events, investigators dismissed them as either nonexistent or illusory. Even worse, many researchers who continued to believe in psychic phenomena bought the idea that paranormal events must exist outside the realm of the physical universe—their reasoning being that only some kind of otherworldly concept, such as spiritualism, could account for these strange forms of communication. As psychologist Lawrence LeShan points out, this sort of explanation is ultimately unsatisfactory, since it doesn't really describe anything:

> It is perfectly useless from a scientific viewpoint to try to "explain" [paranormal events] by saying "spirits do it." Spirits (or "discarnate entities," "people who have passed beyond the plane of existence," or what have you) may or may not exist: that is not the question. Suppose they do exist: the problem remains. We say that the cosmos is put together ("works") in a certain way, and therefore certain things cannot happen. Then we say there is a class of beings who can make these impossible things happen. We have not solved the problem; we have hidden and obscured it. We must still ask—if we accept "spirits" as a factor—"How do the spirits do it? How do they violate the laws of the cosmos and produce impossibilities like clairvoyance and precognition?" We can complicate the question all we wish by adding hypothetical factors like spirits, but the problem and the paradox remain.[8]

The only logical way to explain ESP, LeShan continues, is to *assume* that it does exist within as yet undiscovered laws of science, then to find out what those laws are.

Interestingly, the Russian researchers do not make a distinction between science, on the one hand, and psychic phenomena, on the other. These scientists take the primary view that there must be a logical explanation for everything. If, for example, a Soviet scientist hears that some crazy student who has locked himself in a concrete vault is able to "visualize" events outside the vault, the scientist will immediately begin to search for a physical theory to explain what has happened.

Technically, then, the Russians do not believe in *extrasensory perception*, which implies a method of communication outside the scope of scientific explanation. Rather, they subscribe to the idea of *supersensory perception* (SSP), a way of communicating that is not yet understood but is, in theory, explainable in scientific terms. This assumption—

that psychic phenomena have a physical basis—has led many Soviet scientists to investigate the kinds of strange events that their American counterparts would frequently ignore.

In this context, the chief contribution of biofeedback research to parapsychology in the West is to provide a physicalistic model of ESP. We now know that a person produces electromagnetic body waves which can, with practice, be controlled in such a way as to provide a coded message.[9] We also know that these waves can be transmitted and received at a distant point. For example, Dr. W. A. Schafer, formerly of General Dynamics Life Sciences, has developed a complex of supersensitive electronic instruments with the descriptive but unimaginative name of Field Effect Monitors. Using these devices, he can pick up electromagnetic waves produced by heartbeats at over four feet from the body.[10] When amplifiers are added to the circuit, the distance that body signals can travel is greatly increased.

As a result of biofeedback and other research, five theories of ESP have received serious attention. The most popular, and least likely, is the theory that ESP is transmitted by alpha waves. Why alpha? Of all the brain states, alpha is the easiest to bring under voluntary control. Furthermore, there is some experimental evidence linking alpha to ESP. A few years ago two Philadelphia researchers made some interesting observations. They were studying the brain-wave patterns of two identical twins who were situated in different rooms. When one twin closed his eyes, the EEG machine registered a common alpha response. But something uncommon also happened. Whenever the first twin closed his eyes, the second twin experienced alpha, although his eyes remained open.[11] Despite this evidence, however, the case against alpha as the *sole* cause of ESP is strong. "It must be stressed," writes Dr. Joe Kamiya,

that there is no connection between alpha waves and extra-sensory perception. People tend to associate the two because radio waves are involved in communication, but radio waves are generated at several thousand cycles per second, while brain waves range between a fraction of a cycle and about 100 cycles per second, with most of the energy limited to about 15 cycles per second.[12]

The alpha signal is so weak relative to other energies it is hard to believe that alpha, or at least alpha alone, is the energy source for psychic phenomena.

A more promising variation on the alpha theory holds that ESP is a product of different body rhythms operating in some kind of harmonious pattern. A good way to understand this idea is to consider the following example. Take two metals. Both of them have a particular melting point. If you combine these metals, however, the result is a melting point that is much different from what either of the two had previously.[13] This process of combining a number of different things to achieve a "higher order" result is called a *synergistic effect*. The synergistic theory of ESP holds that psychic communication is really a higher-order effect resulting from the combination of normal body energies, such as brain waves, heart rate, and galvanic skin response, into a synchronous pattern. Tiller believes that biofeedback training will be useful for helping us to synchronize our glands so that psychic phenomena can be controlled systematically and at will.[14]

The third body-wave theory of ESP is the most exotic, though it is not improbable, given what we already know from conventional science. It developed a few years ago when physicist Gerald Feinberg became bored with the idea that Einstein's light speed is the maximum allowed for our universe. Employing some clever mathematical techniques, Feinberg invented a proof for the existence of a faster-than-light particle, which he calls the *tachyon*. Many scientists now believe not only that the tachyon exists but that it is the physical basis of ESP. A fourth and similar theory—

similar in the sense that it posits an as yet undetected physical reality—ties ESP to the existence of a subtle force field,
or *bioplasma*. This bioplasma either acts as a medium for
ESP messages or, more esoterically, expands a person's consciousness such that he can simultaneously experience events
outside his body.[15] And finally, there is Dr. Carl Jung's well-
known theory of *synchronicity*, which holds that two events
—in this case the ESP experience of a given circumstance
and the circumstance itself—can happen simultaneously
without any connection or causal link between them.[16]

If it seems strange to attempt an explanation of ESP with
such scientific-sounding terms as *tachyon*, *bioplasma*, and
synchronicity, we must take pause and remember how truly
bizarre the physicist's view of reality has become within the
last half century. (It is interesting, in this regard, that most
past presidents of the famous British Society for Psychical
Research were physicists, mathematicians, or philosophers
of science; three were Nobel laureates.[17]) Take the world of
subatomic particles. Of the hundred or so elementary particles currently known today, most behave in a fashion so
odd as to make ESP look tame; *strangeness* has, in fact, become a common word in the physicist's jargon. There is, for
example, the funny little electron which often acts like a
particle—except when fired at a screen with two holes in
it, then it seems to go through both openings at once![18] Or
we could ponder what science historian Arthur Koestler calls
the "ghostlike neutrino," which has "virtually no physical
properties: no mass, no electric charge, no magnetic field."[19]
Unaffected by gravity or by the usual force fields that seem
to control our universe, a neutrino could go "clean through
the solid body of the earth as if it were so much empty
space." Last, but certainly not least, we have M. Gell-Mann's
proposal for

a theory of elementary particles which, with acknowledgments to the Buddha, he called "the eightfold way"; and

which enabled him to predict the discovery of yet another
. . . particle called the omega minus—for which he got the
Nobel prize in 1969. Gell-Mann and his co-workers have
even suggested that the "elementary particles" may in fact
not be elementary at all, but may consist of even more elementary entities which they decided to call "quarks"—with
acknowledgments to James Joyce in *Finnegan's Wake*.[20]

Quarks? Neutrinos? The Eightfold Path theory? Such
strangeness, as the physicist would say, does not necessarily
validate ESP; yet it does suggest that the arbitrary distinction between science and parapsychology is unjustified and
that there may already be room within the framework of
established science to allow for psychic phenomena.

ESP TODAY

To scholars of history, the name of Upton Sinclair is usually
associated with *The Jungle*, that classic muckraking book
about the heinous social conditions of the Chicago stock-
yards at the turn of the century. Yet Sinclair had other inter-
ests, including the fact that his wife seemed to possess
so-called psychic abilities. Late in the 1920s the author initiated a sequence of experiments which required Mrs. Sinclair
to identify and reconstruct a total of 290 rough drawings
composed either in secret or at a long distance. Her success,
as reported in the popular 1930 *Mental Radio*, was remarkable. Twenty-three percent of her guesses were correct
"hits"; a total of 53 percent were partial hits; and only 24
percent were inaccurate enough to be classified as
erroneous.[21]

Since Sinclair's pioneering experiment, ESP research
has become more sophisticated, with special emphasis on
statistical rigor and replicability. In a recent and particularly fascinating study, a *sensitive* who had already demonstrated his parapsychological skills in a previous examination
was invited by psychologists Stanley Krippner and Montague

Ullman to spend eight consecutive nights in the dream laboratory of the Brooklyn Maimonides Medical Center.[22]

Unfortunately for him, he wasn't allowed to sleep undisturbed, for every time the sensitive began to dream, as determined by his rapid eye movements, an observer sent a signal by buzzer to a psychologist sitting in a separate, acoustically soundproof room. The psychologist, in turn, randomly selected one of ten envelopes, opened it, and began to concentrate on the picture inside. When his eye movements stopped, the sensitive was awakened and his dreams recorded on tape. He then went back to sleep until another dream began, and the telepathic attempts were repeated.

At the end of the eighth day, a panel of three independent judges was asked to determine the similarities between each of the psychologist's pictures and each of the sensitive's dream recordings. The results were striking indeed: "The judges' ratings," writes Krippner, "indicated that there was a high degree of correspondence ($p < 0.001$) between the art print and the dream transcript on each of the eight experimental nights." A dramatic case in point: on the second night, the psychologist randomly selected Hiroshige's "Downpour at Shono," to which the sensitive responded,

> It's as though I was doing some drawing . . . I had a feeling as though it were in a down position, like a low table. Down on the floor. Seems that's what I meant by "down . . ." Something about an Oriental man who was ill . . . A fountain. Two images and a water spray that would shoot up . . . Walking with someone on the street. Raining . . . It seemed it was raining a little bit and . . . we had to walk out into the street . . . It was raining, and it was night and it had a sort of heavy feeling . . .[23]

Since ESP seems to occur rarely, psychological researchers are also concerned with finding ways to increase its frequency—which gets us back to Russell Targ's ESP teaching

FIGURE 1. "Downpour at Shono," Hiroshige. *Photo: Courtesy Tudor Publishing Company, New York.*

machine. The principle behind the machine is quite simple. For several years ESP researchers have observed what they call the *decline effect,* the phenomenon where a subject in an ESP experiment will start off demonstrating a high clairvoyant ability but will gradually lose that ability. Targ hypothesized that this shift might be due to boredom, since in most ESP experiments a subject is not given knowledge of his results until the experiment is over. For example, if you were asked to guess which cards were being turned up as someone else in another room was going through a deck of them, you would not receive your "score" until all fifty-two cards had been dealt. Targ reasoned that ESP ability could be improved if a subject could get immediate feedback after each ESP attempt. In Targ's words, "the immediate reinforcement gives the subject a feel for what the ESP is like."[24]

Targ's machine looks like a small toolbox with four 35-millimeter transparencies and four corresponding buttons built into the face. When the machine is turned on, it automatically and randomly selects one of the four transparencies. The subject tries to guess what choice the machine has made and then presses one of the four buttons. The correct transparency lights up, and the subject knows immediately if his guess was right or wrong. (By pressing a "pass" button, the subject may also choose to skip a trial if he wishes.) After twenty-four trials the machine places a successful subject's ESP ability in one of four categories with "encouragement lights": "ESP ability present," "useful at Vegas," "outstanding ESP ability," and "psychic medium oracle."

As we indicated earlier, repeated use of the machine increased extrasensory perception in about 30 percent of the people tested. Targ concludes from this that "it is possible to teach and enhance ESP phenomena through techniques of feedback and reward in much the same way as visceral and glandular functions are brought under volitional control."[25]

Aside from feedback, many ESP researchers assert that two other factors—emotional arousal and belief in ESP—facilitate supersensory communication. To test the effects of belief in ESP under the conditions of emotional arousal, UCLA psychologist Dr. Thelma Moss and her colleague Dr. J. A. Gengerelli divided 144 volunteer subjects into 72 teams of two;[26] these teams, in turn, became

> three groups of 24 pairs each: the *ESP Group*, being those who believed in ESP and thought they had such experiences in the past; the *ESP? Group*, those who believed in ESP to some extent but did not believe they had the faculty; and the *Non-ESP Group*, who were convinced that ESP did not exist.[27]

One member of each team, acting as sender, then went into a soundproof room and observed an emotionally charged colored slide while simultaneously listening to relevant sounds; at the same time his partner in another room would try to receive the sender's experience, first by relaxing and recording his impressions on tape then by choosing between two slides, one of which was identical to that seen by the sender. This process was repeated three times for each team with impressive results: The ESP Group registered guesses that had only a 1 in 3,000 probability of occurring by chance, "whereas the other two groups scored no more than chance expectation."[28]

THE ESP TEST

Finally and most importantly, ESP scientists are looking for ways that will allow more people to test themselves for supersensory skills. Dr. R. A. McConnell, a Research Professor of Biophysics and Microbiology at the University of Pittsburgh, has developed a method that enables students in high-school and university classes to test themselves for ESP.[29] We have paraphrased, thereby simplifying, his procedure, which in essence requires only three people: a *subject*—that is, the person to be tested—someone else to act as the *experimenter*, and an *outsider* to perform certain independent tasks.

1. From magazines and other sources, the outsider should secretly gather a large number of pictures selected for distinctiveness, strong lines, striking content.

2. From this collection, the outsider should choose ten pictures which we will now call *targets*, and mark them with a code consisting of the letter T, followed by an identifying number. He then places the targets individually between sheets of aluminum foil and puts each "sandwich" inside an adhesive-flap manila envelope, sealing it.

3. Enter the experimenter, who then codes each target envelope on its outside by the letter R followed by identifying numbers that are unrelated to the T digits inside. He should also be careful to avoid marking the target through the envelope. For the time being, the experimenter must remain ignorant of the pictures within the envelopes, lest he unwittingly give a clue to the subject.

4. The experimenter proceeds to frame each envelope under a sheet of glass so that the R code is showing. The purpose of the glass is to prevent the subject from accidentally pressure marking or pressure reading the target when making his responses.

5. Next the experimenter tapes to the surface of the glass a piece of blank drawing paper, which bears the same R code number that is visible on the envelope.

6. The subject now waits until he is in the proper

mood—that is, until he is relaxed and his mind is clear. Although some psychics are reputed to use exhausting concentration, trying "too hard" may retard a beginner's success.

7. The experimenter introduces the subject to the paper-covered targets and keeps him under surveillance until the drawing part of the experiment is completed.

8. The subject moves from one assembly to the next, drawing his impressions of the targets underneath.

9. The experimenter then gives the ten assemblies to the outsider, who, in seclusion opens each envelope and records the T and R numbers for each target and the drawing that accompanies it. When this is done, the outsider lays aside the empty envelopes, shuffles the target pictures, shuffles the response drawings, and hands the two piles to the experimenter.

10. The experimenter must match the targets and drawings, choosing one response drawing to go with each target picture. The criterion for pairing should be the same as the instructions given to the subject before he started drawing. For example, if the subject had been instructed to create a drawing that "best duplicates" his impressions of the target underneath, the experimenter, in turn, should match drawings to targets on the basis of similarity. When the experimenter has finished this sorting task, he should list his results as pairs of T and R numbers.

11. Finally, a check is made between the experimenter's list of T-R numbers and the outsider's list of actual pairs: Correct matches between these two lists count as "hits," and a couple will happen by chance. However, the probability of additional hits occurring by chance becomes increasingly small, as indicated by the chart below. A high proportion of hits, then, suggests that some "supersensory" communication may have linked the mind of the the subject to the target pictures.[30]

The Number of Hits (Correct Matches)	The Probability That They Occur by Chance[31]
1	.632
2	.264
3	.0803
4	.01899
5	.00366
6	.0006
7	.0000788
8	.0000127
9	—
10	.000000276

SUPERSENSORY PERCEPTION: WHAT'S IN IT FOR US?

I believe that the real impact of psychology will be felt, not through the technological products it places in the hands of powerful men, but through its effects on the public at large, through a new and different public conception of what is humanly possible and what is humanly desirable.—George A. Miller. From his presidential address to the American Psychological Association

If we were to compose a list of the most influential names of the last hundred years, undoubtedly the name Sigmund Freud would rank near the top. His ideas have forcefully shaped present attitudes toward child rearing, sexual behavior, education, politics, and even literary criticism. His influence is even more remarkable when you realize that the validity of Freudian analysis has *never* been adequately demonstrated. Some of Freud's detractors have even suggested that psychoanalysis aggravates, rather than cures, psychological problems.

The point to be made is this: A radical scientific advance such as ESP has consequences far beyond the introduction of a new technique or theory. By changing prevailing conceptions of how man and his universe operate, a new scientific idea can have dramatic and unforeseen political and social consequences. Consider the case of Copernicus. His theory placing the locus of the universe not at the earth but at the sun had repercussions far beyond the province of astronomy. This new idea "did not change the productivity of the fields, turn wine into vinegar, or render less fascinating the pursuit of women or war," notes scholar Garvin McCain wryly, ". . . yet, when a long established and firmly held belief is shattered, life can never be the same."[32] If the experimental evidence for ESP continues to mount, the beneficial consequences for man's own self-concept would be incalculable—this above and beyond whatever technological use we could make of psychic powers. In the words of Sir Alister Hardy, the esteemed British zoologist, "I venture to think that it would have in this century an effect similar in magnitude to that which the acceptance of evolution had in the last."[33]

NOTES

1. We thank Jim Beal of NASA for alerting us to this quote.

2. W. Tiller, Personal communication, 1971.

3. H. Putoff, Personal communication, 1971.

4. C. Tart, Personal communication, 1971.

5. A. Koestler, *The Roots of Coincidence* (New York: Random House, 1972), p. 14.

6. See E. Aserinsky and N. Kleitman, "Regularly Occurring Periods of Eye Motility and Concomitant Phenomena During Sleep," *Science* 118 (1953): 273–274.

7. L. Andrews and M. Karlins, *Requiem for Democracy?* (New York: Holt, 1971).

8. L. LeShan, *The Medium, the Mystic, and the Physicist* (New York: Viking, 1974), pp. 79–80.

9. See, for example, E. Dewan, "Communication by Voluntary Control of the EEG," *Proceedings of the Symposium of Biomedical Engineering* (1966): 349–351.

10. W. Schafer, "Further Developments of the Field Effect Monitor," Life Sciences, Corvair Division of General Dynamics, Report GDC-ERR-AN-1114, October 1967.

11. *Science Digest* (June 1968): 88.

12. J. Kamiya, "Conscious Control of Brain Waves," *Psychology Today* (April 1968): 59.

13. J. Beal, Personal communication, 1971.

14. W. Tiller, Personal communication, 1971.

15. S. Krippner, Maimonides Medical Center, Personal communication, 1974.

16. S. Grof, Maryland Psychiatric Research Center, Personal communication, 1974.

17. Koestler, *The Roots of Coincidence*, pp. 31–32.

18. Ibid., p. 56.

19. Ibid., pp. 61–62.

20. Ibid., p. 60.

21. R. McConnell, *ESP: Curriculum Guide* (New York, Simon & Schuster, 1970), pp. 71–72, 77.

22. LeShan, *The Medium, the Mystic, and the Physicist*, pp. 292–299. Also published as S. Krippner and M. Ullman, "Telepathic Perception in the Dream State," *Perceptual and Motor Skills* 29 (1969): 915–918.

23. Ibid., p. 298.

24. R. Targ, Personal communication, 1971.

25. R. Targ, "Learning Clairvoyance and Precognition with an Extrasensory Perception Teaching Machine." Paper presented at the Parapsychological Association Meeting, Durham, North Carolina, 1971, p. 7.

26. A. Hardy et al., *The Challenge of Chance* (New York: Random House, 1973), pp. 114–116.

27. Ibid., p. 115.

28. Ibid., p. 116.

29. R. McConnell, *ESP: Curriculum Guide*, pp. 95–100.

30. Ibid., pp. 95–97.

31. Ibid., p. 99.

32. G. McCain and E. Segal, *The Game of Science* (Belmont, Calif.: Brooks/Cole, 1969), p. 5.

33. Hardy, *The Challenge of Chance*, p. 7.

SUGGESTED READINGS

KOESTLER, A. *The Roots of Coincidence.* New York: Random House, 1972.

LESHAN, L. *The Medium, the Mystic, and the Physicist.* New York: Viking, 1974.

MCCAIN, G., and SEGAL, E. *The Games of Science.* Belmont, Calif.: Brooks/Cole, 1969.

MCCONNELL, R. *ESP: Curriculum Guide.* New York: Simon & Schuster, 1970.

11

psychology:
what's in the future?

Psychologists have a right to be proud. The science has come a long way since the days when Watson banged a gong near the head of poor little Albert (Chapter1). Nevertheless, the material covered so far, as impressive as it is, does not tell the whole story. Even now newer methods are being developed to augment psychology's role in the service of man. In this final chapter we will discuss some of the more promising approaches:

ON BEING "ROLFED"

As the pain shot through the upper part of his body, Larry grimaced once more.

"Tell me if you want me to stop," said Charles in a sympathetic voice.

"It's OK," Larry gasped. "I don't know why, but the pain goes as quickly as it comes."

Charles nodded knowingly. "Just a little more to go, then we'll be through for the day."

"Right," Larry replied, centering himself on the cloth-covered table. Once again, Charles leaned over the almost-naked body below him and, using all his strength, pushed his fingers in and across the fascial sheaths surrounding Larry's shoulder muscles.

At first there was pain. Intense pain. Even a person as conditioned to "take it" as Larry was couldn't hold it in. He screamed.

Larry screamed louder, but this time it wasn't the pain. At least not *this* pain. He was having vivid flashes to the past. Memories he thought were lost forever. Twenty years ago. The accident. Larry had broken his collarbone. He wanted to cry, but everyone else tried to shut him up. "Be a good boy," said his mother with her characteristically plastic smile. "You want to be a man, don't you?" said the doctor as he shot an anesthetic into Larry's trembling body. Now the repressed pain of the accident seemed to be coming back. For a moment Larry girded himself against the table, fearing that he might be overwhelmed by some intolerable emotion; then he let go, relaxing his body. Immediately the pain was gone. His arms and legs started to vibrate furiously, while jolts of seeming ecstasy spread like waves from his chest to his fingers and toes. He began laughing. "Charlie, I've never felt so good in my life."

"Stand up," said Charles after a few moments.

Larry followed the instructor across the room, then turned to a full-length mirror in disbelief. His normally tight shoulders had actually changed position: They were lower and more relaxed. His neck was straighter and, of all things, his right foot, which normally stuck out at an angle, was now more aligned in a forward position. He walked a few paces backward, then forward. "I feel high," he said, giggling.

"Try moving your shoulders," replied Charles clinically.

"A little sore," said Larry, "but—they feel looser."

"They are!" exclaimed Charles.

Larry got dressed, thanked Charles, and spent the next two hours walking around San Francisco's Union Street and Fisherman's Wharf simply in order to experience what he called his "new body."

What Larry has just experienced is part of a new body therapy called *structural integration*, or *rolfing* (after its inventor, biochemist and physiologist Ida Rolf). This technique is based, in part, on the principle that psychological states are reflections of physiological states, or as Dr. Keith Gilchrist has put it, "Our physical body is the shape of our consciousness."[1] Rolfing is an attempt to change consciousness by altering body structure. In order to understand how and why it works, a small dose of theory is necessary.

In simple physiological terms, all muscular movement is based on the principle of counterbalancing. Whenever a person makes a movement, some muscles contract and thicken, while simultaneously, antagonistic (or counterbalancing) muscles freely stretch and adjust among the adjacent structures. When a person reverses the movement, the first muscles stretch and the second muscles thicken.

Unfortunately, physical damage to the body such as broken bones or even sprains can result in permanent scarring of the muscle tissue; or at best, the muscles work overtime to compensate for the weakness in the damaged part of the body. In either case the muscles at the site of the injury and the fascial sheaths that surround them become permanently thickened and unable to adjust freely to the movements of the counterbalancing muscles. Consequently, other muscles must be used to perform a given action or the movement must remain diminished. "Whatever the solution," notes Rolf, "the result is not satisfactory." The free flow of energy is blocked; awareness, at first painful, is effectively dulled; and obvious distortions of bodily posture are common (e.g., head, stomach, and knees pushed forward; shoulders, feet, and pelvis sticking back).[2]

This type of muscle freezing is not restricted to physical causes. In his classic work *The Stress of Life*, Dr. Hans Selye describes how long-term stress is reflected in alterations of the connective, or fascial tissue. Similarly, Dr. William Schutz has shown how psychological problems can effect permanent contortions of the body structure with parallel changes in consciousness. He cites as an example the common situation of the male child who, when he cries, finds that his behavior is met with parental disapproval.

> After a while, whenever his chin starts to quiver preparatory to crying, he stops it through fear of displeasing his mother [or father]. Psychologically he builds defenses that enable him not to cry so easily. Physically he tenses the muscles of his chin . . . [so that] perhaps he can stop the whole muscular pattern that leads to tears.[3]

The result is that his chin muscles become permanently tense, pulling and altering the muscles around his entire mouth and neck. At first the process is painful, but soon the person becomes numbed to it, effectively diminishing awareness in that part of his body.

Rolf's discovery is simple but important. She has found that a distortion of one muscle group does not exist in isolation; eventually it affects all the other muscles in the body. Therefore, a stretching or massage of the damaged area alone will achieve only temporary unblocking of the body-mind; permanent change requires reorganization of the entire muscular system. "The idea of reorganizing a person's fascial structure as a whole and thereby realigning the entire body seems to have occurred to no one but Ida Rolf," notes Dr. Sam Keen in *Psychology Today* magazine. She realized that only a "systematic integration through manipulation of the fascia in all the major muscle groups allows the recreation of a supple and balanced body."[4]

The actual process of rolfing usually requires ten hours,

or sessions, spaced out over intervals of at least one week's duration. The first seven hours of structural integration are devoted to releasing chronically stressed areas; the last three focus on putting the muscles into a reintegrated pattern. "The rolf practitioner," notes Gilchrist, "will use fingers, knuckles, and occasionally an elbow to stretch or reposition tissue. . . . Each hour, by releasing bound-up areas in a specific sequence, reveals residual tension in unworked areas or deeper levels of structure. The process may be likened to peeling an onion, layer by layer."[5]

The ultimate goal of rolfing is to achieve a posture "organized around an imaginary line drawn through the ear, shoulder, hip bone, knee and ankle. A body so organized will have its major weight blocks—head, thorax, pelvis, legs —distributed in a balanced manner, will be subject to a minimum of stress, and will move in the most economical way."[6]

Until recently most of our knowledge about rolfing came from numerous but isolated reports of rolf practitioners and their subjects. Only now are university studies becoming available. For example, Dr. Valerie Hunt of the Movement Behavior Laboratory at the University of California in Los Angeles conducted a study to measure how rolfing affected muscle action. In a unique experiment she had a group of thirteen people perform a series of motor tests (such as walking, lifting, and sitting) with small electrodes placed on the major muscles of their bodies. Changes in muscle potential were simultaneously and precisely recorded on a multi-channel telemetering system. The subjects then experienced ten hours of rolfing and were retested under the same conditions.[7] Comparisons of pre-rolfing and post-rolfing muscle-potential scores were made, with interesting results. First, she found that after rolfing, people performed different movements with shorter periods of muscle constriction. Second, the amplitude of the energy used was higher during active exercises and lower during shorter ones.[8] In short, people used their energy more efficiently.

A follow-up experiment with the same subjects, conducted by Dr. Julian Silverman of the California Department of Mental Hygiene, measured their EEG patterns in response to an external stimulus (a light) before and after rolfing.[9] Silverman's conclusion: "The data from our tests, combined with those from Dr. Hunt's study, seem to indicate that rolfing creates a more spontaneous, rhythmic reaction to the environment and to one's own kinesthetic and proprioceptive sensations."[10] Dr. E. Gellhorn, reporting in *Psychological Review*,[11] has found a direct relationship between contractions of fascial muscles and neuron firing in the reticular activating system of the brain (the process which is responsible for conscious experiencing). And, finally, in an extensive study conducted jointly by Agnews State Hospital (San Jose, California), the Stanford Research Institute, Langley Porter Neuropsychiatric Institute (San Francisco), and the Esalen Institute, it was found that rolfing dramatically reduced the biochemical indicators of stress in fifteen male subjects. "Changes after structural integration," the experimenters concluded, "show an increased openness and better modulated sensitivity to environmental stimulation."[12]

ROLFING: WHAT'S IN IT FOR US?

There is an excitement among those who study rolfing which is difficult to convey in words, though it is best compared to the sense of enthusiasm that gripped Europe as Sigmund Freud's ideas became known and accepted. Many psychologists, notably Wilhelm Reich, have always suspected a direct relationship between muscle tension and personality, but rolfing is the first process to demonstrate this fact empirically—and to provide a practical therapy at the same time.

Not that rolfing is the only body therapy. Other promising approaches are *bioenergetics*[13] and the Feldenkrais method.[14] Developed by Alexander Lowen, a student of Reich's, bioenergetics is a series of movements or positions that are effective for freeing unconsciously blocked muscles, thereby releasing the person's trapped energy and expanding his awareness. The Feldenkrais method (named for its founder, Israeli Dr. Moshe Feldenkrais) works on a slightly different principle, helping the person through slow and deliberate movements to unlearn the inefficient behavior patterns that mute his feelings and sap his vitality. Both methodologies, however, are united with rolfing in the quest for a greater understanding of the human body-mind. Indeed, what seems to be emerging is nothing less than a "Western yoga": a scientific regimen of physical therapy for heightened consciousness.

DREAMING YOUR TROUBLES AWAY

Swearing to himself, Phil threw the gold-plated pencil, shattering the lead and gashing a small but noticeable hole in the mahogany veneer of his executive desk. Quickly, he rose from the chair, his pear-shaped body rippling like waves on a water bed, and went straight through the den door into the yard. "Perhaps a change of scenery might help," he thought.

A few minutes passed, then Phil dropped into the lawn chair. "Being the best advertising copywriter at the agency isn't as great as I thought," Phil muttered to himself. "Who wants to spend his weekend trying to solve problems that nobody else can? It's already Sunday noon and I still haven't figured out an exciting angle for selling this new detergent."

Finally, Phil knew what had to be done. He called to his wife, Sally, and told her he had decided to go to the neighbor's party after all. That evening he ate a sumptuous meal, told a few old stories, and talked for over two hours with his friend Bob about a sailing vacation in the Caribbean. He even danced with Sally, something he hadn't done in years. Finally, at one o'clock he and Sally wobbled through the front door and upstairs to the bedroom. As she watched curiously, Phil carefully laid a new gold-plated pencil and a large pad of paper by his bedside. Then, without a single overt attempt to solve the detergent problem he had worked on most of the weekend, Phil jumped into bed, dozing off immediately.

Had Phil given up on his responsibilities? Was he planning to retire? Or perhaps escape to an island in the Caribbean? On the contrary, Phil was just getting to work.

That night Phil had a dream. A housewife is in distress, stuck with permanent-press clothes that just wouldn't get clean. Suddenly, a superman figure in white leotards appears with a box of detergent clutched in his powerful arm. Her day is saved. And so is Phil's job. He wakes up briefly, copies down the dream on the pad by his bed, then falls asleep again, confident that his problem is finally solved.

Phil's insight was not a chance event. Nor was it ESP or an act of God. On the contrary, Phil was acting on the results of a scientifically demonstrated technique called *body charting*. Let us take a closer look at how it works.

CHARTING THE BODY-MIND

Most people think of the body as a soft machine, a kind of "mushy" Chevrolet. You take in food-fuel, wash it down the mouth-gas tank into the stomach-engine, where it combusts, giving off nutrition-energy. Weight is considered to be an uncomfortable bulge in the superstructure; indigestion is simply the metal corroding. The body is acknowledged to grow and shrivel with age, but this is a long-term process which does not alter our view of ourselves as hulks.

In fact, the body is quite different from this stereotype. The human organism is a complex of interrelated, clocklike rhythms. These patterns vary so dramatically that a given body which is in a particular physical state at twelve noon may be in quite a different state just a few hours later. States science writer Gay Luce:

Most people don't realize how much they change every 24 hours. They may notice that they get particularly tired at 2:00 A.M., or chilly in the late evening. . . . [However], they remain largely unaware of changing immunity to infection or stress (which drops at night) or the fact that blood pressure, mood, pulse, respiration, blood sugar levels . . . and our ability to handle drugs all rise and fall in a circadian rhythm.[15]

The obvious rhythms are those that parallel the twenty-four-hour cycle. For most of us changes in temperature, hormone levels, and alertness occur at predictable times during the day. However, there are biological rhythms of shorter and longer duration. Breathing through the nose, for example, is an involuntary shifting back and forth between left and right nostrils at three-hour periods. The intestines contract regularly once a minute; the stomach contracts approximately three times per minute. The menstrual cycle, on the other hand, is usually a twenty-eight to thirty-five day period. (Men have less-known monthly cycles, usually slight variations in body weight.) Mood changes, when averaged out, will show cycles as long as three to six months. Even childbirth follows a pattern; most babies are born between midnight and six in the morning.

The fact that the body follows regular cycles allows us to predict what our physical states—and *parallel states of consciousness* (awareness)—will be at given times. If, for example, you note at what periods of the day you feel energetic and at what times you feel drowsy, a pattern will eventually emerge, indicating your daily alertness cycle. Effective body charting should embrace a period of three to six months, but pronounced cycles will often become obvious within a few days.

The purpose of charting your body cycles is simply this: If you learn what your rhythms are, you can plan your activities to best advantage. Some women have already done this by using the rhythm method of birth control, whereby pregnancy is avoided or initiated by a daily charting of fluctuations in body temperature in order to pinpoint ovulation. (This method is not foolproof, however.) If you discovered that your peak alertness period is in the afternoon or evening, you could arrange to do work that demands concentration in the later part of the day. If, on the other hand, you turn out to be an early riser, you could arrange to begin working on important tasks as soon as you get out of bed. By charting your daily and monthly rhythms, you could prepare in advance for low points in the cycle. This would be particularly helpful for businessmen. Important conferences could be arranged for "up" days; unimportant details would be relegated to "down" days. The value of body charting for discovering important biorhythms should not be underestimated. In a *Time* magazine article, it was reported that

> the Swiss have devised a pocket calculator that when individually set will show the owner's "off" days—when he is accident prone, forgetful or in low spirits. In Japan, the Ohmi Railway Company has stored in a computer the biorhythms of each of its 500 bus drivers. At the beginning of each shift, drivers scheduled to have "bad" days are give a card reminding them to be extra careful. In their first biorhythmic year, 1969, Ohmi's drivers achieved a 50% drop in accidents, a downward trend that continued last year.[16]

Fortunately, body charting does not require elaborate machinery. A person simply decides what mood or other state of consciousness he wishes to chart and keeps track of its occurrence on a piece of paper, in a makeshift diary, or on any other recording device. The technique is simple, practical, and available to anyone with a pencil, paper, and a little patience.

The uses of body charting are as varied as the sum of man's moods and motives. Phil, whose problem we discussed at the beginning of the section, had decided to chart his creativity cycle and found that he was unusually creative just before and during sleep. Now, whenever he encounters difficulty in his creative work, he puts it aside until bedtime, frequently coming up with an answer before dawn. Phil's creative cycle is, incidently, a common one. Many artists, writers, and scientists put paper and pencil by their bedside each night, knowing that some of their best ideas come just before falling asleep or in dreams. Physicist Niels Bohr, for example, attributed his conceptual innovations to a dream he had as a student; author Robert Louis Stevenson found "early in his life that he could dream complete stories and even go back to them on succeeding nights to change an unsatisfactory ending."[17]

Other people have employed body charting to keep track of alertness, productivity, anxiety, elation, depression, sensitivity, boredom, and even fantasy cycles. Charting negative moods is particularly useful. Gay Luce writes:

> [With] practice, you will probably discover that your moods change—not just in response to the outside world, but in weekly, monthly, seasonal, or even six-month cycles. . . . So-called moody people . . . can make their lives far smoother by predicting irritation or depression and consequently planning to compensate rather than feel like a victim of the outer world, and victimizing those around them.[18]

BODY CHARTING: WHAT'S IN IT FOR US?

The possibilities for extensive uses of body charting are just beginning to open up. Several companies already advertise predesigned body charts, while others have developed computer systems that allow an individual to chart his cycles with accuracy and ease. To be sure, we may be entering a time when even the average schoolchild will learn the *four R's*: reading, 'riting, 'rithmetic . . . and rhythms.

CREATIVE DISINTEGRATION

Traditionally, psychology has viewed any mental conflict as an intrinsic evil. Whether employing psychoanalysis or conditioning therapies (Chapter 1), the therapist has always tried to rid the patient of dysfunctional symptoms: anxieties, vascillations, hallucinations, and so on. In recent years, however, a small but growing number of mental health professionals has suggested a more radical perspective—namely, that certain forms of psychological disturbance are actually creative attempts by the patient to cope with and resolve personal problems. The goal of the therapist, then, should *not be to eliminate* the "neurotic" symptoms, but to *guide* the patient through them—hopefully to a constructive solution.[19]

How does a psychotherapist guide his client through a mental conflict? One technique rapidly gaining popularity is called *Gestalt therapy.* Developed by Dr. Frederick Pearls, this method encourages the sufferer to "blow up" his problems, engaging the conflicting parts of his personality in a sort of dialogue. To see how this works in practice, let us consider a rather mild example:

A young man comes to a psychologist's office and complains that he cannot decide what he wants to do; part of the time he thinks that he should go immediately to medical school, yet he would also like to spend a few years traveling. What should he do?

The therapist responds by asking the young man to engage his warring "sub-personalities" in a conversation, first pretending that he is the school advocate talking to the wanderer, then being the wanderer talking back to the school advocate, then being the school advocate again, and so on until some kind of conclusion is reached. The young man laughs, for this seems like a silly thing to do, but agrees to try it.

At the beginning the conversation is stilted and indirect,

for the school advocate is accustomed to bludgeoning the wanderer through all manner of devices, including threats of the poverty that will arise from aimless traveling and bribes of a glorious future beyond medical school; the wanderer, for his part, has similar tactics, including threats that medical school will be unbearable drudgery and promises of exhilarating adventures "on the road."

But gradually, as the dialogue continues, each sub-personality comes to treat the other as a real entity with legitimate wants and needs; more importantly, both the school advocate and the wanderer realize that success depends on cooperation, for they inhabit the same body and each has the power to sabotage, through indecision, the efforts of the other. Manipulation and coercion give way to understanding as the two sub-personalities seek and discuss ways to achieve mutual satisfaction.

Furthermore, when a solution *is* agreed upon it turns out to be more than just a superficial compromise. The school advocate learns that he will be happiest as a psychiatrist, for that particular branch of medicine will best satisfy the wanderer's appetite for new and unusual experiences. The wanderer, in turn, discovers that he can rely on the school advocate to be an efficient planner before trips and to be a trusted adviser when encountering difficulties en route. The two sub-personalities realize that each can get what he wants if both grow together.

CREATIVE DISINTEGRATION: WHAT'S IN IT FOR US?

The concept of helping a patient work through, rather than repress (eliminate, decondition), his conflicts is one of the most intriguing—and controversial—notions in contemporary psychology. There is already evidence that acute schizophrenics improve more when they experience the intensity of their "madness" in supportive therapeutic envi-

244

Psychology: What's in It for Us?

ronments than when they take anxiety-reducing drugs.[20]
The problem now is to define with greater precision the
nature of a supportive therapeutic environment. That is, does
Gestalt therapy really help? To what extent? In the meantime the very idea of working through a conflict makes an
important contribution to mental health: It gives those who
suffer from inner conflicts the dignity of knowing that their
struggle is not necessarily a character defect, but a creative,
organic attempt to cope with personal difficulties.

NOTES

1. K. Gilchrist, "An Introduction to Structural Integration," *Bulletin of Structural Integration* 111, No. 3, pp. 4–10.
2. I. Rolf, "Structural Integration," *Journal Institute for the Comparative Study of History, Philosophy and the Sciences* 1 (1963): 9–10.
3. W. Schutz, *Here Comes Every-Body* (New York: Harper & Row, 1971), p. 9.
4. S. Keen, "Sing the Body Electric," *Psychology Today* (October 1970): 58.
5. Gilchrist, "An Introduction to Structural Integration," p. 6.
6. Keen, "Sing the Body Electric," p. 58.
7. V. Hunt, "Tentative Report of Electromyographic Study of Structural Integration," Prepublication manuscript, 1972.
8. Keen, "Sing the Body Electric," p. 88.
9. Ibid.
10. Ibid.
11. E. Gellhorn, "Motivation and Emotion: The Role of Proprioception in the Physiology and Pathology of the Emotions," *Psychological Review* 71 (1964): 457–472.
12. J. Silverman et al., "Stress, Stimulus Intensity Control, and the Structural Integration Technique," *Confinia Psychiatria* 16 (1973): 201.
13. A. Lowen, *Physical Dynamics of Character Structure* (New York: Grune and Stratton, 1958).
14. M. Feldenkrais, *Awareness Through Movement* (New York: Harper & Row, 1972).
15. G. Luce, "Understanding Body Time in the 24-hour City," *New York Magazine*, 15 November 1971, p. 40.
16. *Time*, 10 January 1972, p. 48.
17. S. Krippner and L. Hughes, "Genius at zzz Work zzz," *Psychology Today* (June 1970): 42.

18. Luce, "Understanding Body Time in the 24-hour City," p. 42.

19. See the works of R. D. Laing, in particular *The Politics of the Family* (New York: Pantheon, 1969).

20. J. Silverman, "Altered States of Consciousness: Positive and Negative Outcomes," paper presented at the 19th annual meeting of the American Academy of Psychoanalysis, 1974.

SUGGESTED READINGS

KEEN, S. "Sing the Body Electric," *Psychology Today* (October 1970): 56–58 ff.

LUCE, G. *Body Time.* New York: Pantheon, 1971.

SILVERMAN, J., et al. "Stress, Stimulus Intensity Control, and the Structural Integration Technique." *Confinia Psychiatria* 16 (1973): 201–219.

epilogue

According to common practice, our text should end here. We have examined the various technologies of psychology and, in turn, have explained many of the wondrous ways they can, or will, be used in the service of man.

But we also know that psychology books, particularly those dealing with practical applications, are not always read for strictly academic purposes. Although most introductory psychology courses are structured to present an overall and objective picture of the behavioral sciences, the fact is that many students come to these classes with intense personal needs—for growth, for experimentation, for spiritual enrichment, for guidance, and yes, even for psychotherapy.

Our specific concern is not that you, the student, will abuse or misinterpret the knowledge that we have presented but that, having become excited about some of this material, you might fall prey to others who would abuse it. The recent publicity given to biofeedback training, for example, has spawned innumerable organizations which promise instant nirvana through body-wave training, but do not really use biofeedback equipment at all. Frequently, they will use group pressure combined with subtle hypnotic methods to produce temporary feelings of elation and self-confidence. Not that such experiences are bad, of course—but for the 200-plus dollars that such enterprises usually charge, you could have a better time in Las Vagas. More importantly, you haven't gotten what you really wanted: genuine biofeedback training.

The rise of various psycho-spiritual businesses presents special problems, since many of the techniques they use actually do work, though not for the reasons stated. Advocates of transcendental meditation (Chapter 7), for instance, will with all justification laud the physiological benefits of their discipline. They are unlikely, however, to tell you that the same effects can be achieved by simply relaxing twenty minutes twice each day and that their elaborate initiation ritual, which costs you about seventy dollars, is largely superfluous.

Even this expensive "oversight" is a relatively minor infraction compared to the practices of some other groups claiming to integrate Eastern spiritual enlightenment with the methods of Western psychology. We know of one organization, having an international membership in the thousands, that uses training techniques so authoritarian that they border on dehumanization. How can these businesses prosper? If you are still unsure that psychological methods can be so blatantly distorted, ponder the true story of Leadership Dynamics Institute, a California-based organization which claimed it could make executives more effective managers. A noble goal but implemented with highly questionable methods. At one LDI seminar,[1] held in Ricky's Hyatt House in Palo Alto, California, approximately forty men and women paid 1,000 dollars each for the "privilege" of being subjected to humiliating verbal assaults, forced nudity, and even physical beatings. These students were intelligent adults, yet LDI's persuasive style was so effective that *only one person left*. In the words of a participant:

> We felt, when we arrived, that by [submitting to the leader], we might become better leaders ourselves. As the class began, our acquiesence was replaced by the terror of pain and injury. We were literally terrorized and beaten into submission. Students found it futile to resist, futile to try to escape, futile to speak.[2]

Perhaps we are being a bit dramatic, but we feel one closing point needs to be made: *Psychology is an evolving science and should be treated as such.* The physicist has the awesome power to split the atom, but this does not keep him from probing further into the mysteries of the universe. So it is that, while the psychologist has an impressive technology for changing human behavior, this fact should not cause us to be hypnotized by any and all pronouncements of those who would employ it. The increasingly powerful technology of psychology serves each of us best when we remember science's ultimate and most awesome tool: a healthy skepticism.

NOTES

1. G. Church and C. Carnes, *The Pit* (New York: Outerbridge and Lazard, 1972).
2. Ibid., p. vii.

bibliography

ALLEGRO, J. *The Sacred Mushroom and the Cross*. New York: Doubleday, 1970.

ANDREWS, L., and KARLINS, M. *Requiem for Democracy?* New York: Holt, 1971.

ARDREY, R. *African Genesis*. London: Colins, 1961.

———. *The Territorial Imperative*. New York: Atheneum, 1966.

———. "The Violent Way." *Life*, 11 September 1970, pp. 56B–68.

———. *The Social Contract*. New York: Atheneum, 1970.

ATTHOWE, J., and KRASNER, L. "Preliminary Report on the Application of Contingent Reinforcement Procedures (Token Economy) on a 'Chronic' Psychiatric Ward." *Journal of Abnormal Psychology* 73 (1968): 37–43.

AVON, J. "Beyond Dying." *Harper's Magazine* (May 1973): 56–64.

AYLLON, T. "Intensive Treatment of Psychotic Behaviour by Stimulus Satiation and Food Reinforcement." *Behaviour Research and Therapy* 1 (1963): 53–61.

BACK, K. *Beyond Words*. Baltimore: Penguin, 1973.

BAKAN, P. "The Eyes Have It." *Psychology Today* (April 1971): 64 ff.

BARBER, T., et al., eds. *Biofeedback and Self-Control*, 1971. Chicago: Aldine, Atherton, 1972.

BARD, M. "Alternatives to Traditional Law Enforcement." In *Psychology and the Problems of Society*, edited by F. Korten, S. Cook, and J. Lacey, pp. 128–132. Washington, D.C.: American Psychological Association, 1970.

BARD, M., and ZACKER, J. "The Prevention of Family Violence: Dilemmas of Community Intervention." *Journal of Marriage and the Family*, in press.

BERNAL, M. "Behavioral Feedback in the Modification of Brat Behaviors." *Journal of Nervous and Mental Disease* 148 (1969): 375–385.

BERNSTEIN, D., and BORKOVEC, T. *Progressive Relaxation Training*. Champaign, Ill.: Research Press, 1973.

BONNY, H. *Music and Your Mind*. New York: Harper & Row, 1973.

BROWN, B. "Recognition of Aspects of Consciousness Through Association with EEG Alpha Activity Represented by a Light Signal." *Psychophysiology* 6 (1970): 442–452.

BUDZYNSKI, T., and STOYVA, J. "Biofeedback Techniques in Behavior Therapy and Autogenic Training." (Unpublished manuscript, University of Colorado Medical Center, 1971).

BUDZYNSKI, T.; STOYVA, J.; and ADLER, C. "Feedback-induced Muscle Relaxation: Application to Tension Headaches." *Journal of Behavior Therapy and Experimental Psychiatry* 1 (1970): 205–211.

CALHOUN, J. "Population Density and Social Pathology." *Scientific American* 206 (1962): 139–148.

CHOPRA, A. "Idea Generating Strategies," prepublication manuscript for *Forum*.

CHOROVER, S. "Big Brother and Psychotechnology." *Psychology Today* (October 1973): 43–54.

CHURCH, G., and CARNES, C. *The Pit*. New York: Outerbridge and Lazard, 1972.

CLARK, W. "The Psychedelics and Religion." In B. Aaronson and H. Osmond, *Psychedelics*. New York: Doubleday, Anchor Books, 1970, pp. 188–189.

CLARKE, A. *Profiles of the Future*. New York: Harper & Row, 1963.

COMPTON, D. *Synthajoy*. New York: Ace, 1968.

DABBS, J. "Personal Space When 'Cornered': College Students and Prison Inmates." *APA Proceedings* (1973): 217–218.

DAVISON, G. "Elimination of a Sadistic Fantasy by a Client-controlled Counter-conditioning Technique." *Journal of Abnormal Psychology* 73 (1968): 84–90.

"De-Indexing the Government." *Wall Street Journal*. 6 May 1974, p. 16.

DELGADO, J. *Physical Control of the Mind*. New York: Harper & Row, 1969.

DELGADO, J., et al. "Intracerebral Radio Stimulation and Recording in Completely Free Patients." *Journal of Nervous and Mental Disease* 147 (1968): 329–340.

DICARA, L. "Learning in the Autonomic Nervous System." *Scientific American* 222 (1970): 30–39.

DUNLAP, K. *Habits: Their Making and Remaking.* New York: Liveright, 1932.

EISENDRATH, R. "The Role of Grief and Fear in the Death of Kidney Transplant Patients." *American Journal of Psychiatry* 126 (1969): 381–387.

FELDENKRAIS, M. *Awareness Through Movement.* New York: Harper & Row, 1972.

FENSTERHEIM, H. "Assertive Methods and Marital Problems." *Advances in Behavior Therapy.* New York: Academic, 1972.

FLEMING, J. "Field Report: The State of the Apes." *Psychology Today* (January 1974): 31–46.

FRIEDMAN, M., and ROSENMAN, R. *Type A.* New York: Knopf, 1974.

FULLER, P. "Operant Conditioning of a Vegetative Human Organism." *American Journal of Psychology* 62 (1949): 587–590.

GALLE, O.; GOVE, W.; and MCPHERSON, J. "Population Density and Pathology: What Are the Relations for Man?" *Science* 176 (1972): 23–30.

GARDNER, B., and GARDNER, R. "Comparing the Early Utterances of Child and Chimpanzee," prepublication manuscript.

GARDNER, R., and GARDNER, B. "Teaching Sign Language to a Chimpanzee." *Science* 165 (1969): 664–672.

GELLHORN, E. "Motivation and Emotion: The Role of Proprioception in the Physiology and Pathology of the Emotions." *Psychological Review* 71 (1964): 457–472.

GERARD, R. "Psychosynthesis: A Psychotherapy for the Whole Man," *Psychosynthesis Research Foundation*, No. 14 (1964).

GILCHRIST, K. "An Introduction to Structural Integration." *Bulletin of Structural Integration* 111, No. 3, 4–10.

GOORNEY, A. "Treatment of a Compulsive Horse Race Gambler by Aversion Therapy." *British Journal of Psychiatry* 114 (1968): 329–333.

GORDON, W. *Synectics.* New York: Harper & Row, 1961.

———. *The Metaphorical Way.* Cambridge, Mass.: Porpoise, 1966.

GREEN, E.; GREEN, A.; and WALTERS, E. "Voluntary Control of Internal Stages: Psychological and Physiological." *Journal of Transpersonal Psychology* 2 (1972): 1–26.

GROF, S. "LSD and the Human Encounter with Death," prepublication manuscript.

———. "Theoretical and Empirical Basis of Transpersonal Psychology and Psychotherapy: Observation from LSD Research," *Journal of Transpersonal Psychology* 5 (1973): 15–53.

HALL, E. *The Silent Language.* New York: Doubleday, 1959.

———. *The Hidden Dimension.* New York: Doubleday, 1966.

HALL, E., and WHYTE, W. "Intercultural Communication: A Guide to Men of Action." *Human Organization* 19 (1960): 5–12.

HAMBLIN, R.; BUCKHOLDT, D.; BUSHELL, D.; ELLIS, D.; and FERRITOR, D. "Changing the Game from 'Get the Teacher' to 'Learn.'" *Trans-Action* (January 1969): 20–31.

HARDYCK, C., and PETRINOVICH, L. "Treatment of Subvocal Speech During Reading." *Journal of Reading* 12 (1969): 361–368 ff.

HARDYCK, C.; PETRINOVICH, L.; and ELLSWORTH, D. "Feedback of Speech Muscle Activity During Silent Reading: Rapid Extinction." *Science* 154 (1966): 1467–1468.

HARRIS, T. "Backaches and Personality: Tests Can Save a Useless Operation." *Psychology Today* (May 1974): 27–28.

"Healing: Mind over Matter." *Newsweek*, 24 April 1947, p. 68.

HEATH, R. "Electrical Self-Stimulation of the Brain in Man." *American Journal of Psychiatry* 120 (1963): 571–577.

HENAHAN, D. "Music Draws Strains Direct from Brains." *The New York Times*, 25 November 1970.

HOFFER, A. "Treatment of Alcoholism with Psychedelic Therapy," in B. Aaronson and H. Osmond, *Psychedelics*. New York: Doubleday, Anchor Books, 1970, pp. 357–366.

HOLMES, T., and MASUDA, M. "Psychosomatic Syndrome." *Psychology Today* (April 1972): 71 ff.

HUNT, V. "Tentative Report of Electromyographic Study of Structural Integration," prepublication manuscript, 1972.

HUXLEY, A. *Brave New World.* New York: Doubleday, 1932.

———. *Island.* New York: Harper & Row, 1962.

———. *The Doors of Perception.* Baltimore: Penguin, 1971.

HUXLEY, L. *This Timeless Moment.* New York: Farrar, Straus, and Giroux, 1968.

ITTELSON, W. *An Introduction to Environmental Psychology.* New York: Holt, 1974.

JAMES, W. *Will to Believe.* New York: Longmans, 1896.

———. *The Varieties of Religious Experience.* New York: New American Library, Mentor Books, 1958.

JOHNSTON, J. "Effects of Imagery on Learning the Volleyball Pass." *Dissertation Abstracts International* 32 (1971): 772-A.

KAMIYA, J. "Conscious Control of Brain Waves." *Psychology Today* (April 1968): 56–60.

———. "A Fourth Dimension of Consciousness." *Journal of Experimental Medicine and Surgery* 27 (1969): 13–18.

———. "Operant Control of the EEG Alpha Rhythm and Some of Its Reported Effects on Consciousness." In *Altered States of Consciousness*, edited by C. Tart. New York: Wiley, 1969.

KANELLAKOS, D., and FERGUSON, P. *The Psychobiology of Transcendental Meditation.* Los Angeles: Maharishi University, 1973.

KARLINS, M., ed. *Psychology and Society.* New York: Wiley, 1971.

———. *Psychology in the Service of Man.* New York: Wiley, 1973.

KARLINS, M., and ABELSON, H. *Persuasion.* New York: Springer, 1970.

KARLINS, M., and ANDREWS, L. *Biofeedback: Turning on the Power of Your Mind*. Philadelphia: Lippincott, 1972.

————, eds. *Man Controlled*. New York: Macmillan, Free Press, 1972.

KEEN, S. "Sing the Body Electric." *Psychology Today* (October 1970): 56–58 ff.

KIEFER, D. "Meditation and Bio-Feedback." In *The Highest State of Consciousness*, edited by J. White. New York: Doubleday, Anchor Books, 1972.

KOESTLER, A. *The Roots of Coincidence*. New York: Random House, 1972.

KOREIN, J.; MACCARIO, M.; CARMONA, A.; RANDT, C.; and MILLER, N. "Operant Conditioning Techniques in Normal and Abnormal EEG States." Paper presented at the American Academy of Neurology Meeting, April 1971.

KORTEN, F.; COOK, S.; and LACEY, J., eds. *Psychology and the Problems of Society*. Washington, D.C.: American Psychological Association, 1970.

KRIPPNER, S., and HUGHES, L. "Genius at zzzz Work zzzz." *Psychology Today* (June 1970): 42 ff.

LAING, R. *The Politics of the Family*. New York: Pantheon, 1969.

LANG, P., and MELAMED, B. "Case Report: Avoidance Conditioning Therapy of an Infant with Chronic Ruminative Vomiting." *Journal of Abnormal Psychology* 74 (1969): 1–8.

LENT, J. "Mimosa Cottage: Experiment in Hope." *Psychology Today* (June 1968): 51–58.

LESHAN, L. *The Medium, the Mystic, and the Physicist*. New York: Viking, 1974.

LEUNER, H. "Guided Affective Imagery." *American Journal of Psychotherapy* 22 (1969): 4–22.

LEWIN, K. "Studies in Group Decision." In *Group Dynamics*, edited by D. Cartwright and A. Zander. New York: Harper & Row, 1953.

LEWIS, H., and LEWIS, M. *Psychosomatics*. New York: Viking, 1972.

LIEBERMAN, M.; YALOM, I.; and MILES, M. *Encounter Groups: First Facts*. New York: Basic Books, 1974.

LOWEN, A. *Physical Dynamics of Character Structure*. New York: Harper & Row, 1972.

LOWINGER, P., and DOBIE, S. "What Makes the Placebo Work?" *Archives of General Psychiatry* 20 (1969): 84–88.

LUCE, G. *Body Time*. New York: Pantheon, 1971.

————. "Understanding Body Time in the 24-hour City." *New York Magazine*, 15 November 1971, pp. 37 ff.

LUCE, G., and PEPER, E. "Biofeedback: Mind over Body, Mind over Mind." *The New York Times Magazine*, 12 September 1971, pp. 34 ff.

MAHONEY, M., and THORESEN, C. *Self-Control: Power to the Person*. Monterey, Calif.: Brooks/Cole, 1974.

"Man into Superman: The Promise and Peril of the New Genetics." *Time*, 19 April 1971, pp. 33–52.

MANN, J. *Changing Human Behavior*. New York: Charles Scribner's, 1965.

MARK, V. "A Psychosurgeon's Case *for* Psychosurgery." *Psychology Today* (July 1974): 28 ff.

MAYR, O. "The Origins of Feedback Control." *Scientific American* 223 (1970): 110–118.

MCCAIN, G., and SEGAL, E. *The Game of Science*. Belmont, Calif.: Brooks/Cole, 1969.

MCCLELLAND, D. *The Achieving Society*. New York: Van Nostrand-Reinhold, 1961.

MCCONNELL, R. A. *ESP: Curriculum Guide*. New York: Simon & Schuster, 1970.

MCKIM, R. *Experiences in Visual Thinking*. Monterey, Calif.: Brooks/Cole, 1972.

MEYER, P. "If Hitler Asked You to Electrocute a Stranger, Would You? Probably." *Esquire* (February 1970): 72 ff.

MILGRAM, S. "Behavioral Study of Obedience." *Journal of Abnormal and Social Psychology* 67 (1963): 371–378.

———. "Some Conditions of Obedience and Disobedience to Authority." *Human Relations* 18 (1965): 57–76.

———. "Liberating Effects of Group Pressure." *Journal of Personality and Social Psychology* 1 (1965): 127–134.

MILLER, J. "Relax! The Brain Machines Are Here." *Human Behavior* (August 1974): 16–23.

MILLER, N. "Learning of Visceral and Glandular Responses." *Science* 163 (1969): 434–445.

———. "Applications of Learning and Biofeedback to Psychiatry and Medicine." In *Comprehensive Textbook of Psychiatry*, 2nd ed., eds. H. Kaplan and B. Sadock. Baltimore: Williams and Wilkins, in press.

MORRIS, D. *The Naked Ape*. New York: McGraw-Hill, 1967.

———. *The Human Zoo*. New York: McGraw-Hill, 1969.

NARANJO, C. *The Healing Journey*. New York: Random House, 1973.

OLDS, J. "The Central Nervous System and the Reinforcement of Behavior." *American Psychologist* 24 (1969): 114–132.

OLDS, J., and MILNER, P. "Positive Reinforcement Produced by Electrical Stimulation of Septal Area and Other Regions of Rat Brain." *Journal of Comparative and Physiological Psychology* 47 (1954): 419–427.

OSBORN, A. *Applied Imagination*. New York: Charles Scribner's, 1963.

OSMOND, H. "Foreword," in B. Wells, *Psychedelic Drugs*. Baltimore: Penguin, 1974.

OTIS, L. "The Psychobiology of Meditation." Paper presented at the 1973 APA Convention in Montreal, Canada.

OXENDINE, J. *Psychology of Motor Learning.* New York: Appleton-Century-Crofts, 1968.

PANUSHKA, K. "Games Executives Play," a *Boston Magazine* reprint, p. 3.

PENFIELD, W. "The Interpretive Cortex." *Science* 129 (1959): 1719–1725.

PHILLIPS, D. "Dying As a Form of Social Behavior." Doctoral dissertation, Princeton University, 1969.

PINES, M. *The Brain Changers.* New York: Harcourt, 1973.

PINNEO, L. "Development of a Brain Prosthesis." *Nonhuman Primates and Medical Research.* New York: Academic Press, 1973.

PINNEO, L.; KAPLAN, J.; ELPEL, E.; REYNOLDS, P.; and GLICK, J. "Experimental Brain Prosthesis for Stroke." *Stroke* 3 (1972): 16–26.

PREMACK, D. "The Education of Sarah." *Psychology Today* (September 1970): 55–58.

"Probing the Brain." *Newsweek*, 21 June 1971, pp. 60–68.

RENSBERGER, B. "Computer Helps Chimpanzees Learn to Read, Write, and 'Talk' to Humans." *The New York Times*, 29 May 1974, pp. 43, 52.

ROLF, I. "Structural Integration." *Journal Institute for the Comparative Study of History, Philosophy and the Sciences* 1 (1963): 9–11.

ROSENFELD, A. *Second Genesis.* Englewood Cliffs, N.J.: Prentice-Hall, 1969.

ROSENTHAL, S. "Electrosleep." *World Biennial of Psychiatric Psychotherapy* 2 (1973): 377–389.

RUBIN, R., et al. *Advances in Behavior Therapy.* New York: Academic Press, 1972.

SARGENT, J.; GREEN, E.; and WALTERS, E. "Preliminary Report on the Use of Autogenic Feedback Techniques in the Treatment of Migraine and Tension Headaches" (unpublished manuscript, Menninger Foundation, 1971).

SAVAGE, C., and MCCABE, B. "Psychedelic Therapy of Drug Addiction," in C. Brown and C. Savage, *The Drug Abuse Controversy.* Baltimore: National Educational Consultants, 1971, pp. 145–163.

SCARF, M. "Brain Researcher José Delgado Asks—'What Kind of Humans Would We Like to Construct?'" *The New York Times Magazine*, 15 November 1970, pp. 46 ff.

SCHACHTER, S. "Some Extraordinary Facts About Obese Humans and Rats." *American Psychologist* 26 (1971): 124–144.

SCHUTZ, W. *Here Comes Every-Body.* New York: Harper & Row, 1971.
———. *Elements of Encounter.* Big Sur, Calif.: Joy Press, 1973.

SCHWARTZ, G. "TM Relaxes Some People and Makes Them Feel Better." *Psychology Today* (April 1974): 39–44.

SELIGMAN, M. "Fall into Helplessness." *Psychology Today* (June 1973): 43 ff.

SELYE, H. *The Stress of Life.* New York: McGraw-Hill, 1956.

SHAPIRO, D.; TURSKY, B.; GERSHON, E.; and STERN, M. "Effects of Feedback and Reinforcement on the Control of Human Systolic Blood Pressure." *Science* 163 (1969): 588–590.

SHERIF, M., and SHERIF, C. *Social Psychology.* New York: Harper & Row, 1969.

SILVERMAN, J. "Altered States of Consciousness: Positive and Negative Outcomes." Paper presented at the 19th annual meeting of the American Academy of Psychoanalysis, 1974.

SILVERMAN, J., et al. "Stress, Stimulus Intensity Control, and the Structural Integration Technique." *Confinia Psychiatria* 16 (1973): 201–219.

SINGER, J. *Daydreaming.* New York: Random House, 1966.

SKINNER, B. *Walden Two.* New York: Macmillan, 1948.

———. "Pigeons in a Pelican." *American Psychologist* 15 (1960): 28–37.

———. "Contingencies of Reinforcement in the Design of a Culture." *Behavioral Science* 11 (1966): 159–166.

SOLOMON, G., and AMKRAUT, A. "Emotions, Stress, and Immunity." *Frontiers of Radiation Therapy and Oncology* 7 (1972): 84–96.

SOMMER, R. *Personal Space: The Behavioral Basis of Design.* Englewood Cliffs, N.J.: Prentice-Hall, 1969.

———. "Planning Notplace for Nobody." *Saturday Review,* 5 April 1969, pp. 67–69.

SOUNCHERAY, J. "The Sugarbowl of Rodeos," *TWA Ambassador* 6, No. 9 (1973): 35–38.

STEWART, K. "Dream Theory in Malaya," in C. Tart, *Altered States of Consciousness.* New York: Wiley, 1969, pp. 159–167.

STUDER, R., and STEA, D. "Architectural Programming, Environmental Design, and Human Behavior." *Journal of Social Issues* 22 (1966): 127–136.

STUNKARD, A., and KOCH, C. "The Interpretation of Gastric Motility." *Archives of General Psychiatry* 11 (1964): 74–82.

TALBOTT, J., and TALBOTT, S. "Training Police in Community Relations and Urban Problems." *American Journal of Psychiatry* 127 (1971): 894–900.

TRITES, D. "Influence of Nursing-Unit Design on the Activities and Subjective Feelings of Nursing Personnel." *Environment and Behavior* 2 (1970): 303–334.

"Two Dogs Pass Bomb-finding Test Successfully." *The New York Times,* 8 March 1972, p. 29.

UBELL, E. "How to Save Your Life: The Behavior Control Diet," *New York Magazine,* 3 September 1973, pp. 43 ff.

VERHAVE, T. "The Pigeon As a Quality-Control Inspector." *American Psychologist* 21 (1966): 109–115.

WAGGONER, K. "Psychocivilization or Electroligarchy: Dr. Delgado's Amazing World of ESB." *Yale Alumni Magazine* (January 1970).

WALD, G. "Determinancy, Individuality, and the Problem of Free Will." In *New Views of the Nature of Man*, edited by J. Platt, pp. 16–46. Chicago: University of Chicago Press, 1965.

WALLACE, R., and BENSON, K. "The Physiology of Meditation." *Scientific American* 226 (1972): 84–90.

WATSON, J. *Behaviorism*. New York: People's Institute, 1924.

WATSON, J., and RAYNER, R. "Conditioned Emotional Reactions." *Journal of Experimental Psychology* 3 (1920): 1–14.

WEISS, T., and ENGLE, B. "Operant Conditioning of Heart Rate in Patients with Premature Ventricular Contractions." *Psychosomatic Medicine* 33 (1971): 301–321.

WELLS, B. *Psychedelic Drugs*. Baltimore: Penguin, 1974.

WHITE, J., and TAYLOR, D. "Noxious Conditioning As a Treatment for Rumination." *Mental Retardation* (February 1967): 30–33.

WILLNER, A., et al. "An Analogy Test That Predicts Postoperative Outcome in Patients Scheduled for Open-Heart Surgery." *APA Annual Proceedings* 81 (1973): 371–372.

WITKIN, R. "Bomb Found on Jet Here After $2 Million Demand." *The New York Times*, 8 March 1972, pp. 1 ff.

WOLPE, J. *The Practice of Behavioral Therapy*. New York: Pergamon, 1969.

WYNNE-EDWARD, V. "Population Control in Animals." *Scientific American* 211 (1964): 68–74.

about the authors

Lewis M. Andrews is a Ph.D. candidate in psychology at Union Graduate School in Yellow Springs, Ohio. His current areas of specialization are Clinical Psychology and Theoretical Psychology. In addition to writing *Requiem for Democracy* and *Biofeedback* with Dr. Karlins, he has contributed articles to such publications as *The Nation, Saturday Review,* and the *Wall Street Journal.*

Marvin Karlins is currently Professor of Management at the University of South Florida. He previously taught Psychology at City College of C.U.N.Y. and Princeton University. Dr. Karlins and H. Ableson coauthored *Persuasion.* H. Schroder, J. Phares, and Dr. Karlins wrote *Education for Freedom.* Dr. Karlins and Lewis M. Andrews coauthored *Requiem for Democracy?* and *Biofeedback.* Marvin Karlins edited *Psychology and Society* and *Psychology in the Service of Man.* He has also contributed many articles to such publications as the *Journal of Personality and Social Psychology.*

DATE DUE